TABLE OF CONTENTS

APPENDICES

CITATIONS

Constitution:

Statutes:

Other Authorities:

IN THE SUPREME COURT
OF THE UNITED STATES

October Term, 1977

No. 76-1607

SECURITIES AND EXCHANGE COMMISSION,

Petitioner,

v.

SAMUEL H. SLOAN,

Respondent.

ON WRIT OF CERTIORARI TO THE UNITED STATES COURT OF APPEALS FOR THE SECOND CIRCUIT

BRIEF FOR THE RESPONDENT

OPINIONS BELOW

The opinion of the court of appeals (Pet. App B, pp. 3a-17a), as modified (Pet. App. C, pp. 18a-20a), is reported as 547 F. 2d 152 (2d Cir. 1976). The opinion of the Securities and Exchange Commission (App. 109-110), is reported as *In the Matter of Trading in Securities of Canadian Javelin Ltd.*, 41 Fed. Reg. 17983-17984 (April 21, 1976).

JURISDICTION

The judgment of the court of appeals was entered on November 18, 1976 (Pet. App. A, p. 1a). A timely petition for rehearing was denied on December 27, 1976 (Pet. App. C, p. 18a), and a suggestion that the rehearing be en banc was rejected on January 24, 1977 (Pet. App. F, p. 27a). On March 17, 1977, Mr. Justice Marshall extended the time for filing a petition for a writ of certiorari to and including April 25, 1977, and on April 22, 1977, he granted a further extension to and including May 15, 1977. The petition was filed on Monday, May 16, 1977, and was granted on October 17, 1977. The jurisdiction of this Court is invoked under 28 U.S.C. §1254 (1).

STATUTES AND RULES INVOLVED

Sections 556(d), Pub. L. 89-554, 80 Stat. 386, and 558(c), Pub. L. 89-554, 80 Stat. 388, 5 U.S.C. §556(d) and §558(c) of the Administrative Procedure Act. Sections 12(j) and 12(k), Pub. L. 94-29, 89 Stat. 118, 15 U.S.C. §78*l*(j) and §78*l*(k); Section 15(c)(2), Pub. L. 94-29, 89 Stat. 121, 15 U.S.C. §78*o*(c)(2); Section 25(a)(1), (2), (3),(4) and (5), Pub. L. 94-29, 89 Stat. 158, 15 U.S.C. §78*y*(a)(1),(2),(3),(4), and (5); Section 25(c)(2), Pub. L. 94-29, 89 Stat. 158, 15 U.S.C. §78*y*(c)(2); Section 32, Pub. L. 94-29, 89 Stat. 162, 163, 15 U.S.C. §78*ff;* former Section 15(c)(5), Pub. L. 88-467, 78 Stat. 574, 15 U.S.C. §78*o*(c)(5); and former Section 19(a)(4), 48 Stat. 898, 15 U.S.C. §78*s*(a)(4) of the Securities Exchange Act of 1934. Section 1651(a), 63 Stat. 102, 28 U.S.C. §165(a) of the All Writs Act. Section 2201, Pub. L. 94-455, Title XIII, Section 1306(b)(8), 90 Stat. 1719, 28 U.S.C. §2201 of the Declaratory Judgment Act. Rule 17(a) of the Federal Rules of Appellate Procedure. Rule 15c2-11, 42 Fed. Reg. 13110, 17 C.F.R. §240.15c2-11 of the Rules of the

Securities and Exchange Commission. The text of these statutes and rules are set forth in Appendix A to this brief.

QUESTIONS PRESENTED

1. Did the Securities and Exchange Commission exceed the authority given to it in §12(k) of the Securities Exchange Act of 1934, which authorizes the Securities and Exchange Commission "summarily to suspend trading in any security (other than an exempted security) for a period not exceeding ten days," when it suspended trading in a security for a period of more than a year by issuing a series of thirty-seven successive ten-day suspension orders?

2. Did this case become moot when each of the thirty-seven successive ten-day suspension orders of which review was sought had expired before the time the court of appeals made its decision declaring all but the first order to be invalid?

3. Were each of the successive ten-day trading suspension orders supported by substantial evidence and, if not, must they be vacated?

4. Does §12(k) of the Securities Exchange Act of 1934, which authorizes the Securities and Exchange Commission "summarily to suspend trading in any security" whenever "in its opinion the public interest and the protection of investors so require," constitute an unconstitutional delegation of legislative authority to an administrative agency and does it violate other provisions of the Constitution?

STATEMENT

This case involves a petition for review which was filed in the United States Court of Appeals for the Second Circuit by Respondent, Samuel H. Sloan, seeking review of a total of thirty-seven orders of the Securities and Exchange Commission ("S.E.C."), purportedly issued pursuant to the Securities Exchange Act of 1934 ("Securities Exchange Act"), each of which suspended trading in all securities of Canadian Javelin Ltd. for a ten-day period. Since these orders were issued successively, their total effect was to suspend trading in the securities of Canadian Javelin Ltd. for a continuous period from 3:45 p.m. EDT on April 29, 1975 through May 2, 1976 (App. 11, 110). This was not the first time trading in Canadian Javelin Ltd. had been suspended by the S.E.C. for successive ten-day periods. Prior successive ten-day trading suspension orders had suspended trading in Canadian Javelin Ltd. from March 17, 1971 until April 5, 1971,[1] from March 7, 1972 until August 9, 1972,[2] and from November 29, 1973 until January 26, 1975.[3]

Respondent in this case was a registered broker-dealer in securities from May 10, 1970, when his broker-dealer registration became effective, until April 28, 1975, when his broker-dealer registration was revoked by the S.E.C. and he was barred from being associated with any broker or dealer. During that time, Respondent did business

---

1. See Securities Exchange Act Release No. 9111 (March 17, 1971); Securities Exchange Act Release No. 9124 (March 30, 1971).

2. See Securities Exchange Act Release No. 9528 (March 7, 1972); Securities Exchange Act Release No. 9715 (August 3, 1972).

3. See Securities Exchange Act Release No. 10534, 3 SEC Docket 154 (November 29, 1973); Securities Exchange Act Release No. 11172, 6 SEC Docket 53 (January 9, 1975); Securities Exchange Act Release No. 11178, 6 SEC Docket 78 (January 13, 1975); Securities Exchange Act Release No. 11197, 6 SEC Docket 145 (January 22, 1975). The last of the suspensions is regarded by the S.E.C. as two separate suspensions, the first beginning on November 29, 1973 and ending on January 12, 1975 and the second beginning on January 13, 1975 and ending on January 26, 1975 (See App. 189). This second suspension occurred at the request of Canadian Javelin Ltd., which filed a motion in the United States District Court for the Southern District of New York to enjoin the S.E.C. from lifting its trading suspension..

under the name of Samuel H. Sloan & Co.[4]

During the period in which he was a registered broker-dealer in securities, Respondent's principal and virtually exclusive activity was that of market marker in over-the-counter securities. Respondent at one time or another made a market in approximately one thousand securities, one of them being Canadian Javelin Ltd. Respondent traded heavily in the securities of Canadian Javelin Ltd. and was generally a short-seller, a circumstance which ultimately led to extensive litigation.[5] At

---

4. Samuel H. Sloan & Co. was originally formed as a partnership consisting of two partners. On January 11, 1971, the other partner in this partnership, Harry G. Theodos, withdrew. Respondent immediately thereafter filed an amendment to his broker-dealer registration to reflect the withdrawal of Theodos from the partnership. This amendment was rejected by the S.E.C. Numerous subsequent attempts were made to file an application or amendment reflecting the withdrawal of Theodos from the partnership and to remove the words "& Co." from the name of Samuel H. Sloan & Co., all of which were arbitrarily rejected by the S.E.C., the reason given being that Samuel H. Sloan & Co. was then the subject of investigative proceedings. From September 17, 1973 until April 28, 1975, the S.E.C. refused to allow the withdrawal of the broker-dealer registration of Samuel H. Sloan & Co. for the same reason. Thus, Samuel H. Sloan & Co. was at all times listed on the records of the S.E.C. as a partnership although, in fact, for most of the time in which it was a registered broker-dealer it was a sole proprietorship. Subsequent to April 28, 1975, at the insistence of Harry G. Theodos who by that time had formed his own broker-dealer firm by the name of H. G. Theodos, the S.E.C. agreed to note on its records that Theodos was no longer a partner in Samuel H. Sloan & Co. Although Samuel H. Sloan & Co. was the name listed on the official records of the S.E.C., Respondent, to the extent possible, did business under his own personal name. For example, reference works such as *Securities Dealers of North America,* published by Standard & Poor's Corp., has always listed Samuel H. Sloan under his personal name rather than under the name of Samuel H. Sloan & Co.

5. See *Sloan v. Canadian Javelin Ltd.*, CCH Fed. Sec. Law Rep. ¶ 94, 579 [1973-1974 transfer binder] (S.D.N.Y. 1974), *aff'd* 538 F. 2d 313 (2d Cir. 1976), *cert. denied* 429 U.S. 835 (1976); *S.E.C. v. Canadian Javelin Ltd.*, 64 F.R.D. 648 (S.D.N.Y., 1974), *appeal dismissed* 538 F. 2d 313 (2d Cir. 1976), *cert. denied sub nom. Sloan v. S.E.C.*, 429 U.S. 1023 (1976); *Bonime v. Doyle*, 416 F. Supp. 1372 (S.D.N.Y., 1976), *aff'd* 556 F. 2d 554 (2d Cir. 1977),

the end of all this Respondent wound up holding 13 Canadian Javelin Ltd. shares, which he continues to own to this day.

The controversy which is presently before this Court grew out of a series of suits and countersuits and related administrative proceedings which, at their outset, had nothing to do with trading by Respondent in shares of Canadian Javelin Ltd.[6] On January 11, 1971, Respondent requested from the S.E.C. an extention of time to file his

cert. denied sub nom Sloan v. Bonime, —U.S.— (1977). In the latter case there is presently on file in the United States District Court for the Southern District of New York a proof of claim and supporting documentation consisting of brokers' purchase-and-sale confirmations showing that from the beginning of 1973 until the S.E.C. trading suspension which commenced on November 29, 1973, Respondent sold and purchased 46,810 shares of Canadian Javelin Ltd. This proof of claim also shows that Respondent lost $123,642.51, exclusive of brokerage commissions, as a result. Respondent has been characterized by counsel for Canadian Javelin Ltd. as the largest seller of Canadian Javelin Ltd. stock in 1973, with the exception of the government of Newfoundland.

6. The fact that all of the various court proceedings involving Petitioner and Respondent are inter-related is not in dispute. For example, pp. 2-3 and footnote 1 of the brief filed by the S.E.C. in the court of appeals in *S.E.C. v. Sloan,* Dkt. No. 74-1436, an appeal from the decision reported as *S.E.C. v. Sloan,* 369 F. Supp. 996 (SDNY, 1974), stated the following:

> "This action is the seminal case in a web of litigation involving Mr. Sloan and the Securities and Exchange Commission.[1] Despite the array of proceedings spawned by this initial enforcement action taken by the Commission against Mr. Sloan and despite the profusion of legal theories propounded by Mr. Sloan in an endless stream of motions made before this Court and before various district judges of the Southern District of New York, the substance of the case at bar could not be more routine. Investigators in the Commission's New York Regional Office, after examinations of the books and records of Samuel H. Sloan & Co., then a registered broker-dealer operated by Mr. Sloan as a sole proprietorship, observed that the firm's books and records were not maintained in accordance with the Commission's regulations and, further, that the firm was not in compliance with the Commission's net capital requirements for broker-dealers. Accordingly, the Commission instituted this injunctive action in the United States District Court for the Southern District of New York.

required X-17A-5 report. Commencing the next day and continuing until February 4, 1971, a single S.E.C. staff investigator, Arthur L. Bruder, made several visits to the office of Respondent and reported back to his superiors that at various times Respondent's books and records were "not properly maintained" and that according to Bruder's calculations Respondent had less than the capital required by the S.E.C. net capital rule.[7] On February 4, 1971, without sending a second investigator to confirm Bruder's findings, an S.E.C. staff attorney issued an "order of in-

---

1. In addition to this appeal, Mr. Sloan and the Commissior are adversaries before this Court in four other matters: *Securities and Exchange Commission v. Samuel H. Sloan, individually and d/b/a Samuel H. Sloan & Co.*, No. 75-7056 (appeal from a subsequent preliminary injunction); *Securities and Exchange Commission v. Canadian Javelin, Ltd., et al.*, No. 75-7046 (Mr. Sloan's application for intervention to assert a claim for damages); *Samuel H. Sloan v. Securities and Exchange Commission, et al.*, No. 75-7283 (appeal by Mr. Sloan from dismissal of his suit against the Commission and others seeking declaratory, injunctive and damage relief); *Samuel H. Sloan v. Securities and Exchange Commission*, No. 75-4087 (Mr. Sloan's petition for review of the Commission's order barring him from association with any broker-dealer and revoking the broker-dealer registration of Sloan & Co.). A fifth proceeding *Samuel H. Sloan v. Securities and Exchange Commission*, No. 74-2457 (Mr. Sloan's petition for review of a series of trading suspensions) was dismissed without prejudice on October 15, 1975."

---

7. Internal S.E.C. memoranda obtained in April 1977 by Respondent pursuant to the Freedom of Information Act state that on February 4, 1977, the date of Bruder's last visit to Respondent's office, Bruder determined that Respondent's records were up to date and his capital was in compliance with the S.E.C. net capital rule. This fact was not made known to Judge Ward, who, in his decision reported at 369 F. Supp. 996, 998 ¶ 9, "found" that Bruder observed further record-keeping violations on February 25, 1971 when, in fact, the memoranda of the S.E.C. show that Bruder did not examine Respondent's books and records on that date. Nor, apparently, was this fact revealed to the S.E.C. commissioners who adopted this finding in their decision to bar Respondent for life from being associated with any broker or dealer. See *Samuel H. Sloan*, Securities Exchange Act Release No. 11376, 6 SEC Docket 772, 774 (April 28, 1975).

vestigation," and on February 16, 1971, the Division of Enforcement of the New York Regional Office of the S.E.C. requested authorization by the Commission to commence an injunctive suit against Respondent. This request was denied on April 20, 1971 but the S.E.C. instructed the Division of Enforcement to "warn" Respondent of the "violations." However, the Division of Enforcement did not warn Respondent in writing of the violations but instead on May 14, 1971 went back to the Commission with an urgent request that it reconsider its decision and strongly implied that Respondent had misappropriated $156,000 in cash and securities from another person.[8] Based upon this representation, the Commission

8. The initial memorandum of the S.E.C. requesting permission to institute an injunctive action, the April 20, 1971 memorandum denying this request, and the May 14, 1971 memorandum requesting the S.E.C. to reconsider its decision based upon new facts are included as exhibits A, B and C of document No. 150 of the record transmitted to this Court by the court of appeals Document No. 150 was a motion to stay the order of the S.E.C. pending certiorari. The S.E.C. did not respond to this motion. The figure of $156,000 actually represented the gross dollar value of transactions in the months of February, March and April, 1971 between Respondent and Joseph F. Iny, a securities representative of the New York Stock Exchange member form of Granger & Co., primarily in the shares of Kaiser Steel Corp. Respondent and Iny had engaged in transactions in securities on a "delivery versus payment" basis and Iny had expressed a desire to become partners with Respondent. This relationship terminated in April, 1971, a fact known to the S.E.C. staff because it took Iny's deposition in April, 1971, but not revealed to the S.E.C. in its May 14, 1971 memorandum. Due to the nature of the relationship, Respondent was never in a position where he had the power to misappropriate cash and securities in the amounts suggested by the S.E.C. Division of Enforcement and there was no factual basis for the claim that he had done so. The claim that Respondent had "misappropriated" cash and securities belonging to Iny was also made in court in papers filed on June 17, 1971, in support of a request for a temporary restraining order but was thereafter abandoned. This allegation was useful to the Division of Enforcement in obtaining permission to institute suit against Respondent and in obtaining a temporary restraining order. The memorandum requesting authorization to commence suit also stated that Respondent had failed to disclose on his books certain transactions with an individual by the name of Zia Marashi. Mr. Marashi, however, was a broker-dealer doing business under the name Zimar Company.

gave the Division of Enforcement authorization to commence an injunctive suit. This suit was filed in the United States District court for the Southern District of New York on June 17, 1971. Simultaneous with its commencement of suit, the S.E.C. filed a request for a temporary restraining order and stated that this request was necessary in view of the failure of Respondent to provide the S.E.C. with a copy of his April, 1971 trial balance and the fact that Respondent had misappropriated $156,000 in cash and securities belonging to another. The S.E.C. also requested the appointment of a temporary receiver. At a conference in Judge McLean's chambers, Respondent consented to the temporary restraining order on condition that he be permitted to consummate all existing contractual commitments. This provision was incorporated in the terms of the temporary restraining order which was signed by Judge McLean on June 21, 1971. However, immediately upon leaving Judge McLean's chambers the attorneys for the S.E.C. violated this agreement by seizing Respondent's bank account, thereby causing Respondent to bounce approximately 40 checks totaling approximately $80,000 which had been written to various broker-dealers in settlement of securities trades. On June 23, 1971, Respondent and his counsel met with the attorneys for the

---

All transactions with Zimar Company were properly recorded on Respondent's books, a fact which the Division of Enforcement did not see fit to mention in its request for permission to institute suit. No claim of impropriety by Respondent in his dealings with Mr. Marashi was ever made in any court or administrative proceeding but again had this claim not been made in the May 14, 1971 memorandum, the S.E.C. probably would not have given its staff authorization to institute suit. Similarly, the earlier memorandum requesting authorization to institute suit stated that on November 24, 1970 Respondent was notified that his request for an extension of time to file his X-17A-5 report was denied. In fact, Respondent was never given such notification and believed, until he received the memorandum in April, 1977, that this request had been granted. An examination of the material obtained under the Freedom of Information Act shows that no order denying this request, as required by S.E.C. rules, was ever issued or mailed to Respondent.

S.E.C. in Judge McLean's court and at that time the S.E.C. offered to return the money which had been seized from Respondent's bank account and to abandon its request for a temporary receiver and all other claims against Respondent and to permit Respondent to return to doing an active business as a securities broker-dealer provided that Respondent would "consent" to a permanent injunction. After a lengthy colloquy, Respondent refused to consent to a permanent injunction but agreed to consent to a preliminary injunction with the understanding that he would get his money back and have the opportunity to be vindicated at a trial on the merits. The S.E.C. staff agreed to this and the preliminary injunction was formally entered on June 24, 1971.

In the ensuing months, the S.E.C. enforcement staff made repeated requests that Respondent consent to a permanent injunction in order to spare the Division of Enforcement the effort and expense of having to bring its case to trial. Eventually, the S.E.C. staff advised Respondent that if he did not consent to a permanent injunction, an administrative proceeding would be brought against him. Respondent refused at all times to consent to an injunction and the threatened administrative proceeding was, in fact, commenced on April 25, 1972. The Division of Enforcement then offered to settle the administrative proceeding with a suspension of sixty days provided, again, that Respondent would consent to a permanent injunction. Although Respondent did not object to the sixty-day suspension he continued to refuse to consent to an injunction, as a result of which no settlement agreement was ever reached.

An administrative hearing was scheduled and, after several postponements by the S.E.C., the hearing was actually conducted from October 30, 1972 until November 1, 1972. An initial decision was filed by an administrative law judge on April 24, 1973 and that decision was appealed to the Commission where the matter remained pending for the next two years. Meanwhile, the injunctive suit which had been filed in the district court had been assigned to Judge Ward, upon the death of Judge McLean, and in early 1973 Judge Ward became impatient with the length of time that case had been sitting dormant on his calendar and scheduled a pre-trial conference where he directed the parties to proceed with discovery and prepare the case for trial. There were no discovery proceedings by either side and, after a period of time had passed, Judge Ward directed the parties to be prepared to go to trial on December 10, 1973. The trial actually commenced on December 11, 1973 and continued until December 22, 1973, following which Judge Ward on January 7, 1974 made a decision in favor of the S.E.C. An injunction was entered on January 18, 1973, even before the court reporter had completed making a transcript. Judge Ward's decision is reported as *S.E.C. v. Sloan,* 369 F. Supp. 996 (S.D.N.Y. 1974).

On June 27, 1974, with an appeal from Judge Ward's decision pending in the United States Court of Appeals for the Second Circuit and an appeal from the decision of the administrative law judge pending before the S.E.C., and no sign of a decision in either case being immediately forthcoming, Respondent commenced suit against the S.E.C. The original complaint filed in that suit alleged that the S.E.C. had acted arbitrarily, illegally, unconstitutionally, and without just cause in suspending trading in a number of securities owned by Respondent, one of them being Canadian Javelin Ltd. The complaint also alleged that the S.E.C. had acted illegally and improperly in its application of Rule 15c2-11 by refusing to permit the resumption of quotations in the pink sheets published by the National Quotation Bureau, Inc. of securities which had previously been suspended by the S.E.C. and that Rule 15c2-11 was constitutionally invalid. The S.E.C. answered with a number of affirmative defenses, some of which were pleaded and others of which were set forth in a conference before Judge Griesa, to whom the case had been assigned. The S.E.C. contended, (1) that the S.E.C. cannot be sued in its own name, (2) that the suit as it pertains to the submission of quotations after a trading suspension had been terminated was more properly brought against the National Quotation Bureau, Inc. since it was the National Quotation Bureau and not the S.E.C. that was refusing to publish quotations for these securities in the pink sheets, (3) that Respondent's sole remedy with respect to his claims regarding Rule 15c2-11 was to violate the rule and wait for the Commission to institute enforcement proceedings, and (4) that Respondent's exclusive remedy with regard to the trading suspension orders was to file a petition for review in a United States Court of Appeals. The S.E.C. also claimed that Respondent lacked standing to sue and that most of his claims with regard to the impropriety of trading suspension orders had become moot since, with the exception of Canadian Javelin Ltd., the suspension of trading in all of the securities set forth by Respondent in the complaint had expired. At a conference in chambers, after reading the complaint and hearing the arguments of the S.E.C., Judge Griesa directed Respondent to file an amended complaint setting forth facts in greater detail concerning the trading suspension orders issued by the S.E.C., the manner in which Respondent has sustained injury as a result of these suspensions, and other matters. The amended complaint which Respondent thereafter filed set forth in detail 28 securities which had been suspended by the S.E.C. and which suspensions had adversely affected Respondent in that Respondent had either been a stockholder or a market maker or a short-seller prior to the trading suspension. In addition, the amended complaint alleged that as a result of the trading suspension in Triex International Corp. plus a retroactive application by the S.E.C. of Securities Exchange Act Release No. 10209 (June 8, 1973), which required broker-dealers to deduct "fails to deliver" in suspended securities from their net capital, the S.E.C. had found Respondent to be in violation of the net capital rule retroactively to May 24, 1973 due to the fact that Respondent had been a short seller of Triex International Corp. and had $11,000 in fails to deliver in that security. The amended complaint also joined as additional parties the National Quotation Bureau, Inc., publisher of the pink sheets, and the owner and operator of another inter-dealer quotation system known as NASDAQ and alleged violations of antitrust law as well as violations of the Securities Exchange Act and the Constitution. That suit was ultimately dismissed by the district court and this dismissal was affirmed by the court of appeals, which characterized the suit as "frivolous." See *Sloan v. S.E.C.*, 535 F. 2d 676 (2d Cir. 1976), *cert. denied* 429 U.S. 885 (1976).[9]

A further outgrowth of the affirmative defenses set forth by the S.E.C. was two other actions taken by Respondent. The first was a petition for review filed by Respondent in the United States Court of Appeals for the Second Circuit on November 8, 1974, which sought review of the then current orders suspending trading in Canadian Javelin Ltd., which, as noted previously, was the only security which Respondent owned which continued to be the subject of a current trading suspension order. The second was that in the latter part of December, 1974, Respondent submitted at least 293 applications on Form 211, a form promulgated in accordance with the S.E.C.

9. That case was filed in this Court under Docket No. 76-58. Page 4, n. 3 of the brief in opposition filed by the S.E.C. states that a copy of the appendix in the court of appeals in that case "is being lodged in this Court." The appendix contains a copy of all pleadings, transcripts, and pertinent court filings.

Rule 15c2-11, requesting permission to resume quotations in various securities which had previously been suspended by the S.E.C. The National Quotation Bureau, in accordance with an agreement it had worked out with the S.E.C. with regard to the filing of Forms 211, forwarded all of these listing applications to the S.E.C., which responded by filing a suit in the district court which requested an injunction on the grounds that Respondent was threatening to violate Rule 15c2-11 and to publish quotations in securities which had previously been suspended by the S.E.C.[10] Rather than file this suit with the clerk of the

10. The complaint filed by the S.E.C. had two counts: one count dealing with listing applications filed for previously suspended securities and the other count dealing with a letter written by Respondent to the S.E.C. dated November 6, 1974, which stated that henceforth Respondent would refuse to show his personal books and records to the S.E.C. and which cited the Fourth Amendment as the basis for his refusal. Memoranda released to Respondent pursuant to the Freedom of Information Act including the memorandum in which the S.E.C. staff requested permission to institute suit make it clear that the decision to sue was actually triggered by the listing applications. Subsequently, however, that aspect of the suit dealing with Respondent's refusal to show his personal books and records to the S.E.C. became more important because the temporary restraining order which Judge Ward signed on December 30, 1974 effectively extinguished Respondent's listing applications and therefore mooted that part of the case. The affidavit of Ira Spindler filed by the S.E.C. in support of its request for a temporary restraining order, stated, in part, the following:

> "7. On December 18, 1974, the NQB, publishers of the Pink Sheets, forwarded to this office applications submitted by Sloan to quote the shares of Franklin New York Corp. ('Franklin') and Triex International Corp. ('Triex'). Each of these issues had been suspended from trading in the over-the-counter market by the Commission. Franklin was suspended for the period May 13, 1974 through October 31, 1974 and Triex for the period December 15, 1972 through December 19, 1973. There apparently is no current financial information available either.
>
> **********
>
> 15. Defendant Sloan & Co. and Sloan are and have been in violation of the requirements for initiating over-the-counter quotations of the Exchange Act and Rule promulgated thereunder. Sloan's submission for publication of quotations, for securities for which he does not possess reasonable information under Rule 15c2-11, places the public in jeopardy. Unless defendant Sloan & Co. and Sloan are enjoined, members of the public may become victims of an unscrupulous scheme."

Southern District of New York in the normal manner, where it would have been assigned by lot to a judge in accordance with Rule 4(A) or the Calendar Rules of the Southern District of New York and most likely thereafter would have been reassigned to Judge Griesa before whom the other case was pending and where the S.E.C. had requested several extentions of time and was adopting delaying tactics, the S.E.C. took its complaint directly to Judge Ward's chambers and asked him to take jurisdiction over that case since he had been the judge in the previous case brought by the S.E.C. against Respondent. Judge Ward agreed to do so and the same day signed a temporary restraining order. Subsequent attempts by Respondent to disqualify Judge Ward on the grounds of bias and prejudice and on the grounds that this case had not been properly assigned in accordance with the Calendar Rules of the Southern District of New York proved unsuccessful. After Judge Ward signed the temporary restraining order, he entered a preliminary injunction on January 14, 1975, without an evidentiary hearing, and subsequently found Respondent to be in "civil contempt" for failing to produce his books and records in a place "easily accessible" to the S.E.C., as a result of which the United States Court of Appeals for the Second Circuit dismissed three appeals which had been taken by Respondent from injunctions obtained by the S.E.C. *See S.E.C. v. Sloan,* 538 F. 2d 313 (2d Cir. 1976), *cert. denied* 429 U.S. 1023 (1976). Although no reason was given by the court of appeals for that decision it appears from the case which the court cited that it determined *sua sponte* that Respondent was a "fugitive from justice" in view of his continuing to be held in civil contempt for failure to make his books and records easily accessible to the S.E.C.[11]

11. Assuming that was, in fact, the basis for the decision of the court of appeals, and the Solicitor General claimed it was in a brief filed in this Court in opposition to the Petition for Writ of Certiorari in *Sloan v. S.E.C.,* No.

Although three appeals which had been filed by Respondent were dismissed *sua sponte* by the court of appeals, a number of other appeals which were also pending during the period in which Judge Ward had adjudged Respondent to be in "civil contempt" were unaffected. One of these was the petition for review of the orders suspending trading in Canadian Javelin Ltd. which, as noted previously, was filed on November 8, 1974. That appeal was decided on October 15, 1975, at a time when Respondent was just as much in contempt of court as he was on January 6, 1976, when a different panel of judges dismissed three other appeals. The decision of the court of appeals is reported as *Sloan v. S.E.C.*, 527 F. 2d 11 (2d Cir. 1975), *cert. denied* 426 U.S. 935 (1976). Why the court of appeals summarily dismissed three appeals on January 6, 1976 and yet made a decision on another appeal on October 15, 1975 and allowed four other appeals to remain on the calendar unaffected has never been explained.

At the time of the decision of the court of appeals dated October 15, 1975, the orders suspending trading in Canadian Javelin Ltd. which the petition dated November 8, 1974 ask to be reviewed, had long since expired. Those orders had been superseded by subsequent orders which had the effect of continuing the trading suspension until January 26, 1975. The S.E.C. initially announced that it was going to terminate the trading suspension on January 12, 1975, but at the earnest request of Canadian Javelin Ltd. and a number of its stockholders, the S.E.C. agreed to extend the trading ban until the January 26th date.[12]

76-365, although the S.E.C. did not make this or any other contention in the court of appeals, the decision of that panel of the court of appeals is in conflict with a decision of another judge of that court with regard to what constitutes being a "fugitive from justice." See *United States v. Salzmann*, 548 F. 2d 395, 403 n. 2 (2d Cir. 1976) (Feinberg, J., concurring).

12. These developments are described in the Securities Exchange Releases listed in footnote 3, *supra*.

Canadian Javelin Ltd. even went so far as to file a motion for a temporary restraining order and a preliminary injunction enjoining the S.E.C. from lifting its trading suspension in a suit before Judge MacMahon in the Southern District of New York entitled *S.E.C. v. Canadian Javelin Ltd.*, 73 Civil 5074. After Judge MacMahon signed an order to show cause staying the S.E.C. from lifting its trading suspension and setting the matter down for a hearing, the S.E.C. agreed to extend the trading suspension and Canadian Javelin Ltd. withdrew its motion by stipulation. The reason given in the motion papers filed by Canadian Javelin Ltd. for its request of the extention of the trading suspension was that it needed time to prepare an "orderly market." Ironically, after giving officials of Canadian Javelin Ltd. time to prepare an "orderly market", the S.E.C. subsequently filed an injunctive suit alleging that a market manipulation took place when trading was allowed to resume. See *S.E.C. v. Doyle, et al*, Civil Action No. 76-1882 (S.D.N.Y.).

On February 3, 1975, eight days after the S.E.C. lifted its trading ban it filed in the court of appeals a "suggestion" that the court of appeals dismiss the petition for review of the trading suspension orders filed by Respondent as "moot." This suggestion was not in the form of a formal motion but rather was filed in response to a motion by Respondent for various relief including an order requiring the S.E.C. to file in the court of appeals the original record rather than a certified list. The S.E.C.'s claim that the case was moot was based on the assertion that there was then no order suspending trading in Canadian Javelin Ltd. currently in effect. The court of appeals took no action on the S.E.C.'s "suggestion," although on February 21, 1975 it denied the motion to require the S.E.C. to file the original record, which by that time the S.E.C. had filed anyway.

Subsequently, on April 29, 1975 at 3:45 p.m. EDT, the S.E.C. resuspended trading in Canadian Javelin Ltd. This development forced the S.E.C. to come up with a new argument on the point of mootness. In its brief filed in the court of appeals on the merits, the S.E.C. argued that although there was then in effect an order suspending trading in Canadian Javelin Ltd., that order was not part of the same series of orders which included the orders that the petition for review had challenged. In addition, argued the S.E.C., the reason for the first series of suspension orders was different from the reason for the second series of suspension orders as a result of which the question of the propriety of the first series of suspension orders was moot. The S.E.C. did not, however, offer any evidence showing the reason for the second series of trading suspension orders. Although the brief filed by the S.E.C. devoted considerable attention to its mootness argument, the decision subsequently handed down by the court of appeals did not discuss the question of mootness. However, by dismissing the petition for review "without prejudice", the court of appeals made it clear that it regarded the mootness argument as meritless.

The decision of the court of appeals to dismiss the proceeding "without prejudice" came as a result of a statement made by counsel for the S.E.C. during the course of oral argument to the effect that the S.E.C. was willing to grant Respondent some sort of administrative hearing. This statement constituted a substantial concession at the time because at the outset of the oral argument the first question from the bench was, "What remedy does Mr. Sloan have?" and the reply by counsel for the S.E.C., Michael J. Stewart, Esq., was, "He doesn't have any." This statement precipitated a series of further questions from the panel as a result of which it became apparent that unless the S.E.C. changed its position it was going to be faced with an immediate adverse ruling by the court. This led counsel for the S.E.C., in effect, to offer Respondent the opportunity for an administrative hearing. Whether the attorney for the S.E.C. was authorized to make this offer is not clear.[13]

Immediately upon receipt of the decision of the court of appeals dated October 15, 1975 Respondent wrote to the S.E.C. and requested the promised administrative hearing. A copy of this request is included as Appendix B to this brief.[14] The Secretary of the S.E.C., George A. Fitzsimmons, Jr., responded with a statement that this letter would not be acted upon because it was not verified or properly formulated. A copy of this response is included as Appendix C to this brief.[15] Respondent thereafter submitted to the S.E.C. a "verified petition for review" in ac-

13. The practice of the United States Court of Appeals for the Second Circuit is to make a tape recording of all oral arguments. These tapes are retained for the convenience of the judges and the parties to the case are not permitted to hear a tape or order a transcript. Dissatisfaction with this state of affairs led Respondent to file in this Court a motion for leave to file apetition for a writ of mandamus. See *Sloan v. Mulligan, mandamus denied* 429 U.S. 1059 (1977). In the case at bar, the result might turn on the contents of these tapes and consequently Respondent hereby requests this Court to ask the court of appeals to transmit the tape of the oral argument described above.

14. The procedure of including documents such as this in the appendix to a brief is admittedly irregular. However, in this case the proceedings before the S.E.C. were not contested in the normal sense and consequently Respondent was not allowed to participate in the decision of what should be included in the record. With the exception of one document, which is a verified petition for review filed by Respondent, the record consists entirely of trading suspension orders issued by the S.E.C. and memoranda requesting their issuance. Thus, the exchange of correspondence between Respondent and the Secretary of the S.E.C., although germane to the issues involved in this case and although referred to in the opinion of the court of appeals (Pet. App. B, p. 10a), are not part of the formal record. They were, however, available to the court of appeals because copies of this correspondence was forwarded to the court of appeals by the parties and included in the file maintained by the court of appeals under Docket No. 74-2457, which was the first petition for review. Thus, Appendix B to this brief is a document which the court of appeals read and relied upon and its inclusion in this brief is not improper since otherwise this Court would not be able to read it.

15. This letter is included in this brief for the same reasons as those given in footnote 14, *supra*.

cordance with the requirements set forth in the letter from George A. Fitzsimmons, Jr. (App. 114-118). The S.E.C. states that this petition was received on March 15, 1976 (App. 120). The S.E.C. did not act on this petition immediately but instead issued four more trading suspension orders and held off a decision so as to coincide with the issuance of the last trading suspension order. That order was issued on April 21, 1976 and suspended trading in Canadian Javelin for ten more days from April 23, 1976 until May 2, 1976 (App. 109-110).

On April 23, 1976, the day Respondent received the April 21, 1976 order and also the first day of the last ten-day trading suspension period, Respondent filed a petition for review in the United States Court of Appeals for the Second Circuit and simultaneously filed a proposed order to show cause and a motion for a stay of the order of the S.E.C., for an expedited review, and for an order requiring the S.E.C. to file the record forthwith (App. 123-127). This motion was not acted upon by the court of appeals. Respondent later learned from Edward Guidaro, the motion clerk for the court of appeals, and from his deputy clerk, Art Heller, that the reason no action was taken on this motion was that an attorney from the Office of General Counsel of the S.E.C. had called them and informed them that trading in Canadian Javelin Ltd. was going to be allowed to resume at the termination of the then current ten-day trading suspension order and that no action should be taken on Respondent's motion for that reason. However, Respondent himself was not informed that the trading suspension would terminate until the S.E.C. publically announced this six days later.[16]

16. See Securities Exchange Release No. 12394, 9 SEC Docket 509 (April 29, 1976). Had Respondent or anyone else learned the plans of the S.E.C. prior to this public announcement, they could have made a substantial profit by buying shares of Canadian Javelin Ltd. on the Vancouver Stock Exchange since the market price, predictably, nearly doubled when the S.E.C. announced that its trading suspension was about to terminate.

Under Rule 17(a) of the Federal Rules of Appellate Procedure, the S.E.C. had 40 days to file the record with the court of appeals. However, the S.E.C. did not file the record but instead filed a certified list on June 4, 1976, two days later than the time permitted by the rule.(The appendix filed by the S.E.C. in this Court includes what is purported to be a docket sheet which contains an entry that on June 4, 1976 "Documents comprising the record" were filed (App. i). In fact, the actual docket sheet in the court of appeals states that on June 4, 1976 a "certified list of documents comprising the record" was filed). A brief was filed by Respondent but the S.E.C. moved for an extension of time to file its answering brief (App. 128). This motion was granted but the court of appeals did not give the full amount of time requested by the S.E.C. The S.E.C. then filed a motion to dismiss the appeal on the ground of mootness and requested that if the motion be denied the court grant a second extension of time to file its brief and that the court adjourn the oral argument, which had by that time been scheduled (App. 129-130). The court of appeals, however, treated the motion in part as a motion for an extension of time and denied that part of the motion and set the motion to dismiss on the grounds of mootness for argument on the same date as the argument of the appeal (App. 131). Thus, the S.E.C. was forced to file a brief, which it did on October 12, 1976, the day before the oral argument and well after the time which had been set by the court for the filing of its brief had expired. The shortness of time between the filing of the S.E.C.'s brief and the date of the oral argument before the court of appeals precluded Respondent from putting in a reply brief.

When the time came for the oral argument of the appeal, the attorney who appeared to argue on behalf of the S.E.C., David Ferber, insisted on sitting at the table on the left hand side facing the bench so as to go first and argue his motion to dismiss the appeal as moot and asked the court to decide that motion prior to hearing the argument of the appeal. The court, however, denied the request of counsel for the S.E.C. that he be permitted to argue first but allowed him to sit at the table on the left hand side, there being no objection on that point from Respondent. The court then heard argument on the two cases which had been scheduled for argument at that time. The first was Case No. 75-4087, which was an appeal from an order of the S.E.C. revoking Respondent's broker-dealer registration and barring Respondent from being associated with any broker or dealer. The second was Case No. 76-4110, which was a petition for review of a series of 37 consecutive trading suspension orders. Treating these cases as having been consolidated, the court subsequently rendered a decision which is reported as *Sloan v. S.E.C.*, 547 F. 2d 152 (2d Cir. 1976).

On the case concerning the decision of the S.E.C. to revoke Respondent's broker-dealer registration and to bar Respondent from being associated with any broker or dealer, the court apparently did not review the 1,286-page-long record and determine whether or not the findings of the S.E.C. were supported by substantial evidence. Instead, it based its decision on the entry of two injunctions by Judge Ward, one of which had subsequently been vacated when the underlying case was dismissed as moot, the two injunctions being an injunction entered on January 18, 1974 which pertained to record-keeping and net capital violations found to have been committed by Respondent in the years 1971-1973 and a preliminary injunction which had been entered without an evidentiary hearing on January 14, 1975, which enjoined Respondent from publishing quotations in certain securities which had been previously been suspended by the S.E.C. and which ordered Respondent to produce his books and records for inspection by the S.E.C. in "an easily accessible place." With respect to these two injunctions, the court of appeals said (Pet. App. B, p. 7a):

> "Each of these injunctions was in itself a sufficient ground to support the revocation of Sloan's broker-dealer license under §15(b)(5)(c)of the 1934 Act."

With respect to the case which sought review of a series of 37 consecutive trading suspension orders, the court rejected the S.E.C.'s contention that the case had become moot with the expiration of the last order and decided that all but the first of these orders had been issued illegally. The court therefore vacated all but the first order. After determining that the practice followed by the S.E.C. was illegal and that all but the first order should be vacated, the court of appeals stated (Pet. App. B, p. 17a):

> "The S.E.C. is, therefore, directed to discontinue forthwith its adoption and use of successive ten-day suspension orders to order the suspension of trading in a security for an extended period, i.e. in excess of 10 days.
>
> Is is so ordered."

Both sides petitioned for a rehearing and suggested that the rehearing be en banc. Due to the objections by the S.E.C. to certain language in the decision, the court of appeals struck certain passages as "not necessary to the decision in the case" and modified the decision accordingly (Pet. App. B, p. 20a). Otherwise, the petitions for rehearing and suggestions that the rehearing be en banc were denied. Both sides then petitioned this Court for certiorari. The petition for certiorari filed by Respondent was denied but the petition for certiorari filed by the S.E.C. was granted. A subsequent petition for rehearing filed by Respondent was also denied.

SUMMARY OF ARGUMENT

The court of appeals had the authority to enjoin future successive trading suspension orders. This case is not moot as to Respondent whether viewed narrowly in his capacity as a stockholder of Canadian Javelin Ltd. or viewed in Respondent's capacity as an investor generally, or viewed in Respondent's capacity as a frustrated short-seller, or even viewed in Respondent's capacity as a former market maker and broker-dealer in securities specializing in trading in shares of Canadian Javelin Ltd. The harm to a person in the position of Respondent would clearly be one which is "capable of repetition, yet evading review" and Respondent would be without remedies were this case to be declared moot. Even were that not true, the S.E.C.'s delaying tactics precluded review of the trading suspension orders while they were in effect and the S.E.C. should not be permitted to benefit from its own delays. Moreover, the arguments presented by the S.E.C. in this Court on the subject of mootness are totally different and alien from the arguments presented by the S.E.C. to the court of appeals and the S.E.C., in its position as a defeated party, is barred from asserting new arguments in this Court which it did not assert in the court of appeals. Moreover, assuming *arguendo* that this case is moot, that would not entitle the S.E.C. to the relief it is seeking, which is a vacatur of the decision and order of the court of appeals. Rather, the petition would be dismissed and the decision of the court of appeals would stand as a declaratory judgment barring the S.E.C. from resuming its practice of issuing successive ten-day trading suspension orders.

The contentions of the S.E.C.. regarding statutory construction must be rejected. The principles cited by the S.E.C. regarding statutory construction only apply when the statute itself is ambiguous, which is not the case here since the statute expressly limits the authority of the S.E.C. to suspending trading in a security "for a period not exceeding ten days." Most of the cases cited by the S.E.C. deal with the deference which must be given to the agency's construction of its own rules. The "administrative deference rule" only applies when the administrative agency has issued binding, consistant, official interpretations of the statute over a long period of time which has not occurred here. The S.E.C. has never issued a formal opinion explaining the legal basis for its practice of issuing successive trading suspension orders and this Court is not permitted to accept the rationalization by appellate counsel for the S.E.C.'s actions. None of the cases cited by the S.E.C. stand for the proposition that an agency can expand its own jurisdiction as the S.E.C. has attempted to do here. Even the S.E.C. does not contend that when Congress passed the Securities Exchange Act in 1934 and incorporated the trading suspension power therein, it intended to give the S.E.C. the power to suspend trading in a security for an indefinite time period. The statute, when read as a whole, makes it clear that the determination by the court of appeals of the intent of Congress is correct and it is apparent that when it created the trading suspension power Congress omitted the notice and hearing requirements found in analogous sections of the Securities Exchange Act because it intended the summary trading suspension power to be an emergency power to be used only for periods of short duration, i.e. ten days or less. The S.E.C.'s claim that it is necessary to have the power to suspend trading for an extended period is appropriately addressed to Congress and not to the courts.

The record of this case establishes that the S.E.C. abused its authority and acted with improper motives and that the suspension of trading for a period of more than one year did not serve the public interest and only served the interests of the S.E.C. Assuming *arguendo* that there exist circumstances under which the S.E.C. may legally follow a ten-day trading suspension order with another ten-day trading suspension order, these circumstances were not present in this case. The record of this case establishes that the orders of the S.E.C. were not supported by substantial evidence or, for that matter, any evidence at all. Thus, even if there is some merit to the contentions advanced by the S.E.C., the court of appeals acted correctly in vacating the trading suspension orders which are the subject of this case.

Finally, notwithstanding the above, assuming *arguendo* that the exercise of the trading suspension power in this case was valid on statutory and evidentiary grounds, the issuance of successive ten-day trading suspension orders so as to suspend trading in a security for an indefinite time period is unconstitutional. For that matter, even a single summary trading suspension order without notice or a hearing violates the Constitution. The trading suspension power is an unconstitutional delegation of legislative power because Congress has provided no standards to the administrative agency and because Congress may not delegate to an administrative agency the broad authority to decide what is in the "public interest" and "for the protection of investors" without standards on which to base that decision. No important governmental interest is served by a securities trading suspension, particularly by the trading suspensions which are the subject of this case, and the interference with property rights which a trading suspension entails without notice and the opportunity for a hearing is unconstitutional. In addition, the exercise of the summary trading suspension power is unconstitutional as being arbitrary and capricious.

ARGUMENT

I

THE COURT OF APPEALS HAD THE AUTHORITY TO VACATE PAST TRADING SUSPENSION ORDERS AND TO ENJOIN FUTURE SUCCESSIVE TRADING SUSPENSION ORDERS

The order of this Court granting certiorari specifically requested the parties to brief and argue the question of the possibility of mootness (App. 213) and for that reason the bulk of the argument in this brief will be devoted to that question. However, the reply brief filed by the S.E.C. in support of the petition for a writ of certiorari raised a question of such fundamental importance that it should be addressed first. That reply brief stated (pp. 1-2):

> "This case arose on petition for review of a series of 10-day suspension orders issued by the Commission (Pet. App. B, p. 8a). On petition for review of an order of the Commission, the reviewing court's jurisdiction is limited to the power 'to affirm or modify and enforce or to set aside the order ***.' Section 25(a)(3) of the Act, 48 Stat. 902, as amended, 15 U.S.C. (Supp. V) 78y(a)(3). The court of appeals, however, did not limit its relief to the orders before it. Instead, the court in its opinion 'directed (the Commission) to discontinue forthwith its adoption and use of successive ten-day suspension orders to order the suspension of trading in a security for an extended period, i.e., in excess of ten days' and concluded '(i)t is so ordered' (Pet. App. B, p. 17a).
>
> ---
>
> 1. The judgment could not have been intended merely to set aside particular suspension orders, for the series of such orders that respondent challenged had terminated even before oral argument was heard (see Pet. 11)."

Essentially, the contention of the S.E.C. is that the decision and order of the court of appeals was unlawful in that it exceeded authorized judicial power. It should be noted that the S.E.C. did not make this claim in the petition for rehearing and suggestion that the rehearing be en banc it filed in the court of appeals nor did it make this claim in the petition for a writ of certiorari or in its brief on the merits. Thus, it seems possible that the decision to raise this argument was hastily made and has since been reversed.[17] Nevertheless, this argument raises questions of such importance that it must be addressed.

The S.E.C. misreads, or, to put it more accurately, misrepresents § 25(a)(3) of the Securities Exchange Act when it states that this section limits the jurisdiction of the court of appeals to the power to affirm, modify, enforce or set aside the order. Nowhere in §25(a)(3) is the word "limit" or any equivalent term to be found. It is true that §25(a)(3) does not specifically authorize a court of appeals to enjoin future orders, but it need not do so, because that authority is provided in other sections of the United States Code and in the inherent equitable power of the courts.

For example, the All Writs Act, 28 U.S.C. §1651(a), provides that, "all courts established by Act of Congress may issue all writs necessary or appropriate in aid of their respective jurisdictions." The application of this statute to the instant case is clear. The court of appeals found that the practice of the S.E.C. of issuing consecutive summary trading suspension orders was illegal. It also found that the harm to Respondent was one "capable of repetition, yet evading review." Faced with this situation, it had no

17. Indeed, were the S.E.C. to prevail on this claim, its so-called "enforcement program" wherein it often seeks what is called "ancillary relief" not specifically authorized by the Securities Exchange Act, cf. *S.E.C. v. General Host Corp.*, 438 F. Supp. 105, 109 (S.D.N.Y. 1977) (a request that a district court order the donation of certain funds to charity), might suffer a severe setback.

choice but to issue a judgment which would prevent the illegal activities of the S.E.C. from recurring. This judgment was "necessary in aid of" the jurisdiction of the court of appeals. Had the court of appeals stopped short of what it did and merely vacated the by then expired trading suspension orders, the S.E.C. could simply have started a new series of trading suspension orders, and had Respondent successfully challenged that series of orders, it could have started yet another series and so on. Thus, if the S.E.C. were correct that a court of appeals lacks the power to enjoin future successive trading suspension orders, the result would be that the courts would be powerless to halt a clearly illegal practice.

The authority of the court of appeals to act as it did can also be found in the Declaratory Judgment Act, 28 U.S.C. §2201. This statute provides, "In case of actual controversy within its jurisdiction . . . any court of the United States may declare the rights and other legal relations of any party seeking such declaration. . . . Any such declaration shall have the force and effect of a final judgment . . . ." In its opinion, the court of appeals stated (Pet. App. B, pp. 16a-17a):

> "We declare that the successive roll-over ten-day suspension procedure erroneously adopted by the S.E.C. was improperly pursued and was contrary to the statutory provisions for summary suspensions in force April 30, 1975 to May 2, 1976."

This statement had the effect of a declaratory judgment. In that section of its brief dealing with mootness, the S.E.C. contends that the court of appeals lacked jurisdiction to make this statement. However, the court of appeals merely declared the rights and legal relations of the parties, something it was empowered by statute to do.

The authority of the court of appeals to do what it did may be found in other statutory provisions as well, such as §703 of the Administrative Procedure Act, 5 U.S.C. §703, and even §21(e) of the Securities Exchange Act, 15 U.S.C. §78 *u*(e). In the latter case, it has been established through *J.I. Case Co. v. Borak,* 377 U.S. 426, 432 (1964) that a private litigant, as well as the S.E.C., can sue for equitable relief under this section. Moreover, §3(a)(9) of the Securities Exchange Act, 15 U.S.C. §78*c*(a)(9), defines a "person" as "a natural person, company, government, or political subdivision, agency, or instrumentality of a government." Since the S.E.C. is a government agency and therefore a person as defined by the Securities Exchange Act and since §21(d), 15 U.S.C. §78*u*(d), authorizes the bringing of injunctive suits against "persons" for violations of the Securities Exchange Act, in this case the violation being the suspension of trading in a security for a period exceeding ten days in violation of §12(k) of the Act, it follows that the S.E.C. can be enjoined from threatened future conduct under §21(d) and §21(e) of the Securities Exchange Act.

When the S.E.C. argues that the court of appeals lacked jurisdiction to vacate past consecutive trading suspension orders and at the same time the court of appeals lacked the power to enjoin future consecutive trading suspension orders, what it is really saying is that the question of whether or not it is legal for the S.E.C. to issue consecutive trading suspension orders is of no moment because in any event the courts are powerless to do anything about it or even to make a declaration as to whether the practice is legal. It is submitted that this claim must be rejected.[18]

18. It must be remembered that the other possible remedy available to Respondent, namely a suit against the S.E.C. for declaratory and injunctive relief and money damages was already tried and there the S.E.C. prevailed as the result of a number of arguments, one of them being that Respondent's "exclusive remedy" if he felt aggrieved by a trading suspension order was to file a petition for review in a court of appeals.

II

THIS CASE IS NOT MOOT

A

When this case was argued in the court of appeals and the attorney for the S.E.C. stood up and commenced his argument that this case was moot, Judge Gurfein asked, "But isn't this just like the old Southern Pacific Terminal case?" The attorney for the S.E.C. was unable to respond to the question. In this Court as well, the S.E.C. does not respond to the statement made in the decision of the court of appeals, which said (Pet. App. B, p. 16a):

> "Because of the S.E.C.'s continuing policy of roll-over ten-day suspension orders, the harm to him was 'capable of repetition yet evading review.' *Southern Pacific Terminal Company v. ICC,* 219 U.S. 498 (1911)."

Neither the petition for a writ of certiorari nor the brief for the S.E.C. on the merits cite or make any reference to the authoritative *Southern Pacific Terminal* decision where this Court stated that "short term orders, capable of repetition, yet evading review" would not be declared moot. 219 U.S. at 515. Instead, the S.E.C. discusses other decisions cited by the court of appeals such as *Sosna v. Iowa,* 419 U.S. 393 (1975) which, it says, is distinguishable because that was a class action. The S.E.C. also studiously avoids another decision of this Court more recent than any of the cases it cites, namely *Nebraska Press Association v. Stuart,* 417 U.S. 539, 546-547 (1976), which is contrary to the position of the S.E.C. Returning to Judge Gurfein's remark that this case is "just like the old Southern Pacific Terminal case", it can be seen that the facts of this case are far more similar to the facts of that case than any of the intervening cases cited by the S.E.C. of the point of mootness. This is not surprising since the petitioner in the instant case assumed many of the powers of the type vested in the Interstate Commerce Commission, which issued the "short term orders" which were the subject of that case. There, the Interstate Commerce Commission issued numerous short term orders which expired by their terms before judicial review could be obtained and, consequently, these orders would have been unreviewable had any attempt to seek review been declared moot upon expiration of the order. Hence, this Court declared in that case that attempts to seek review of "short term orders, capable of repetition, yet evading review" would not be declared moot and that decision clearly controls here. Ergo, this case is not moot.

The case presented here is even less susceptible to a mootness argument than *Southern Pacific Terminal v. ICC*. There, the order being challenged had a life span of two years. Here, the orders being challenged had each a duration of only ten days. In other respects, the cases are quite similar. There, this Court noted that although the government was contending that the case was moot, the government was not like a private litigant which can settle a controversy at any time, because it has no power "as a substantial trustee for the public under the act of Congress" to extinguish the rights of the public. 211 U.S. at 516. It also said that "the object of the suit is to have declared illegal an order of the Interstate Commerce Commission [and that] the defendants should be enjoined for the future" from issuing such orders and this "broader consideration" defeated any claim that the case was moot. 211 U.S. at 515. The instant case was instituted for the same reason and is thus indistinguishable from *Southern Pacific Terminal v. ICC* and cannot be declared moot. Of course, the S.E.C. neatly avoids this problem by not even mentioning *Southern Pacific Terminal* in its entire brief, although purporting to brief and argue the question of mootness.

B

As this case has wended its way through various court proceedings, the S.E.C. has concocted a variety of arguments which seem to be designed to confuse the issue in order to avoid the irrefutable logic set forth above. In this Court, for example, on page 19, note 9, of its brief, the S.E.C. proffers a mathematical formula which it claims supports its conclusion that this case is moot. This formula was not presented to the court below nor were any of the arguments made on pages 17-19 of the S.E.C.'s brief made previously. It is a well established judicial rule that a defeated litigant may not present to an appellate court arguments which were not presented to the court below and the S.E.C. has violated that rule here. Conversely, the prevailing litigant is allowed to present to an appellate court arguments which he did not make previously. However, in this case, Respondent, unlike the S.E.C., is entirely satisfied with the arguments he made in the court below and therefore will not present new arguments here. Since the S.E.C. is bound by the arguments it presented to the lower court, it is appropriate to look at the arguments the S.E.C. made there and see how they contrast and conflict with the arguments the S.E.C. now presents to this Court.

As noted previously, the first proceeding instituted by Respondent to challenge the validity of S.E.C. trading suspension orders was a suit filed in the United States District Court for the Southern District of New York on June 27, 1974. The complaint in that action complained of trading suspensions in a total of nine different securities.[19] The securities in question were Old Town Corp. common,

19. As noted in footnote 9, *supra*, the appendix in the court of appeals to that case was lodged in this Court by the office of the Solicitor General. If it is still here, the pleadings are thus available to this Court.

Sheffield Watch Corp. convertible debentures, Applied Devices Corp. common, Sav-On Inc. common, Seaferro Inc. common, Canadian Javelin Ltd. common, Stirling Homex preferred, Stirling Homex common and Triex International Corp. common. The complaint alleged that Respondent owned all of these securities with the exception of Triex International Corp. in which Respondent had a short position of 800 shares. However, at a pre-trial conference held in Judge Greisa's chambers on September 18, 1974, counsel for the S.E.C. contended that the case was moot with respect to all securities except for Canadian Javelin Ltd. since the suspension of trading in all of the other securities listed in the complaint had by then expired. In addition, counsel for the S.E.C. repeated an argument which was set forth as the "Third Affirmative Defense" in the answer filed by the S.E.C. which stated:

> "19. The complaint purports to state a claim against the Securities and Exchange Commission. Congress has never declared that the Commission can be sued in its own name apart from having its orders reviewed in courts of appeal. Accordingly, this Court does not have jurisdiction of the claims made against the Securities and Exchange Commission, *eo nomine.*"

On November 8, 1974, Respondent filed a petition for review in the United States Court of Appeals for the Second Circuit which sought review of the then current orders which suspended trading in Canadian Javelin Ltd.[20] Upon the filing of this petition, the S.E.C. had 40 days under Rule 17(a) of the Federal Rules of Appellate Procedure to file the record in the court of appeals. As is its custom, the S.E.C. did not comply with the time re-

20. The petition for review was filed on November 8, 1974. It sought review of orders dated November 29, 1973, September 5, 1974, September 15, 1974, September 25, 1974, October 5, 1974, October 15, 1974, October 25, 1974, and November 4, 1974. A copy of the petition is included as Appendix D to the petition for a writ of certiorari filed in *Sloan v. S.E.C.*, No. 75-1507.

quirements of this rule.[21] On December 23, 1974, the S.E.C. did file something but rather than file the record, it filed a certified list. On January 22, 1975, Respondent then moved for an order requiring the S.E.C. to file the full record and while this motion was pending the series of orders suspending trading in Canadian Javelin Ltd. terminated. Eight days later, the S.E.C. filed a "suggestion" that the petition for review be dismissed as moot.

At that point the S.E.C. claimed that the case was moot because no order suspending trading in Canadian Javelin Ltd. was currently in effect. However, on April 29, 1975, the S.E.C. was forced to come up with a new argument because on that date the S.E.C. resuspended trading in Canadian Javelin Ltd. When the time came for the S.E.C. to file its brief, it argued that the case was moot in spite of the fact that there was then in effect an order currently suspending trading in Canadian Javelin Ltd., because that order was part of a different series of orders from the series of orders which included the orders which Respondent had challenged in his petition for review. Furthermore, argued the S.E.C., the reason for the second series of suspension orders was different from the reason for the first series of suspension orders (in spite of the fact that the reason for the second series of suspension orders had at that point not been publicly announced).[22]

---

21. Characteristically, in this Court as well, the S.E.C. was twelve days late in filing its brief, in spite of the generous period of 45 days given by the rules of this Court, and no permission for this late filing was either requested or obtained.

22. Securities Exchange Act Release No. 11383, 6 SEC Docket 780 (April 29, 1975), which announced the first of the second series of trading suspension orders states:

> "The Commission instituted the suspension pending dissemination of information concerning regulatory action by Canadian authorities."

The release is included as Appendix D to the brief for Samuel H. Sloan in response to the petition for a writ of certiorari. The reason given in the brief filed by the S.E.C. for the second series of trading suspension orders, however, was different from that reason.

In the decision subsequently rendered, the court of appeals did not discuss the mootness arguments advanced by the S.E.C. for the obvious reason that the court considered these arguments to be frivolous. This is apparent from the fact that the court dismissed the petition "without prejudice" and, in effect, directed the S.E.C. to give Respondent "some sort of administrative hearing." Had the court of appeals agreed with the S.E.C. that the case was moot, it simply would have dismissed the petition.

The S.E.C. prevailed in that first action largely as a result of its own delaying tactics and its attempts to frustrate the judicial process. Had the S.E.C. complied with the time requirements of Rule 17(a) of the Federal Rules of Appellate Procedure, it would have filed a record by December 18, 1974. Assuming Respondent filed his brief immediately thereafter and the S.E.C. departed from its usual practice of asking for an extension of time to file its brief, final briefs would have been filed and the case could have been argued prior to January 26, 1975, when the first series of trading suspension orders terminated.[23] The record filed by the S.E.C. consisted of photocopies of trading suspension orders and excised memoranda, the latter of which purported to set forth the reasons for the trading suspensions. In fact, the excised memoranda had significant portions deleted and these deletions were signified by blank white spaces at a place which had obviously been occupied previously by a paragraph or sentence and the names of all employees of the S.E.C. were deleted. Thus, as the court of appeals aptly noted,

23. This brief has adopted the consistent practice of referring to the trading suspension which lasted from November 29, 1973 until January 26, 1975 as the first series of trading suspension orders. However, as noted previously, this was actually the third series of trading suspension orders since trading in Canadian Javelin Ltd. was previously suspended from March 17, 1971 until April 5, 1971 and again from March 7, 1972 until August 9, 1972.

the record filed by the S.E.C. was "insurmountably sparse." Faced with this record, which did not come close to qualifying as "substantial evidence" under §556(d) of the Administrative Procedure Act, 5 U.S.C. §556(d), but apparently unwilling abruptly to cut off the S.E.C.'s exercise of its trading suspension power, the court of appeals, incorrectly, it is submitted, dismissed the proceeding without prejudice, thereby giving the S.E.C. the opportunity to construct a proper administrative record to facilitate review of the trading suspension orders.

The decision made by the court of appeals stemmed from the argument advanced by the S.E.C. that Respondent had "failed to exhaust his administrative remedies," coupled with a statement made by the S.E.C. attorney who argued the appeal orally that the S.E.C. was willing to grant Respondent "some sort of administrative hearing." The decision of the court of appeals was an unfortunate one and was clearly incorrect since it said that it was making its decision for the purpose of "satisfying any possible exhaustion requirements" and stated, "We do not suggest, nor need we decide, that such a requirement necessarily exists," 527 F. 2d at 12, whereas the court of appeals had acquired jurisdiction over the case and had before it the question of whether an exhaustion of remedies requirement existed and it was duty bound to decide that question rather than dismiss the proceeding without prejudice. As a result of this erroneous decision of the court of appeals and as a result of further delaying tactics adopted by the S.E.C. both when Respondent sought an administrative hearing before the Commission and later when the second petition for review was filed in the court of appeals, the S.E.C. was able to continue for another year its illegal practice of suspending trading in securities for periods exceeding ten days.

Following the decision of the court of appeals, Respondent wrote to the S.E.C. and requested the promised administrative hearing and, in addition, petitioned this Court for writ of certiorari to review the decision of the court of appeals. In opposition to this petition for writ of certiorari, the Solicitor General filed a brief on behalf of the S.E.C. which stated:

> "No order of the Commission suspending trading in CJL stock is now in effect. Whether or not the Commission might ever again suspend trading in CJL stock is purely a matter of conjecture, as is the question whether petitioner, if that event should occur, would again claim to be aggrieved. Cf. *Securities & Exchange Commission v. Medical Committee for Human Rights,* 404 U.S. 403, 406. Accordingly, this case probably is moot.[8]
>
> ---
>
> 8. Because each suspension lasts but 10 days, a challenge to a single suspension might survive the suspension's expiration if it raised issues 'capable of repetition, yet evading review.' *Weinstein v. Bradford,* 423 U.S. 147, 148-149; *Southern Pacific Terminal Co. v. Interstate Commerce Commission,* 219 U.S. 498. The suspensions of CJL stock have aggregated lengthy periods however. Petitioner's reluctance to present his complaint to the Commission in the first instance, not the short duration of the Commission's orders, has frustrated effective judicial review here."

The exhaustion of remedies argument advanced by the S.E.C. which led to the first decision of the court of appeals was essentially fictitious. As the attorney for the S.E.C. stated at the beginning of oral argument in the court of appeals, there was no remedy available to a person in the position of Respondent. In addition, the brief filed by the S.E.C. in the court of appeals argued that Respondent lacked standing to challenge a trading suspension order and that the federal courts "probably" lack jurisdiction to review a trading suspension. Both arguments were rejected by the first panel of the court of appeals but had the S.E.C. succeeded with either of them, it would not have been obliged to give Respondent or, for that matter, anyone else a hearing. During the course of the oral argument before the court of appeals, when the attorney for the S.E.C. perceived which way the wind was blowing, he realized that he had better change his position if he wanted to avoid an immediate curtailment of the S.E.C.'s exercise of its trading suspension power. Thus, he began to speak in terms of giving Respondent an administrative hearing. Back at the Commission, however, the appropriate persons were unwilling to make any concessions which might infringe on the S.E.C.'s arbitrary exercise of its trading suspension authority. Thus, when Respondent wrote to the S.E.C. and requested an administrative hearing, he was predictably rebuffed. Thereafter, Respondent filed a verified petition for review of the trading suspension orders. At this point, knowing that Respondent was likely to go back to the court of appeals if the S.E.C. did not act on his petition favorably, the S.E.C. concocted a procedure which would enable it later to state to the court of appeals that a remedy was available and which at the same time would spare the S.E.C. the burden of having to conduct an administrative hearing and to allow it to maintain a shroud of secrecy over the reasons for its trading suspensions. This procedure, which is not authorized by any provision of the Securities Exchange Act, was publicly announced in the Securities Exchange Act Release No. 12361, 9 SEC Docket 482 (April 22, 1976) and is included as Appendix E to the petition (Pet. App. E, p. 24a). This procedure requires that, although the S.E.C. customarily does not give the reason for a continued trading suspension, a person seeking to have a trading suspension terminated must "set forth with particularity the facts upon which petitioner relies" after which the S.E.C. would determine if "there is a genuine issue as to any material fact." As Respondent pointed out in his verified petition to the S.E.C. (App. 114-115), this procedure is inadequate because:

> "To this date the S.E.C. has given no reason for its suspension of trading in Canadian Javelin Ltd. and since I do not know why the S.E.C. persists in suspending trading in Canadian Javelin Ltd. I cannot disprove any 'facts' upon which the suspensions are based. As I understand the Court of Appeals decision, the hearing which I have demanded should commence with testimony by the S.E.C. for the purpose of meeting the burden of proof which is properly on the S.E.C. to demonstrate that the suspensions of trading are legal. Only after cross-examination of the S.E.C.'s witness will I be in a position to know why the S.E.C. has suspended trading in Canadian Javelin Ltd. in the first instance and only then will I be in a position to rebut this testimony.

As §556(d) of the Administrative Procedure Act states:

> "Except as otherwise provided by statute, the proponent of a rule or order has the burden of proof . . . A sanction may not be imposed or rule or order issued except on consideration of the whole record of those parts thereof cited by a party and supported by and in accordance with reliable, probative and substantial evidence."

Since it is the S.E.C. that is the proponent of the rule or order in the case of a trading suspension order, it is clear that at a proper administrative hearing the S.E.C. would have the burden of proof and would be required to go first and produce evidence supporting the trading suspension. In this case the S.E.C. could not have done so because, as far as Respondent has been able to determine, no such evidence exists.

The procedure announced by the S.E.C. was also qualified by the following provision:

> "The Commission will not be disposed to grant any such petition if the petitioner or anyone affiliated with the petitioner shall fail to cooperate in supplying relevant information to the Commission or shall in any way obstruct any inquiry by the Commission into the relevant facts."

It should be noted that the decision of the S.E.C. administrative law judge to revoke Respondent's broker-dealer registration and bar him for life from being associated with any broker or dealer cited as a reason for this severe sanction "Sloan's uncooperative attitude." (See Pet. No. 76-1547, App. D, p. 19a). Respondent is not aware of what, if anything, the administrative law judge was referring to because he was at all times fully cooperative with the S.E.C. and its staff investigators at least during the period in which he was actively engaged in the business of being a securities broker-dealer.[24] The point is that what constitutes a cooperative or uncooperative attitude is clearly a subjective determination and by insisting that a person who wishes to petition the S.E.C. to terminate its trading suspension must fully cooperate with the S.E.C., the S.E.C. has revealed that the "remedy" it claims to have created is nothing more than a sham. It might be added that the S.E.C.'s typical response in analogous situations has been to retaliate against any person seeking to challenge the S.E.C.'s exercise of power. Considering the record the S.E.C. has established, it would not be surprising if the S.E.C. would retaliate against any person who requested the S.E.C. to terminate its trading suspension in a security. A characteristic sort of retaliation would be a claim that the person was somehow

24. On August 16, 1973, subsequent to the decision of the administrative law judge, Respondent voluntarily stopped doing an active securities business and ceased being a market maker in over-the-counter securities. This was due to the lack of trading volume in the over-the-counter market and financial losses relating to a meteoric rise in the price of Canadian Javelin Ltd. shares, in which Respondent held a substantial short position. Thereafter, the S.E.C. refused to allow Respondent to withdraw his broker-dealer registration, thereby burdening Respondent with the requirement to adhere to the recordkeeping and net capital requirements for registered broker-dealers which in turn prohibited Respondent from obtaining employment in other fields and developing outside sources of income. This circumstance led Respondent to write a letter to the S.E.C. dated November 6, 1974, referred to in footnote 10 *supra*, advising that he would no longer cooperate with the S.E.C. staff.

involved in the wrongdoing which brought about the trading suspension and accordingly an investigation or prosecution of him. Respondent, of course, did not have to worry that the S.E.C. was going to institute proceedings against him in retaliation for his challenge to the trading suspension orders, inasmuch as the S.E.C. was already prosecuting him to the fullest extent possible. It does seem, however, that the decision of the S.E.C. to invoke the Draconian penalty of a lifetime bar upon Respondent from "being associated with any broker or dealer" was in direct retaliation for remarks by Respondent which were critical of the S.E.C. and for his challenges to the S.E.C.'s exercise of power as opposed to any actual wrongdoing on the part of Respondent. See e.g. Pet. No. 76-1547, App. E, p. 28a-29a and n. 28.

After Respondent submitted his verified petition for review to the S.E.C., the S.E.C. had a number of strategic choices. It could have simply ignored the petition and allowed the trading suspension eventually to terminate, but in that case Respondent would no doubt have complained to the court of appeals that the S.E.C. had reneged on its promise to the court of appeals to grant Respondent "some sort of administrative hearing," and perhaps that court would have instituted disciplinary or other proceedings against the S.E.C. and its staff. It could have scheduled an administrative hearing, but this was an action it was apparently not prepared to take. It could have denied the petition and allowed the trading suspension to continue, in which case Respondent would have gone back to the court of appeals and the S.E.C. would not have been able to argue that the case was moot. Finally, the S.E.C. could have done what it did, which was to adopt the tactic best suited to depriving Respondent of the opportunity for an administrative hearing while at the same time placing the S.E.C. in the most favorable possible position to defeat any attempts at obtaining judicial review. The S.E.C. waited until it had decided to terminate the trading suspension, and in so doing issued four trading suspension orders after the receipt of the verified petition for review, and then denied the petition while simultaneously issuing its last trading suspension order. By so doing, the S.E.C. made certain that the series of trading suspension orders would terminate by the time the court of appeals could possibly pass upon their validity. The reason for this is that under Rule 17(a) of the Federal Rules of Appellate Procedure, the S.E.C. again had 40 days to file the record, whereas the last trading suspension order was due to expire in ten days. Thus, except in the unlikely event that the court of appeals was prepared to pass upon the validity of the trading suspension orders without seeing the orders themselves or the record upon which those orders were based, and except in the equally unlikely event that the court of appeals was prepared to convene, receive briefs, hear oral arguments and hand down a decision, all within the ten-day period during which the order would be in effect, the order would terminate before the court of appeals would be able to make a decision and consequently the S.E.C. would be able to argue that the case is moot. With regard to the first of the above considerations, the court of appeals may not even have had jurisdiction to decide the case prior to the filing of the record by the S.E.C. Section 15(c)(2) of the Securities Exchange Act, 15 U.S.C. §78*o*(c)(2), provides:

> "After the filing of a petition under this section, the court, under whatever conditions may be required and to the extent necessary to prevent irreparable injury, may issue all necesary and appropriate process to stay the order or rule or to preserve the status or rights pending its review; but . . . no such process may be issued by the court before the filing of the record or the material set forth in subsection (b)(2) of the section unless: (A) the Commission has denied a stay or failed grant requested relief, (B) a

reasonable period has expired since the filing of an application for a stay without a decision by the Commission, or (C) there was reasonable ground for failure to apply to the Commission."

Respondent, due to prior experience, was familiar with the tactics customarily adopted by the S.E.C. and did the only thing he could possibly do to obtain review of the last trading suspension order while it was still in effect, which was to file a proposed order to show cause with the court of appeals which asked that (1) the S.E.C. be ordered to file the record of this proceeding forthwith, (2) the current order of suspension of trading in Canadian Javelin Ltd. be stayed, and (3) the court of appeals grant expedited review (App. 123). It was necessary for the Respondent to request an order to show cause because the next regular motion day scheduled by the court of appeals would have come too late to permit review of the order of trading suspension within the ten-day period. Respondent's affidavit in support an order to show cause stated (App. 125):

> "The last time I presented this question to this court, the specific suspension orders I was protesting had long since expired by the time briefs were filed. This led the S.E.C. to contend that my petition for review was moot and that I had failed to exhaust my administrative remedies with respect to the orders which were then current. At the present time, however, the S.E.C. can make neither objection. On the other hand, if this court does not act expeditiously, the current order will expire on May 2, 1976, and after that date the S.E.C. will no doubt make the same argument which permitted it to prevail previously."

It is noteworthy that because of the shortness of time this effort could have succeeded if and only if a judge of the court of appeals had been prepared to sign the order to show cause. Had a judge signed the order to show cause, the S.E.C. would have been ordered to file the record forthwith and as soon as, but not until, it complied with this order, the court of appeals would have had exclusive jurisdiction to stay, modify or vacate the orders suspending trading in Canadian Javelin Ltd. Thus, had the order to show cause been signed, the court of appeals could conceivably have decided the case within ten days. There have been some cases, although few in number, where a court of appeals has acted this expeditiously. Even had the S.E.C. responded to the request for an order to show cause by filing written opposition, it might have felt constrained to make a concession which would foreclose a subsequent claim of mootness. Instead, the S.E.C. did something highly improper which Respondent was not told about until it was too late for Respondent to attempt to seek a remedy. Specifically, an attorney in the S.E.C. Office of General Counsel made an *ex parte* telephone call to the office of the motion clerk of the court of appeals, conveyed the secret information that the current order suspending trading in Canadian Javelin Ltd. was to be the last order, and asked that Respondent's request for expedited review not be granted for that reason. In this manner, the S.E.C. frustrated the last ditch attempt to obtain review of an order suspending trading in Canadian Javelin Ltd. while that order was still in effect.

In its petition for a writ of certiorari and again in its brief, the S.E.C. argues:

> "The court of appeals also erred in not dismissing Respondent's petition as moot. The suspension of trading in CJL stock had been terminated in May, 1976, prior to argument below and more than five months before the decision in this case."

The passage of five months between the time of the termination of the trading suspension and the date of the decision of the court of appeals was not due to any lack of diligence on the part of Respondent, however. The petition for review was filed in the court of appeals on April 23, 1976, the first day that the last order suspending trading in Canadian Javelin Ltd. was in effect. Then not only did the S.E.C. not file the record within ten days so as to make possible expedited review but it did not even comply with the forty-day filing requirement set forth in Rule 17(a) of the Federal Rules of Appellate Procedure or with the scheduling order entered by the clerk of the court of appeals which ordered the S.E.C. to file a record by June 1, 1976. The S.E.C. subsequently filed two motions for an extension of time to file its brief (App. 128-129). The first was granted; the second was denied (App. 131). The S.E.C. then failed to comply with the time for filing set by the court, once extended, and did not file its brief until October 12, 1976, one day prior to the scheduled oral argument, which precluded Respondent from putting in an answering brief. The court of appeals itself took five weeks to decide the case (Pet. App. B, p. 3a). Thus, most of the five month period to which the S.E.C. refers in making its mootness argument passed because of delays by the S.E.C.

It is axiomatic that a government agency, or for that matter a private litigant, should not be permitted to take advantage of its own delays and its own improper attempts to frustrate the judicial process. Numerous improprieties have been committed by the S.E.C. in the course of this case going back to the first brief filed by the S.E.C. which stated that Respondent had "failed to exhaust his administrative remedies," when, in fact, no administrative remedies were available, following which the S.E.C. told the court of appeals that the S.E.C. was "willing in fact to grant Sloan some sort of administrative hearing" whereas the record establishes that the S.E.C. had no intention of doing so. Had the S.E.C. not committed these and other improprieties, the question of the legality of the S.E.C.'s exercise of the trading suspension power would have been decided long ago and at a time when there was in effect an order currently suspending trading in Canadian Javelin Ltd. The S.E.C. should be satisifed that it succeeded in obstructing and delaying judicial resolution by the court of appeals for as long as it did and clearly is forclosed from arguing that this case is moot.

However, assuming that the S.E.C. had made an extraordinary departure from its usual practice and not acted improperly, during the course of this litigation, its claim that this case is moot would still be meritless. To begin with, it should be noted that the S.E.C. does not wish this Court to declare this case presently to be moot, since that would result in the dismissal of the petition and leave the decision of the court of appeals standing as a declaratory judgment. Instead, it wants this Court to declare that the court of appeals should have delcared this case to be moot and further asks this Court to vacate the order of the court of appeals and extinguish any precedental value the decision of that court has. The reason it asks for this extraordinary relief is that it wishes to revert to its practice of issuing series of consecutive trading suspension orders so as to suspend trading for periods of indefinite duration, and it is now prohibited from doing so by the decision of the court of appeals declaring this practice to be illegal. The hope of the S.E.C. is that the decision of the court of appeals will be vacated and the legality of the practices of the S.E.C. will remain unsettled so that even if the practice of issuing consecutive trading suspension orders is illegal, the S.E.C. will be able to violate the law with impunity.

The attempt by the S.E.C. to obtain the judicial authorization of this Court for its plans to violate the law cannot be permitted to succeed for several reasons. It is useful, again, to look at what the S.E.C. said in the court below. In support of its motion to dismiss this case as moot, the S.E.C. filed a six-page memorandum. Subsequently, when ordered to do so, the S.E.C. filed its brief which, on the point of mootness, repeated almost verbatim the statements made in the six-page memorandum. The brief for the S.E.C. stated (footnotes omitted):

> "A *The Issues Presented by the Petition for Review are Moot.*
>
> The series of trading suspensions sought to be reviewed here terminated on May 2, 1976, and, accordingly, there is no Commission order in effect which prevents petitioner from purchasing or selling shares of CJL stock. In addition, the series of trading suspension orders for which review is sought cannot be regarded in any sense as a reoccurrence of the Commission's previous suspensions of trading with respect to CJL stock, since they were entered in a wholly different factual context and for reasons totally independent of those which led the Commission to order the previous suspensions.
>
> Courts do not sit 'to decide abstract, hypothetical or contingent questions . . . or to decide any constitutional question in advance of the necessity for its decision. . . .' *Alabama State Federation of Labor v. McAdory,* 325 U.S. 450, 461 (1945); *Thorpe v. Housing Authority of the City of Durham,* 393 U.S. 268, 284 (1969); See also *Socialist Labor Party v. Gilligan,* 406 U.S. 583 (1972). In addition, constitutional questions 'must be presented in the context of a specific live grievance.' *Golden v. Zwickler,* 394 U.S. 103, 110 (1969).
>
> It is true that an exception to the 'mootness' principle has been recognized in controversies where the action complained of is 'capable of repetition, yet evading review. . . .' *Southern Pacific Terminal Company v. Interstate Commerce Commission,* 219 U.S. 498, 515 (1911). If petitioner were seeking review of an active series of trading suspensions and his efforts were frustrated by the ten-day duration of the Commission's orders, that exception might well have force here. But the series of trading

suspensions entered in conjunction with the Commission's enforcement action against CJL ended five months ago, and, since no suspension is now in effect or planned, any complaint which petitioner wishes to air with respect to the propriety of past suspensions is purely hypothetical. The Supreme Court has held that a case is moot where the possible recurrence of allegedly illegal conduct is speculative and the recurrence of the controversy 'purely a matter of conjecture.' *Securities & Exchange Commission v. Medical Committee for Human Rights,* 404 U.S. 403, 406 (1972).

Petitioner's brief cites *United States v. W.T. Grant Co.*, 345 U.S. 6729, 632 (1953), for the proposition that a voluntary cessation of allegedly illegal conduct does not make a controversy moot. That case was limited, however, by *Medical Committee* to apply only in cases where the allegedly illegal conduct is likely to be repeated. 404 U.S. at 406. At this point, whether there might be a future suspension of trading in CJL stock is bare speculation.

Citing *Roe v. Wade,* 410 U.S. 113 (1973) and *Sosna v. Iowa,* 419 U.S. 393 (1975), petitioner claims this case is one of those not moot because they would otherwise be 'capable of repetition yet evading review.' Petitioner ignores the fact that *Sosna* and *Roe* were class actions. The class nature of the suit was a major factor in the Court's decision in *Sosna* (419 U.S. at 401) . . . *Roe,* involving abortion laws, was found not moot because the court took judicial notice that 'preganancy *often* comes more than once to the same woman. . . .' 410 U.S. at 125. (emphasis added).

Finally, petitioner refers to *Sibron v. New York,* 392 U.S. 40 (1968) and *United States v. Schrimsher,* 493 F. 2d 842 (C.A. 5, 1974). These cases are both criminal cases, where the usual rules concerning mootness do not apply. . . The court in Sibron, 392 U.S. at 53-58, gave examples of the collateral consequences of criminal convictions that change the usual rules concerning mootness . . . These considerations do not apply in this case."

This is all that the S.E.C. said on the subject of mootness to the court of appeals. It is readily apparent that the arguments presented to this Court by the Solicitor General are dissimilar to the arguments presented to the court of appeals by the S.E.C. in a number of respects. The main thrust of the Solicitor General's argument to this Court is grounded on this Court's decision in *Weinstein v. Bradford*, 423 U.S. 147, 149 (1975). That case was not even cited in the brief filed by the S.E.C. in the court of appeals even though it knew or should have known of that case since it was cited by the Solicitor General in footnote 8 of the brief in opposition to the first petition for a writ of certiorari, No. 75-1507, quoted *supra.*

The S.E.C. makes extensive use of canned briefs, presumably because of large number of regional offices and branch offices of the S.E.C. and the large number of attorneys in each office, any or all of whom may be involved in extensive litigation, and its perceived need to have control over what all of these attorneys say. Thus, the S.E.C. can be seen to be filing the same brief over and over again in a variety of diverse circumstances and surprisingly often the cases cited by the S.E.C. stand for precisely the opposite proposition from that which it is asserting. In the instant case, the S.E.C. cited three decisions as primary authority on its claim that the case is moot: *Alabama State Federation v. McAdory, 325 U.S. 450 (1945); Thorpe v. Housing Authority, 393 U.S. 268 (1969);* and *Socialist Labor Party v. Gilligan, 406 U.S. 583 (1972).* All three of these cases were cited in the brief filed in the court of appeals by the S.E.C. in another case, *S.E.C. v. Sloan,* Dkt. No. 75-6106, which was an appeal from various orders including an order adjudging Respondent to be in civil contempt. That appeal resulted in a decision reported as *S.E.C. v. Sloan,* 535 F. 2d 679 (2d Cir. 1976), *cert. denied 430 U.S.* 966 (1977). There is no similarity whatever between the two cases except that in both cases the S.E.C. was claiming that the appeal was moot. It is hard to imagine three cases more worthless than those cited by the S.E.C. As Respondent stated in opposition to the motion to dismiss as moot (App. 137):

> ". . . Incidentally, in the first sentence of the second paragraph of page 4 of its memorandum, the S.E.C. again cites three cases which it cited in its brief in *S.E.C. v. Sloan,* Dkt. No. 75-6106. In that appeal, I filed a reply brief which pointed out that all three of these cases are wholly irrelevant and two of them do not even deal with mootness. Since it persists in citing these three cases, it is obvious that the S.E.C. is merely copying from its previous court filings and did not even bother to look up these cases prior to filing its memorandum in this Court. As I noted previously, none of the cases cited by the S.E.C. in *S.E.C. v. Sloan,* Dkt. No. 75-6106, were relied upon by this Court when it made its decision in that appeal."

After wasting the time and judicial resources of the court of appeals by filing a canned brief which cited wholly irrelevant cases and did not rely on, except to distinguish, any recent or relevant cases, the S.E.C., when confronted with an adverse decision, comes before this Court and complains that the holding of the court appeals "on the issue of mootness is sufficiently contrary to this Court's recent decisions to warrant summary reversal" (Pet. 12, n. 8). It is submitted that the S.E.C. is foreclosed from making this argument.

It is also appropriate to examine what the S.E.C. said on the subject of mootness when the predecessor case (No. 74-2457) was before the court of appeals. The brief of the S.E.C. stated (Brief pp. 12-13):

"ARGUMENT

I. THIS PETITION FOR REVIEW IS NOT PROPERLY BEFORE THIS COURT.

A. *The Issues Presented by the Petition for Review Are Moot.*

The series of trading suspensions sought to be reviewed here terminated in January 1975. While it is true that the Commission again suspended trading in the securities of CJL in April of this year and has entered orders continuing that suspension, these orders were for reasons wholly independent of the factual basis upon which the suspensions challenged in this Court were ordered. The Commission orders suspending trading in CJL stock beginning in April 1975 were not sought to be reviewed here; nor can these orders be regarded in any sense as a reoccurrence of the Commission's previous actions with respect to Canadian Javelin, since they were entered for a wholly different reason. See p. 4, n.5, *supra.* Moreover, any CJL stock owned by the Petitioner when the earlier orders were entered could have been sold during the period from January 26, 1975, through April 29, 1975.

Courts do not sit 'to decide abstract, hypothetical or contingent questions . . . or to decide any constitutional question in advance of the necessity for its decision. . . .' *Alabama State Federation of Labor v. McAdory,* 325 U.S. 450, 461 (1945); *Thorpe v. Housing Authority of the City of Durham,* 393 U.S. 268, 284 (1969); see, also, *Socialist Labor Party v. Gilligan,* 406 U.S. 583 (1972).

It is true that an exception to the "mootness" principle has been recognized in controversies where the action complained of is "capable of repetition, yet evading review." *Southern Pacific Terminal Company v. Interstate Commerce Commission,* 219 U.S. 498, 515 (1911). If Petitioner were seeking review of an active series of trading suspensions and his efforts were frustrated by the ten-day duration of the Commission's orders, that exception might well have force here. But the series of trading suspensions entered in conjunction with the Commission's enforcement action against CJL ended six months ago, and any complaints which Petitioner wishes to air with respect to that series of suspensions are purely hypothetical at this point."

This is the full text of what the S.E.C. said to the first panel of the court of appeals on the question of mootness. Page 4, n. 5, to which the above quoted passage refers, stated:

"5/ The Company did not mail its annual report to the shareholders for the year ending December 21, 1973, until August 1974. Its quarterly reports required to be filed with the Commission on Form 10-Q for 1974, were not filed with the Commission until December 12, 1974. (Securities Exchange Act Release No. 11172, January 9, 1975, p. 2). On December 16, 1974, CJL sent a report to its shareholders and distributed it to the public. (*Id.*, p. 2.) On January 9, 1975, the Commission announced that trading would resume in CJL shares on January 12, 1975 (*id.*, p. 1). However, at the request of the Amex and CJL itself an additional ten-day suspension was entered on January 13 to permit the preparation of an orderly over-the-counter market for the shares in view of the fact that Amex was not yet ready to permit trading to resume. Finally, on January 22 at the request of the Amex and CJL a suspension order of four more days was entered so that trading on Amex and in the over-the-counter market could resume simultaneously. (Securities Exchange Act Release No. 11197, January 22, 1975).

While Petitioner notes (Pet. Br. 3) that trading in the securities of CJL was again suspended by the Commission on April 29, 1975, and the suspension has been continued by additional orders, this later suspension arises in a wholly different factual context and for reasons totally independent of the Commission's previous injunctive action and the previous suspensions. The later suspension was intended to permit dissemination of information concerning regulatory action against CJL by Canadian authorities.

(Securities Exchange Act Release No. 11383, April 29, 1975.)"

It should be noted that there are obvious discrepancies between what the S.E.C. said to the court of appeals in the first case and what it said to the court of appeals in the second case and even greater discrepancies between what the S.E.C. said to the court of appeals in both those cases and what it now says to this court. Essentially, what the S.E.C. said in the first case was that a challenge to a series of trading suspension orders becomes moot when that series of orders is allowed to terminate, even when a new series of trading suspension orders is initiated shortly thereafter. In the second case, it retreated from that position, since it had no need to do otherwise, and said that a challenge to a series of trading suspension orders is moot when there is no order currently in effect suspending trading at the time the case is argued before the court of appeals. In this Court, the S.E.C. takes a different approach which focuses on the status of Respondent. The brief for the S.E.C. states that in the court of appeals it viewed Respondent "merely in his capacity as a holder of the particular security initially at issue" (Brief p. 17). This statement is false. As an examination of the above quoted passages in the briefs filed by the S.E.C. in the court of appeals demonstrates, the S.E.C. said nothing about the status of Respondent to the court of appeals, at least not with regard to the question of mootness, nor could it have done so because at the time these cases were presented to the court of appeals the status of Respondent was different from that of "an investor generally". In particular, Respondent was a broker-dealer in securities whose registration had been revoked by the S.E.C. and the question of the validity of that revocation was then before the court of appeals. Had the court of appeals reached a different decision and reversed the order of the S.E.C. revoking Respondent's broker-dealer registration, Respondent would have been able to go back into business and the arguments which the S.E.C. presents to this Court regarding mootness would have been foreclosed. This is because a broker-dealer in securities in the normal course can be expected to do business in a large number of securities and any time the S.E.C. suspends trading in a security, a large percentage of all broker-dealers are likely to be adversely affected. A broker-dealer would not have to own the security to be adversely affected. For example, a broker-dealer which has a customer who holds the security in a margin account which becomes unsecured as a result of a trading suspension, a broker-dealer which has a fail to receive or a fail to deliver with another broker that refuses to complete its contractual obligations because of the trading suspension, and a broker-dealer which has recommended the stock to its customers and has come under a cloud as a result of the trading suspension, all would be adversely affected by an order of the S.E.C. suspending trading. Thus, if Respondent were a registered broker-dealer, as he was at the time of the orders suspending trading which were challenged in the first petition for review, there could be no claim that a challenge to the trading suspension orders had become moot under the standards set forth on pp. 17-19 of the S.E.C.'s brief in this Court. Therefore, the S.E.C. was forced to make a different argument when this case was pending before the court of appeals. It is submitted that the S.E.C. is now foreclosed from making a new argument to this Court. It should also be pointed out that to divert attention from the status of Respondent as a broker-dealer whose registration has been revoked, the S.E.C., as of this writing, has refused to certify the full record of this case to the court of appeals for transmission to this Court. This occurred because following the decision of the court of appeals, that court returned the entire administrative record to the S.E.C. When this Court granted certiorari, the Clerk of this Court wrote to the clerk of the court of appeals and requested that court to transmit the record to this Court. The court of appeals then wrote the S.E.C. and requested the transmission of the record to that court. However, the S.E.C. refused to certify the record of the administrative proceeding which resulted in the revocation of Respondent's broker-dealer registration and which were part of the record when this case was before the court of appeals. And as a result, this Court does not have access to the full record which was before the court of appeals.

Referring again to the above-quoted passages from the briefs filed by the S.E.C. in the court of appeals, it should be noted that the "reasons" given by the S.E.C. for the trading suspensions are not in conformity with the record of the releases which the S.E.C. cites. Indeed, the briefs of the S.E.C. never cited the record, even though the record supposedly provided the reasons for the trading suspensions, and the facts set forth in footnote 5 quoted above as the reasons for the suspension were not set forth in the record of that appeal.

Ignoring all of the above, the brief of the S.E.C. in this Court focuses upon *Weinsten v. Bradford, supra.* However, that case did not represent the breaking of new ground with respect to the law of mootness. Rather, this Court simply expounded in somewhat greater detail on the principle stemming from *Southern Pacific Terminal v. I.C.C., supra,* that controversies which are "capable of repetition, yet evading review" will not be declared moot. This is clear from the subsequent decision of *Nebraska Press Association v. Stuart, supra,* a case involving judicial "gag" orders, where this Court stated that the case was not moot because (427 U.S. at 546-547):

> "The Nebraska Supreme Court's decision authorizes state prosecutors to seek restrictive orders in appropriate cases. The dispute between the State and the petitioners who cover events throughout the State is thus 'capable of repetition.' Yet, if we decline to address the issues in this case on the ground of mootness, the dispute will evade review, or at least considered plenary review in this Court, since these orders are by their nature short lived."

As noted previously, the S.E.C.'s brief ignores this case, and with good reason since it demonstrates the meritlessness of the S.E.C.'s mootness argument. If the arguments advanced by the S.E.C. here and in the court below were correct, then in order to defeat the claim of mootness it would have been necessary for the Nebraska Press Association to show that there was a "substantial likelyhood" that the same judge would issue the same gag order in the same case for the same reason and that a member of the Nebraska Press Association would be aggrieved and seek review of that order, obviously an impossible requirement. Analogies to other authoritative decisions dealing with mootness equally demonstrate the meritless character of the S.E.C.'s mootness argument. Consider the case of *Roe v. Wade,* 410 U.S. 113, 125 (1973). That case involved a pregnant woman who wanted an abortion and sought a declaration that the anti-abortion laws were unconstitutional. By the time that case reached this Court, more than two years later, it was obvious that the same woman was not still pregnant with the same child. Nevertheless, this Court held that the case was not moot. In the instant case, the brief for the S.E.C. states (Brief, p. 19):

> "If respondent submits an affidavit stating the precise number of publicly traded issues he owns, and the number of those that are listed on the New York Stock Exchange or are of large banks and insurance companies, and further shows that he will continue to hold approximately as many

similar securities in the next five years, we can then make an adequate assessment whether there is a 'reasonable expectation that respondent, in his capacity as an investor, will be subjected to the same action again'."

It is noteworthy that in this paragraph the S.E.C. asks Respondent to file an affidavit which predicts the future. If the same standard had been applied in *Roe v. Wade,* Roe would have been required to submit an affidavit stating not only that was she pregnant and wanted abortion but that after her pregnancy was terminated there was a "reasonable expectation" that she would become pregnant a second time and would want an abortion again. Of course, in actuality, Roe did not and could not have filed an affidavit of any kind, the plaintiff being anonymous and the name Roe being a pseudonym. It is also noteworthy that the 266-day human gestation period was sufficiently short to defeat a claim of mootness in *Roe,* even though it is much longer in duration than the ten-day trading suspension orders which are the subject of the instant case.

In the court below, Respondent was not content to rely entirely on his argument that this case was "capable of repetition, yet evading review" and set forth a number of alternative grounds, relying on cases such as *Sibron v. New York,* 392 U.S. 40, 51-58 (1968); and *United States v. Schrimsher,* 493 F.2d 842, 843 (5th Cir. 1974). The court of appeals, correctly, it is submitted, did not need to reach these alternative arguments. Since these arguments also bear on the question of whether this case is "capable of repetition, yet evading review" they will be repeated here. With the exception of the last of these arguments, which is addressed for the first time on pages 17-20 of the S.E.C.'s brief, none of these arguments have been responded to by the S.E.C. either here or in the court below.

C

One of the principles regarding mootness set forth in *Sibron v. New York, supra,* 392 U.S. at 57, is that for the government to sustain a claim that a case is moot, it must meet the burden of showing that no possible collateral legal consequences could arise as a result of the challenged orders. Here, the government, in this case the S.E.C., has not attempted to and clearly could not meet that burden of proof for a number of reasons which were set forth in Respondent's affidavit in opposition to the motion to dismiss this case as moot (App. 140-144). It should be noted that the S.E.C. never responded to any of the points made in Respondent's affidavit in opposition in the court of appeals nor does it do so in this Court. In the court of appeals, the S.E.C. was satisfied to limit its presentation to a certificate from the Office of Reports and Information Services which stated that there was no order currently in effect suspending trading in Canadian Javelin Ltd.[25] Not only did the S.E.C. not attempt to meet the affirmative burden of showing that no collateral legal consequences could arise as a result of the trading suspension orders, but

---

25. The S.E.C.'s designation of documents to be included in the Appendix to this appeal did not include any of the papers filed in the court of appeals. in order to enable this Court to have ready access to the papers the S.E.C. filed in the court of appeals and to demonstrate that the S.E.C.'s presentation to this Court was different from its presentation to the court of appeals, Respondent cross-designated a number or documents including the S.E.C.'s motion to dismiss this appeal as moot. By cross-designating this motion Respondent obviously intended that all of the papers filed by the S.E.C. in support of its motion to dismiss the appeal as moot would be included in the Appendix. However, the S.E.C. foiled this plan by including nothing more than a notice of motion (App. 129). It also failed to include the complete docket sheet of the court of appeals, although cross-designated by Respondent, thereby frustrating Respondent from demonstrating by documentary evidence such significant facts as the fact that the S.E.C. did not file its brief in the court of appeals until October 12, 1976, one day before the oral argument, and the fact that the S.E.C. filed only a certified list of documents comprising the record and even this list was filed three days late.

it failed to refute or even to address the specific collateral legal consequences which have arisen as a result of S.E.C.'s trading suspension orders which were set forth in Respondent's affidavit in opposition to the motion to dismiss this appeal as moot. One noteworthy collateral legal consequence is that as a result of the orders suspending trading in Canadian Javelin Ltd., trading in Canadian Javelin Ltd. has not been permitted to resume to this very day. This arises because of the arbitrary authority which the S.E.C. has assumed to prevent securities regarded as undesirable by the S.E.C. from being quoted in any inter-dealer quotation system including the pink sheets published by the National Quotation Bureau, Inc. The S.E.C. claims to derive this authority from Rule 15c2-11, the text of which is included in Appendix A to this brief. In practice, however, in the case of Canadian Javelin Ltd., the S.E.C. will not permit brokers to publish quotations even if Rule 15c2-11 has been complied with fully. A simple telephone call to the National Quotation Bureau, over which the S.E.C. has the authority to exercise jurisdiction as a result of the 1975 amendments to the Securities Exchange Act, specifically §11A(b), 15 U.S.C. §78k-1(b), is sufficient to prevent brokers from publishing quotations in Canadian Javelin Ltd. That is precisely one of the points of the lawsuit brought by Respondent against the S.E.C. in 1974 and the S.E.C.'s countersuit against Respondent later the same year.

Rule 15c2-11 was promulgated by the S.E.C., ostensibly under the authority of §15(c)(2) of the Securities Exchange Act, the text of which is also included in Appendix A. It should be noted that under this Court's decision in *Ernst & Ernst v. Hochfelder*, 425 U.S. 185, 212-213 (1976), Rule 15c2-11 is patently unconstitutional. Section 15(c)(2) of the Securities Exchange Act prohibits brokers and dealers from making "any fictitious quotation" and authorizes the S.E.C. to define by rules and regulations "such quotations as are fictitious." Given the authority to define "such quotations as are fictitious," the S.E.C. has gone off on a tangent known as Rule 15c2-11 which defines "fictitious" in a manner totally alien to the dictionary definition and the generally accepted meaning of the term and affirmatively requires brokers who wish to publish a quotation in a security to file information regarding that security with the National Quotation Bureau, Inc. The National Quotation Bureau, Inc., which has no use for nor interest in this information, simply transmits all submitted material directly to the S.E.C. The S.E.C. then decides whether or not it will permit the security to be quoted in the pink sheets and if its decision is negative, it calls the broker and asks him to "withdraw" the quotation application. In the rare case in which the broker declines to withdraw his application, the S.E.C. simply calls the National Quotation Bureau and directs it not to publish the quotation. Respondent has spoken with Mr. Edward Lubensky, who is head of the library department of the National Quotation Bureau and the person in charge of handling these quotation applications, and Mr. Lubensky has advised Respondent that a large number of brokers have submitted applications to quote Canadian Javelin Ltd. and in all cases the S.E.C. has directed the National Quotation Bureau not to publish the quotations. The S.E.C. has also obtained an agreement from the National Quotation Bureau whereby the National Quotation Bureau refuses to accept any listing applications which are submitted without a proposed bid or ask quotation. This agreement is necessary to the success of the S.E.C.'s efforts to prevent Canadian Javelin Ltd. and other securities regarded by the S.E.C. as undesirable from being traded. This is because § 15(c)(2) of the Securities Exchange Act and Rule 15c2-11 only speak of actual bid and ask quotations. Thus, the S.E.C. has no jurisdiction to prevent any security from being listed in the pink sheets providing the listing broker does not publish a bid and ask quotation. See *Rothchild Securities Corp.*, CCH Fed. Sec. Law Rep. ¶79,593 [1973-74 Transfer Binder]. However, by coercing the National Quotation Bureau into an agreement not to publish any initial listings of a security without a bid or ask quotation, the S.E.C. has closed this potential loophole, thereby preventing any security from being quoted in the pink sheets which has not been expressly approved by the S.E.C.

A copy of Form 211, which is the submission required under Rule 15c2-11, is included as Appendix D to this brief. It can be seen that in the case of Canadian Javelin Ltd., a broker could easily complete Form 211 and meet the listing requirements of Rule 15c2-11. At a minimum, a broker can comply with Rule 15c2-11 by submitting certain specified information, including the names of the members of the board of directors, the location of the principal office of the company, and the company's most recent balance sheet and profit and loss and retained earnings statement and similar information for the two preceding years. In the case of Canadian Javelin Ltd., all this information is currently on file with the S.E.C. inasmuch as Canadian Javelin Ltd. has a current 10-K and 10-Q report on file there. Thus, it can be seen that a broker could easily comply with Rule 15c2-11 and the S.E.C.'s refusal to permit a listing in Canadian Javelin Ltd. is arbitrary and capricious.

The point is that were it not for the trading suspension orders which have now expired, the S.E.C. would not have been able in the first instance to invoke Rule 15c2-11 to prevent the quotation of shares of Canadian Javelin Ltd. This is because paragraph (f)(3) of Rule 15c2-11 provides that the rule shall not apply to the "publication or submission of a quotation respecting a security which has been the subject of both bid and ask quotations. . . with no more than four business days in succession without such a two-way quotation." Thus, any security, including Canadian

Javelin Ltd., which has been quoted on a continuous basis would not become subject to Rule 15c2-11 except in the event that the S.E.C. suspended trading in the security for a period of more than four business days. Conversely, any security, including Canadian Javelin Ltd., which has been suspended by the S.E.C. for a period of more than four business days, automatically becomes subject to Rule 15c2-11 and this gives the S.E.C. the power to exercise the arbitrary authority to prevent future trading in that security. In this case, the S.E.C. has exercised that power. Were this Court to declare all of the 37 consecutive trading suspension orders to be invalid,[26] then it would follow that the S.E.C. could not invoke Rule 15c2-11 and it would be forced to permit trading in Canadian Javelin Ltd. to resume. Hence, this case is not moot. This point is further illustrated by the fact that the release announcing that the suspension of trading in Canadian Javelin would terminate, Securities Exchange Act Release No. 12394, 9 SEC Docket 509 (April 29, 1976), stated the following:

---

26. The S.E.C. may, and very likely will, argue that this Court cannot determine the validity of the first of the 37 trading suspension orders because the court of appeals refused to vacate that order and this Court denied the petition filed by Respondent for a writ of certiorari to review that order. However, this argument, if made, will be without merit. As Respondent pointed out on pp. 21-22 of his petition for a rehearing of the denial of his petition for a writ of certiorari, Article III of the Constitution limits this Court in cases such as this to the exercise of appellate jurisdiction. Thus, except in the instance where intervening circumstances have arisen since the decision of the court of appeals, which is not the case here, this Court must view this appeal from the same posture as did the court of appeals. In other words, if this Court were to assume the validity of the first trading suspension order or, for that matter, the order revoking Respondent's broker-dealer registration, it would alter the character of this case and would be exercising original rather than appellate jurisdiction. This is not to say that this Court must determine the validity of the initial trading suspension order, only that it has jurisdiction to do so and must do so if a determination of the validity of that order is necessary to the proper outcome of this appeal.

"Furthermore, brokers and dealers should be alert to fact that, pursuant to Rule 15c2-11 under the Exchange Act, at the termination of the suspension, no quotation may be entered unless and until they have strictly complied with all of the provisions of said rule. If any broker or dealer has any questions as to whether or not he has complied with said rule, he should not enter any quotation but immediately contact the staff of the S.E.C. Division of Enforcement in Washington, D.C. If any broker or dealer is uncertain as to what is required by Rule 15c2-11, he should refrain from entering quotations relating to the securities in question until such time as he has familiarized himself with said rule and is certain that all of its provisions have been met. If any broker or dealer enters any quotation which is in violation of said rule, the Commission will consider the need for prompt enforcement action."

The above paragraph would seem to contain a virtual admission that Rule 15c2-11 is unconstitutional under this Court's decision of *Connally v. General Construction Co.*, 269 U.S. 385, 391 (1926). In any event, it is apparent that the S.E.C. is using the now-expired trading suspension orders as a basis for preventing future trading in Canadian Javelin Ltd. It is noteworthy that this point was made in Respondent's affidavit to the court of appeals in opposition to the motion to dismiss this case as moot (App. 141), in the brief Respondent filed in the court of appeals, and on page 9 of the brief filed by Respondent in this Court in opposition to the petition for a writ of certiorari and at no time has the S.E.C. addressed itself to this point. It should also be added that at this very moment Respondent would like to be able to buy and sell stock in Canadian Javelin Ltd. and is prevented from doing so by the S.E.C. as an collateral consequence of the now expired trading suspension orders.

Going further on the point of collateral legal consequences, it has been held by the courts that the stigmatizing effect of S.E.C. action in itself gives an adversely affected party standing to seek review. See e.g. *Buchman v. S.E.C.*, 553 F. 2d 816, 823 (2d Cir. 1977). In the instant case there is a definite stigma resulting from the trading suspension and this stigma is likely to adversely affect Respondent. Shares in Canadian Javelin Ltd. have now been suspended by the S.E.C. during four distinct time periods. As a result, Canadian Javelin Ltd. and its officers and directors have been branded as evil-doers in the minds of the investing public.[27] Members of the investing public are likely to be wary of purchasing Canadian Javelin Ltd. shares and, in fact, the compliance department of most major stock brokerage firms has issued directives prohibiting their registered representatives from soliciting either purchase or sales orders in Canadian Javelin Ltd. Indeed, some brokers refuse to make security transactions in Canadian Javelin Ltd. under any circumstances. There is good reason for this, since past history demonstrates that an individual who decides to purchase Canadian Javelin Ltd. shares runs the substantial risk that trading in Canadian Javelin Ltd. will be suspended at some time in the forseeable future. Since public investors are likely understandably to be reluctant to purchase these shares, it follows that even assuming these shares were allowed to trade in the United States, they would trade at a severly depressed price. This adversely affects Respondent, who is a stockholder in Canadian Javelin Ltd., since the stigmatizing effect of the past trading suspensions will result in Canadian Javelin Ltd. trading at a lower price

---

27. An example of the stigmatizing affect can be seen in the article "John Doyle—Evil Genius," *Barron's*, August 16, 1976, p. 3, which, in accusatory fashion, cites the trading suspensions of the S.E.C.

than it would have traded had it not been suspended for lengthy time periods.

In addition to being stigmatized, there are other direct adverse collateral consequences flowing from the trading suspension. There is presently pending in the District Court for the District of Columbia a suit against Canadian Javelin Ltd. and its board of directors and principal stockholder. In this suit, *S.E.C. v. Canadian Javelin Ltd., et al.* Civil Action No. 76-2070 (D.D.C.), the S.E.C. is using the past late filings which, the S.E.C. alleges, resulted in suspensions of trading in Canadian Javelin Ltd., as the basis for seeking injunctive relief. This phenomenon was described in the article by Goldman and Magrino, both of whom formerly held the position of Chief Interpretive Attorney of the New York Regional Office of the S.E.C., entitled *Suspension of Trading in Securities: Some Observations on Sections 15(c)(5) of the Securities Exchange Act of 1934*, 15 N.Y.L. Forum 638, 654 n. 96 (1969), which stated:

> "It would appear that at times due perhaps to an excess of zeal, this has taken on the trappings of a boot-strap operation wherein an order of suspension is entered and is used as the basis for seeking an injunction—which is often consented to by the respondents in order that trading may be resumed."

Indeed, the suit in the District for the District of Columbia is in itself being used as a basis for preventing trading in Canadian Javelin Ltd. to resume. The original complaint in that action alleged that Canadian Javelin Ltd. was delinquent in filing its 10-K report.[28] The S.E.C. subsequently amended the complaint to allege that the 10-

---

28. See Litigation Release No. 7642, 10 SEC Docket 948 (November 10, 1976).

K report filed by Canadian Javelin Ltd. was improper and contained false and misleading statements.[29] This seems to be the basis for the S.E.C.'s present refusal to allow trading in Canadian Javelin Ltd. to resume. Under Rule 15c2-11, the S.E.C. must allow trading to resume in a security if the issuer of that security is up to date in filing its 10-K and subsequent reports. However, the theory of the S.E.C. apparently is that since the 10-K report contains "false and misleading statements," it is a nullity and, therefore, trading in Canadian Javelin Ltd. may not resume. This suit, unlike prior suits against Canadian Javelin and its officers and directors,[30] is being contested. To give an idea of how far the S.E.C. intends to carry this particular suit against Canadian Javelin Ltd., Respondent understands that in the course of settlement negotiations the suggestion has been made that Canadian Javelin Ltd. agree to the voluntary deregistration of its shares under §12(j) of the Securities Exchange Act, 15 U.S.C. §78 *l* (j). If that were to occur, brokers and dealers would be forever prohibited from making "use of the mails or any means or instrumentality of interstate commerce to effect any transaction in, or induce the purchase or sale of", shares of Canadian Javelin Ltd.

It can also be seen that the statement in the petition (Pet. 12, n. 7) which is quoted on page 15 of the S.E.C.'s brief, that "there is no reason to believe that it will be necessary to suspend trading in Canadian Javelin Ltd. again," is simply a lie. Of course, in the opinion of Respondent, who is a proponent of the free enterprise system and the law of supply and demand, it is not likely that it would ever be "necessary" to suspend trading in

29. See Litigation Release No. 7779, 11 SEC Docket 1772 (February 14, 1977).

30. See *S.E.C. v. Canadian Javelin Ltd.*, 1958 Civil Action file 138-85 (S.D.N.Y.); *S.E.C. v. Canadian Javelin Ltd.*, Docket No. 73 Civil 5074 (S.D.-N.Y.); *S.E.C. v. Doyle et al, supra.*

Canadian Javelin Ltd. However, any objective viewer of the situation will almost certainly conclude that the time will someday come when the S.E.C. will, in fact, again suspend trading in Canadian Javelin Ltd., that is if trading in Canadian Javelin Ltd. is ever allowed by the S.E.C. to resume and if this Court reverses the decision of the court below.[31] When a corporation becomes delinquent in filing its 10-K report, the S.E.C., in recent years, has adopted the practice of almost routinely suspending trading in its securities. See e.g. Securities Exchange Release No. 10732, 4 SEC Docket 82 (April 11, 1974) which announced that the S.E.C. was simultaneously suspending trading in securities

---

31. If this Court affirms the decision of the court below, the S.E.C. will presumably retain the power to issue a single, i.e. non-consecutive, trading suspension order at some time in the future. However, a single trading suspension order would not serve the purposes for which the S.E.C. has suspended trading in Canadian Javelin Ltd. in the past. In the case of Canadian Javelin Ltd., the S.E.C. has used the trading suspension power as a sanction to force Canadian Javelin Ltd. to take certain action such as issue a press release, consent to an injunction, file a report with the S.E.C. or cooperate with the S.E.C. staff. A single ten-day suspension order would presumably not accomplish these purposes. The article by Goldstein & Magrino, *supra*, addresses this point as follows (15 N.Y.L. Forum at 655):

> "What is confusing is that in the absence of any affirmative requirement by the Commission or undertaking by [the corporation whose securities are suspended from trading] such as the dissemination of new or corrective financial or other information, it is rather difficult to comprehend the purpose served by a mere ten day suspension period. We have noted that in previous instances the announcement of suspension has served this reasonable purpose and the length of the suspension period was specifically geared to the time interval necessary.
>
> What is pointed up here is the ambivalent role played by the suspension device. It would, at times, appear that suspension of trading is used to perform and promote the function of full disclosure. In such instances, the length of its duration may be reasonable and corrective. Yet, in other instances, especially where the ten day periods multiply, it would seem to be used in the nature of a sanction—and such has never been authorized by Congress (for the simple reason that the persons most likely to suffer ultimately are the public shareholders)."

of 48 corporations for reason of a delinquency in a 10-K filing and Securities Exchange Act Release No. 12360, 9 SEC Docket 481 (April 22, 1976) in which the S.E.C. stated that it was simultaneously suspending trading in 34 securities for the same reason. In the case of Canadian Javelin Ltd., however, when it became delinquent in its 10-K filing, the S.E.C. took the unusual action of instituting suit to compel the filing but did not suspend trading, in contrast to what it has done on all comparable occasions. The obvious reason for this is that the S.E.C.'s suit was filed on November 8, 1976, just 26 days after the S.E.C. had argued orally before the court of appeals that it had no plans to suspend trading in Canadian Javelin Ltd. and, as it turned out, just ten days before the court of appeals made its decision (Pet. App. B, p. 3a). It is clear that the S.E.C. did not suspend trading in Canadian Javelin Ltd. on November 8, 1976 because to do so would have been to extinguish its mootness argument in the case then *sub judice* in the court of appeals and also because the S.E.C. had invoked Rule 15c2-11 to prohibit trading in Canadian Javelin Ltd. from resuming and, therefore, a suspension of trading was unnecessary.[32]

---

32. In many cases, curiously enough, the S.E.C. has suspended trading in a security in which there was no trading. One such instance took place on November 29, 1973, when the S.E.C. suspended trading in securities of Canadian Javelin Ltd. although trading in those securities had been suspended by the American Stock Exchange since October 25, 1973, as a result of an unfavorable article published in *The Wall Street Journal* on that date, and an over-the-counter trading market had not developed. *The Wall Street Journal* article was entitled, "Now You See It: Canadian Javelin Doesn't Have Gold Rights In Panama, Nation Says; Firm Disputes That." A second unfavorable article appeared in *The Wall Street Journal* on October 30, 1973. An example of a security which was suspended from trading by the S.E.C. although it never traded either on a national securities exchange or in the pink sheets or any other inter-dealer quotation system for at least the preceding five years is Dumont Corp., which was suspended from trading by the S.E.C. on April 11, 1974, simultaneously with 47 other securities (App. 190). This anomaly is not inconsistent with the policies of the S.E.C. since many corporations are

With further regard to the S.E.C.'s assertion that "there is no reason to believe that it will be necessary to suspend trading in Canadian Javelin Ltd. again," the attention of the Court is directed to the article entitled "John Doyle—Evil Genius," *Barron's*, August 16, 1976, p. 15, which records the reaction of Stanley Sporkin, the chief of the Division of Enforcement of the S.E.C., to a special stockholder's meeting of Canadian Javelin Ltd. held on July 30, 1976, in accordance with an order of a justice of the Quebec Superior Court (App. 160-162):

> " 'We are not going to take this lying down,' barked Sporkin. 'There were brazen acts conducted in Canada. The American stockholders are being put upon here.' "

Any one reading this statement would assume that at the time of the statement there was excellent reason to believe that it was likely that the S.E.C. was about to suspend trading in Canadian Javelin Ltd. again. Yet at the very moment this statement was made, which was some time after the July 30, 1976 meeting and some time before the August 16, 1976 *Barron's* article, the S.E.C. was telling the court of appeals that "there is no reason to believe that it will be necessary to suspend trading in Canadian Javelin Ltd. again." It is noteworthy that Mr. Sporkin has never denied making the statement, and he would be expected to have done so if he had been misquoted. Of course, when the S.E.C. says that "there is no reason to believe that it will be necessary to suspend trading in Canadian Javelin Ltd. again" it is not really saying, not could it say, that an

---

required to register with the S.E.C. pursuant to 12(g)(1) of the Securities Exchange Act, 15 U.S.C. §78 *l*(g)(1), even though there has never been a public trading market for any of their securities. These companies, therefore, sometimes become delinquent in their 10-K filings and are "suspended from trading" for that reason.

objective outside observer would reach this conclusion. What it must be saying is that as long as the instant case is pending, and as long as the order of the court of appeals prohibiting it from issuing consecutive orders suspending trading in Canadian Javelin Ltd. stands, it has reached the conclusion that it will not be necessary to suspend trading in Canadian Javelin Ltd. again. Should the occasion arise where the S.E.C. decides to suspend trading in Canadian Javelin Ltd. even before the instant case has been decided, it will still have in reserve the argument which it used when the first case was pending before the court of appeals and which it can always use, due to the policy of the S.E.C. of not announcing to the public the reasons for continuing a trading suspension, that the current trading suspension order was issued for a different reason than the prior trading suspension orders and hence the question of the validity of the prior trading suspension orders is "moot." It should also be pointed out that the attorneys from the Office of General Counsel of the S.E.C. who are appearing before this Court in the instant case are proporting to speak for the S.E.C., although they can hardly do so. The S.E.C. consists of five commissioners who are political appointees and who come and go. Since the date of the decision of the court of appeals, one commissioner has resigned and two new commissioners have been sworn in. There have been many cases in which the S.E.C. Division of Enforcement, in the course of litigation, has taken a position directly contrary to the official pronouncements of the S.E.C. itself. It appears that the Division of Enforcement and the Office of the General Counsel of the S.E.C. act pretty much independently from the S.E.C. commissioners, or at least they claim to do so. The S.E.C. often releases statements to the effect that the opinions of the staff and even the opinions of the individual commissioners cannot be taken to be the opinions of the S.E.C. Therefore the attorneys appearing in the instant case are not authorized to state what the S.E.C. itself plans to do or not to do.[33]

In addition to the foregoing, at least one collateral legal consequence may flow as a result of a favorable decision of this Court. It must be remembered that Respondent originally instituted suit against the S.E.C. seeking a declaration that the S.E.C.'s exercise of its trading suspension power was invalid, at a time when the S.E.C. was prosecuting two proceedings against Respondent. Respondent sued the S.E.C. in the belief that if he were successful in his attempts to have a court declare the exercise of the trading suspension power to invalid, he might well upend the S.E.C.'s prosecution of him. This conclusion is still justified and this alone demonstrates that Respondent has a vital interest in the outcome of this controversy and this case is not moot. To begin with, had it not been for the S.E.C.'s exercise of the trading suspension power, Respondent would likely not have been barred from the securities business and conversely if he prevails in this Court, Respondent's position in any proceedings he might institute to have that bar lifted will be greatly strengthened.[34] For example, the decision in *S.E.C. v.*

---

33. Of course, it appears from the memoranda which comprise the record of this case that it is the S.E.C. staff and the Secretary of the S.E.C., and not the S.E.C. itself, which makes the actual decision of whether or not to suspend trading. As page 32 of the brief in response to the petition points out, the memoranda in the record are uniformly addressed from the Division of Enforcement to the Commission and are dated usually several days after their respective trading suspension orders and are clearly prepared for the purpose of explaining to the S.E.C. why the S.E.C. staff decided to suspend trading in the security. From this it is obvious that the commissioners themselves play no active role in the process of deciding whether or not trading should be suspended, and therefore perhaps the S.E.C. staff is in a position to tell this Court and the court of appeals what the S.E.C. will and will not do.

34. In spite of this Court's denial of the petition for a writ of certiorari to review that part of the decision of the court of appeals which affirmed the revocation of Respondent's broker-dealer registration, there are still avenues available to obtain review and/or reconsideration. The S.E.C. itself recently

Sloan, 369 F. Supp. 996, 1001, ¶28 (S.D.N.Y. 1974) contains a finding that on May 24, 1973 Respondent had a net capital deficiency in the amount of $4,383. An injunction based in part on this finding was cited as a basis for the decision to revoke Respondent's broker-dealer registration. Moreover, the finding itself was specifically cited by the S.E.C. as establishing a recurrance of violations of the net capital rule. See *In the Matter of Samuel H. Sloan*, Securities Exchange Act Release No. 11376, 6 SEC Docket 772, 775, n. 19 (Pet. in 76-1547, App. 32a, n. 19). However, this figure was arrived at by deducting from the capital of Respondent the sum of $11,000, which represented the gross dollar amount of fails to deliver by Respondent in shares of Triex International Corp., a security then the subject of a series of consecutive ten-day trading suspension orders which had the effect of suspending trading for more than one year (App. 207). The basis for the S.E.C.'s deduction of $11,000 was a release, dated June 8, 1973 and applied 15 days retroactively in

---

stated: "so-called lifetime bars are actually bars of indefinite duration." *In the Matter of Steadman Security Corp.*, Securities Exchange Act Release No. 13695, 12 SEC Docket 1042, 1064 n. 100 (June 29, 1977). For that matter, as footnote 26 of this brief has pointed out, this Court presently has jurisdiction to review the order revoking Respondent's broker-dealer registration, notwithstanding the denial of certiorari. The reason for this is that the decision and order of the court of appeals involved a consolidated case wherein Respondent sought review of the order revoking his broker-dealer registration and a series of thirty-seven trading suspension orders. The court of appeals upheld two of the orders and vacated the other thirty-six orders. Although this Court granted the S.E.C.'s petition and denied Respondent's petition, the record of the entire case, and not just the record of the thirty-six orders which the court of appeals vacated, is required to be transmitted to this Court. This Court has the discretionary authority to pass upon the validity of the order revoking Respondent's broker-dealer registration much as if, in a case where this Court grants certiorari but limits the argument to certain specified questions, it may, in reaching a decision, pass upon other questions, either with or without hearing reargument. Admittedly, it seems unlikely that this Court will pass upon the validity of the order revoking Respondent's broker-dealer registration, but the fact remains that it has jurisdiction to do so.

order to penalize Respondent, entitled *Interpretation of Rule 15c3-1 Respecting the Net Capital Treatment of Securities Positions and Transactions in Suspended Securities*, Securities Exchange Act Release No. 10209, 1 SEC Docket, No. 19 (June 8, 1973). This release was issued in accordance with the S.E.C. practice of making a substantive change in a rule by issuing an "interpretation" of the rule which interprets the rule to mean something different from what it says. In this case, Rule 15c3-1, the S.E.C. net capital rule, provides that fails to deliver are counted as an asset and fails to receive are counted as a liability, the logic of this being that fails to deliver represent accounts receivable which are due upon the delivery of securities and fails to receive represent accounts payable due upon the receipt of securities. In the double entry bookkeeping system, every asset is offset by a liability. However, Securities Exchange Act Release No. 10209 upset this equation by its "interpretation" that fails to deliver in suspended securities were not an asset. It so happened that Respondent had a short position of 800 Triex international Corp. shares, and these shares were represented by fails to deliver in that security to various brokers. Under Securities Exchange Act Release No. 7920 (July 19, 1966), explained in Goldman and Magrino, *Suspension of Trading in Securities: Some Observations on Section 15*(c)(5) *of the Securities Exchange Act of 1934*, 15 N.Y.L. Forum 633, 638-643 (1969), brokers are not obliged to accept delivery in suspended securities while the suspension is still in effect. The result of this plus the standard treatment of items under Rule 15c3-1 is that a broker who is short a suspended security is required to carry the short position on his books marked at the full market value at the time trading was suspended and to deduct from his capital a haircut of 30% of that evaluation while at the same time is required to carry long positions in suspended securities at zero and is required to write off to zero any offsetting fails to deliver in suspended securities. This result is illogical and directly contrary to the express language of Rule 15c3-1. The point is that had the S.E.C. not suspended trading in Triex International Corp. for a period of more than one year by the use of consecutive ten-day trading suspension orders which the court of appeals in the instant case declared to be illegal, Respondent would not have been found to be in violation of the net capital rule on May 24, 1973 and, hence, might not have been barred from the securities business. From this it follows that if Respondent prevails in the instant case in this Court, he might be able to use this as a basis to reopen successfully the proceedings against him, since the S.E.C. cannot be permitted to use its own illegal orders as the basis for imposing sanctions against Respondent under the "fruit of the poisonous tree" and related doctrines.[35] Hence, this case is not moot.

D

As noted previously, all of the above points were briefed and argued by Respondent in the court of appeals and in response to the petition for a writ of certiorari and the S.E.C. has remained silent. Therefore, the S.E.C. is foreclosed from raising new objections in this Court. However, there is one argument which Respondent made in the court of appeals which the S.E.C. did not respond to there but which, nevertheless, the S.E.C. has addressed in its brief to this Court. That concerns statements made in paragraph 5 of the affidavit filed by Respondent in op-

35. Even the reversal of one of the findings against Respondent would be sufficient to require reconsideration by the S.E.C. See *NLRB v. Pipefitters*, 429 U.S. 507, 522 n. 9 (1977); *Todd & Co. v. S.E.C.*, 557 F. 2d 1008, 1014 (3rd Cir. 1977). Therefore, if this Court does not reverse the decision of the court of appeals with regard to trading suspensions, it should remand that part of this case dealing with the revocation of Respondent's broker dealer registration to the S.E.C. for reconsideration in light of this Court's decision.

position to the motion of the S.E.C. to dismiss the appeal is moot (App. 153). The statement concerns the number of securities owned by Respondent. The conclusion stated by Respondent in his affidavit was (App. 153):

> "An elementary knowledge of probability theory establishes that based upon this, the likelihood is miniscule that the S.E.C. will never again suspend trading in any security in which I have an interest. Thus, even under the standard proposed by the S.E.C., this case is not moot."

Although the S.E.C. said nothing about this to the court of appeals, in its brief to this Court, the S.E.C. has addressed the point made by Respondent and has siezed upon an obvious typo as the basis for launching a general attack on Respondent's credibility. In order to do so, page 16 of the brief filed on behalf of the S.E.C. in this Court quotes a sentence from Respondent's brief which stated (Br. in Response, p. 18):

> "As Respondent set forth in an affidavit filed with the court of appeals . . . Respondent continues to own stock in nearly 400 publically traded corporations . . ."

However, the affidavit in question actually said 200, rather than 400, corporations (App. 153). Therefore, the obvious fact is that there was an error in the brief filed by Respondent in this Court with regard to the number of securities.[36] However, rather than simply point out this

36. The S.E.C. has not been without errors of its own. For example, the complaint filed by the S.E.C. in 1971 alleged that Respondent was "not permitting" violations of the Securities Exchange Act of 1934. When Respondent understandably moved to dismiss for failure to state a claim, the

error, the S.E.C. has made a great issue of this, stating (Brief p. 18), "the number of publically traded corporations in which respondent owns shares is now in doubt. . . . A more accurate count is necessary before a meaningful assessment of probability bearing upon mootness may be made."

It so happens that there are substantial problems in making an "accurate count" of the securities owned by Respondent. The vast majority of securities owned by Respondent were purchased when Respondent was an active broker-dealer in securities. Due to the nature of the type of securities most often dealt in by Respondent, namely low-priced securities traded over-the-counter, a broker, after selling the security to Respondent, would sometimes discover that there was no longer a transfer agent and the delivery of shares in good negotiable form could not be made. Rather than antagonize the broker in

---

S.E.C. stated that this was a "typographical error," and the words "not permitting" should have read "now permitting." Judge Ward accepted this explanation and denied the motion (See Pet. 76-365, p. 17a). In addition the papers filed by the S.E.C. stated that Respondent had never provided the S.E.C. with a copy of his April, 1971 trial balance, a charge vehemently denied by Respondent. After resisting discovery motions, subpoenas and other court process to compel the S.E.C. to produce the trial balance, the S.E.C., during the course of the trial before Judge Ward in December, 1973 searched its files and produced two copies of the April, 1971 trial balance, after having been ordered by Judge Ward to do so. The S.E.C. admitted that these documents had been delivered to the S.E.C. on May 20, 1971, and on June 18, 1971, but stated that they had been lost in the files of the attorney assigned to the case due to an "oversight." Material subsequently obtained by Respondent pursuant to the Freedom of Information Act includes a 1971 memorandum by the same S.E.C. attorney discussing the documents in question, however. Meanwhile, and S.E.C. investigator testified at the administrative hearing before the S.E.C. and again at the trial before Judge Ward that Respondent never submitted an April, 1971 trial balance and this charge was included in proposed findings of fact filed with the Administrative Law Judge and with Judge Ward and this testimony has never been withdrawn. Other "errors" committed by the S.E.C. include the misreading or misquotation of transcripts introduced for impeachment purposes during the course of the trial before Judge Ward.

question, which was most often a major firm, and risk losing its business, Respondent did not issue a buy-in notice and instead allowed the firm to hold the securities in question on account. Since the S.E.C. apparently now wishes to verify the exact number of securities owned by Respondent, presumably by a physical inspection of these securities, Respondent, for the purposes of this appeal, has made a list of securities he owned at the time of the decision of the court of appeals dated November 18, 1976 and were or are now in his physical possession. Respondent intends to produce these securities for inspection by the S.E.C. and the Solicitor General and, if the S.E.C. refuses to agree to this inspection,[37] to produce them at the time this case is

---

37. In analogous situations in the past the S.E.C. has refused to agree to an inspection. For example, during the course of events which led to the decision reported as *S.E.C. v. Sloan*, 369 F. Supp. 996, and in the parallel administrative proceeding, in response to claims by the S.E.C. staff that Respondent's books and records "were not properly maintained," Respondent made numerous offers to produce his books and records at the offices of the S.E.C. for inspection by members of the S.E.C. staff superior to Bruder and Kanoff, the two staff investigators who examined Respondent's records in his office, and the S.E.C. staff refused to agree to an inspection. On January 18, 1971, Respondent brought all of his records to the offices of the S.E.C. and they were examined by Alan Rashes, the staff attorney then assigned to the case, but the S.E.C. subsequently refused to acknowledge that this examination had taken place. See e.g. *In the Matter of Samuel H. Sloan, supra*, 6 SEC Docket 772, 774 where the S.E.C. found that on January 18, 1971 Respondent "submitted something." Subsequently, in January, 1976 when Respondent was found in "contempt of court" for failing to produce his books and records "in an easily accessible place," Respondent's mother, who had physical possession of the records (Respondent was in Iceland at the time), called Thomas L. Taylor III, the attorney in the S.E.C. Office of General Counsel assigned to the case, and offered to produce the records for inspection by the S.E.C. staff but Mr. Taylor, on behalf of the S.E.C., refused to agree to an inspection. Again, the S.E.C. staff has since refused to acknowledge that this conversation took place (and Mr. Taylor has since left the S.E.C.). There were obvious strategic reasons for these decisions. Had a supervisory person in the S.E.C. Division of Broker-Dealer Inspection examined Respondent's books in the period 1971-1973 and found, contrary to his subordinates, that Respondent's books and records were properly maintained, the S.E.C. staff would have been forced to abandon its

argued before this Court.[38] The securities in question form a stack several feet high.

Included as Appendix E to this brief is a list of security positions held by Respondent on November 18, 1976, the date of the decision of the court of appeals. Appendix E also gives the date the security was suspended, if it has ever been the subject of an S.E.C. suspension. A remarkable

---

prosecution of Respondent, something it clearly did not wish to do. Similarly, had Mr. Taylor, in January, 1976, agreed to an inspection of Respondent's books and records by the S.E.C. staff, the S.E.C. would have been forced to discontinue contempt proceedings against Respondent and in turn the three appeals taken by Respondent to the court of appeals would not have been subject to dismissal and the injunctions obtained by the S.E.C. might have been reversed. (The S.E.C. staff ultimately did examine Respondent's records but only after having been ordered to do so by Judge Ward and only then after Respondent had spent two days in jail.) Thus, there is reason to believe that the S.E.C. might refuse to examine the actual stock certificates owned by Respondent, for strategic reasons, although in this Court the S.E.C. is required to act through the Office of the Solicitor General, which has a better reputation for integrity than the S.E.C. staff.

38 The procedure of producing physical items, in this case stock certificates, may seem unorthodox, but Respondent has used it before. In the first district court case, in view of the claim by the S.E.C. staff that Respondent's records were "not available for inspection," Respondent produced all of his records in court and they remained on his table throughout the duration of the trial. In spite of the S.E.C. staff's specious claim that they were eager to examine Respondent's records, they made no attempt to do so. Most of these records were then offered into evidence by Respondent, and the S.E.C. staff still did not examine them even then. To this day, these records are in the custody of the Clerk of the Southern District of New York, and, as far as Respondent is aware, have never been examined by the S.E.C. (Inexplicably, although he acknowledged the presence of these records in the courtroom (Trial Transcript p. 295), Judge Ward found that "at no time since August 16, 1973, has Sloan made his books and records available for inspection by the Commission," 369 F. Supp. at 999, ¶ 20 even though Respondent, through counsel, had offered to turn his records over to the S.E.C. in toto, and no testimony or evidence had been offered by the S.E.C. at trial in support of Judge Wards' finding). Similarly, at the oral argument of the instant case before the court of appeals, Respondent produced for inspection by the court his 13 shares of Canadian Javelin Ltd., in order to prove that he owned the actual securities rather than a mere photocopy (App. 179-181).

thing about this list is the number of securities held by Respondent which at some time have been the subject of an S.E.C. suspension. An explanation for this can be found from the circumstances which often arise as the result of a trading suspension. As noted previously, Respondent at one time or another was a market maker in approximately one thousand securities. Normally, whenever Respondent stopped making a market in a security, he would sell out whatever position he held. However, in cases where the S.E.C. suspended trading in the security, Respondent had no chance to sell and was left holding whatever inventory he happened to have on hand at the time the suspension was announced. Moreover, after the termination of the suspension, Rule 15c2-11, which has been discussed previously, came into play. In order for a previously suspended security to start trading again, it is necessary for a broker to file a Form 211. Even if all of the information required by Form 211 is readily available, the vast majority of brokers are unwilling to risk the potential liability entailed in the filing of the form. In addition, many of the securities held by Respondent were suspended by the S.E.C. from trading for the very reason of a delinquency in a 10-K filing. Because of the S.E.C.'s application of Rule 15c2-11, which is at variance with what the rule itself says, unless and until a corporation is up to date in filing its 10-K reports, the filing of a Form 211 will not be accepted by the S.E.C. Most of the corporations suspended by the S.E.C. for delinquency in filing a 10-K report have never brought their 10-K filings up to date and the S.E.C. has not allowed trading in their securities to resume for that reason, even though in all cases the order suspending trading expired long ago. Therefore, Respondent has never had the opportunity to sell these securities and he continues to own them to this day.

This does not entirely explain the fact that Respondent is a stockholder in so many corporations whose securities have been suspended from trading by the S.E.C. Many securities presently held by Respondent were suspended from trading by the S.E.C. before Respondent purchased them, such as Baylock Instrument Corp., which was suspended from trading by the S.E.C. in 1965, years before Respondent was even in business. However, it should be noted that there are at present an average of 10,000 securities quoted daily in the pink sheets, which includes listings for securities which are traded in the "third market" and are primarily traded on a national securities exchange.[39] The S.E.C. states in its petition (Pet. 9) that subsequent to the 1964 amendments to the Securities Exchange Act and prior to the decision of the court of appeals dated November 18, 1976, the S.E.C. used the suspension power with respect to a total of 941 securities. Even not considering the fact that when the S.E.C. suspends trading, it normally suspends trading in "all securities" of the offending corporation, and thus many of these 941 suspensions resulted in a suspension of all common, preferred, warrant, debenture and other issues, the S.E.C. has suspended trading in 9.41% of all over-the-counter securities. Of course, this is by no means a precise calculation, since many securities which have in the past been suspended from trading by the S.E.C. may have since ceased to be outstanding as a result of a merger, liquidation, bankruptcy reorganization, or any one of a number of other possible events. However, the point is that assuming even that the securities owned by Respondent con-

---

39. Respondent obtained the figure of 10,000 securities from Ed Lubensky, Head of the Library Department, and from Dave Burnett, Vice President of the National Quotation Bureau, Inc. The figure of 10,000 as being the number of securities listed in the daily pink sheets can also be found in numerous published sources. In reaching this number, if, for example, a corporation has an issue of common, an issue of preferred, and an issue of warrants outstanding, this is treated as three securities listed in the pink sheets. Thus, the number of corporate *issuers* which have securities listed in the pink sheets is significantly less than 10,000.

stituted a random sample of all over-the-counter securities, a substantial percentage of them would at some time in the past have been suspended from trading by the S.E.C.

As noted previously, Appendix E is a list of security positions held by Respondent on the date of the decision of the court of appeals and either then or now in his possession. The choice of the November 18, 1976 date seems most appropriate, since the S.E.C.'s argument to this Court is that the decision of the court of appeals was erroneous because on the date of that decision, this case was moot. Of course, this perceived error in the decision of the court of appeals is based upon facts which the court of appeals did not and could not have known. The S.E.C. did not question the number of securities held by Respondent when the case was pending before that court and did not suggest that Respondent should prove the number of securities he owned at that time. One reason for this is that the S.E.C. already knew that Respondent owned a large number of securities. Of course, it did not know the exact number of securities owned by Respondent on a particular date, although it could easily have ascertained this information, but it did know that Respondent owned an exceptionally large portfolio of securities. As Respondent stated in his affidavit to the court of appeals (App. 153):

> "I also own securities of more than 200 corporate issuers. On February 4, 1976 Ralph Pernick and Alexander Worobec of the S.E.C. staff examined the stock certificates representing my ownership in these securities."

In addition to that, Respondent, over the years, has submitted a large number of trial balances and capital computations to the S.E.C., many of which are included in the record of the administrative proceeding before the S.E.C. which is, or should be, included in the record of this appeal, and each of these trial balances and capital computations has contained a list of securities owned by Respondent. Moreover, in the course of various broker-dealer inspections of Respondent, members of the S.E.C. staff have conducted several "box counts" of the securities owned by Respondent. Thus, the S.E.C. staff knew that Respondent owned a large number of securities and that raising an issue in the court of appeals with regard to the number of securities owned by Respondent was not going to help the position of the S.E.C. Of course, it should be pointed out that the argument contained on pp. 17-19 of the S.E.C.'s brief in this Court was apparently conceived by the Solicitor General's office and the Solicitor General does not have the first-hand knowledge that the S.E.C. has of the number of securities owned by Respondent.

The list of securities included in Appendix E to this brief would not be the same as a list of securities held by Respondent on the date of his affidavit to the court of appeals nor the list of securities held by Respondent on the date he filed his brief in response to the petition for writ of certiorari in this Court, nor presumably will be the same as the list of securities held by Respondent on the date this appeal is argued and on the date this appeal is decided by this Court. This is not surprising since Respondent is a professional securities trader and his securities portfolio is subject to frequent changes. However, considering the list which is included in Appendix E, a number of observations can be made. The list contains securities of a total of 150 corporate issuers. In several cases Respondent owns more than one security of the same issuer. Fifty-five of these corporate issuers have had all of their securities suspended by the S.E.C. at one time or another since the 1964 amendments to the Securities Exchange Act. Although Appendix E does not indicate this, twelve of these have been the subject of a series of consecutive trading suspension orders.[40] Of the securities listed in Appendix E, only one is listed on the New York Stock Exchange, that being Playboy Enterprises, Inc. Two are listed on the American Stock Exchange, Applied Devices Corp. and Canadian Javelin Ltd. However, Respondent sold his shares in Applied Devices Corp. in early 1977, shortly after that security resumed trading on the American Stock Exchange after having been suspended from trading on that exchange for almost six years. Canadian Javelin Ltd., while it has continued to be listed on the American Stock Exchange, has been suspended from trading on that exchange since April 30, 1975, one day after the S.E.C. invoked its trading suspension.

On page 19, n. 8 of its brief, the S.E.C. proffers a mathematical formula with regard to the probability of a future trading suspension adversely affecting Respondent. Respondent concedes the mathematical accuracy of this formula, but does not concede that the arguments advanced by the S.E.C. are properly raised for the first time at this late date. At any event, Respondent is prepared to argue that even under the premises upon which this mathematical formula is based, this case is not moot. To begin with, it should be pointed out that according to the S.E.C.'s calculation, there is a probability of "approximately .740" that one of the securities held by Respondent will be subject to consecutive trading suspension orders within the next five years. This would seem to constitute a virtual admission that this case is not moot under

---

40. These are Applied Devices Corp., Canadian Javelin Ltd., Electrospace Corp., Four Seasons Nursing Centers of America, Inc., Franklin National Bank, Lilac Time Inc., Old Town Corp., Phoon Inc., The Seabord Corp., Topper Corp., Triex International Corp., and Baylock Instrument Corp. Since the date of the decision of the court of appeals, Respondent has sold his stock in Applied Devices Corp.

Roe v. Wade, 410 U.S. 113, 125 (1973). Recognizing this, the S.E.C. claims it needs to make a "more accurate count" of the securities held by Respondent. Accordingly, it is appropriate to substitute a few numbers into the mathematical formula offered by the S.E.C. in order to determine how the substitution of these numbers is likely to affect the computation of the probability that one of the securities held by Respondent will be subject to a suspension order or a series of consecutive suspension orders at some time within the reasonably immediate future.

First, it should be noted that the numbers suggested by the S.E.C. are wrong. It claims that "the Commission's staff has estimated that between 25,000 and 30,000 corporations have publically traded stock." No authority is given for this self-serving statement. Respondent regards himself as something of an expert in obsolete and obscure securities, and must state that the numbers suggested by the S.E.C. are high by any reasonable calculation. As noted previously, there are approximately 10,000 securities listed daily in the pink sheets, and that includes in many cases different issues of securities by the same corporate issuer. The National Stock Summary, which is an authoritative volume published by the National Quotation Bureau, Inc., lists approximately 20,000 securities. However, this volume lists all securities which have been quoted at any time in the past seven years and includes many securities which have been the subject of a name change, have been merged out of existence, or called or are no longer outstanding for any one of a number of reasons. Indeed, with the exception of securities which have been at one time or another suspended from trading by the S.E.C., in which case the S.E.C. has invoked Rule 15c2-11 to prevent trading in most of these securities from resuming, the vast majority of all securities which have traded during the past seven years and which are still in existence, are listed in the daily pink sheets. The most recent issue of the *Directory of Companies Required to File Annual Reports With the Securities and Exchange Commission Under the Securities Exchange Act of 1934,* which is dated June 30, 1977 and is published by the Superintendent of Documents, lists 9,447 companies required to file reports. Even this list includes many corporations which do not have equity securities trading in public markets. In short, the number of "corporations who have publically traded stock" is much less than what the S.E.C. claims it to be for the purposes of this appeal.

In order to arrive at the inflated figures set forth in its brief, the S.E.C. has no doubt included the large number of banks which have stock outstanding. The *E-Z Directory of Brokers and Banks* sells a list of 15,500 banks in the United States. Almost every country bank in the United States has publicly traded stock, in the sense that members of the local community own shares in the bank and buy and sell them from time to time. Many larger banks are listed in the pink sheets but most of these are regarded as inactive issues. It seems virtually certain that at least half of the "25,000 to 30,000 corporations" that have publicly traded stock are banks. The problem with including banks in the list of all publicly traded corporations is that the S.E.C. does not have the authority to suspend trading in a security issued by a bank. This is because §12(i) of the Securities Exchange Act, 15 U.S.C. §78*l*(i), vests that authority in the Comptroller of the Currency, the Board of Governors of the Federal Reserve System, the Federal Deposit Insurance Corporation, or the Federal Home Loan Bank Board, depending on the nature of the bank.[41] Thus, the universe of "30,000 publically traded

41. In a recent celebrated instance, the Comptroller of the Currency suspended trading in the National Bank of Georgia. On p. 13, n. 25 of the

issues" posited by the S.E.C. in its brief is much too large and the actual number of publically traded issues which might be the subject of an S.E.C. trading suspension is almost certainly no larger than 10,000 or 15,000.

The S.E.C. also relies on the assertion that it has issued consecutive suspension orders suspending trading in an average of twenty securities during the past twelve years. However, many of these securities were suspended more than once, a prime example of this being Canadian Javelin Ltd., which has been the subject of consecutive trading suspension orders on four distinct occasions. In addition, many securities were suspended from trading for a period of more than one year, the best known example of this being Continental Vending Machine Corp., which was suspended from trading for a period of more than 13 years. Thus, although it is presumably true that the S.E.C. has issued consecutive trading suspension orders with respect to 234 different corporate issuers during the past twelve years as it claims, it is not correct simply to divide the number 234 by 12, which equals 19.5, rounded off by the S.E.C. to 20, to arrive at the number of securities which are the subject of a consecutive series of trading suspension orders within the average year. In addition, the S.E.C. treats a series of orders as though it were one order. If one calculated the number of consecutive trading suspension orders issued by the S.E.C., it would

---

S.E.C.'s petition for rehearing in the court of appeals, it states, "The Comptroller of the Currency issued orders which continuously suspended trading in the stock of Mercantile National Bank of Atlanta, Georgia, from May 13, 1976, to July 23, 1976 (31 Fed. Reg. 20592 (May 19, 1976); 41 Fed. Reg. 29436 (July 16, 1976)). The Federal Deposit Insurance Corporation has suspended trading in the securities of Farmers Bank of the State of Delaware from March 9, 1976, through June 15, 1976 (41 Fed. Reg. 10713 (March 12, 1976); 41 Fed. Reg. 23228 (June 9, 1976)), and in the securities of the Unity State Bank of Dayton, Ohio, from July 7, 1976, through July 26, 1976 (41 Fed. Reg. 28583 (July 12, 1976); 41 Fed. Reg. 30213 (July 22 1976))."

be much higher. Continental Vending Machine Corp. alone was the subject of 484 separate trading suspension orders. Canadian Javelin Ltd. has been the subject of a total of 100 separate orders during the four periods in which it has been suspended from trading. Furthermore, it is not correct simply to count the number of securities which have the subject of a series of consecutive trading suspension orders. In the instant case, Respondent challenged the validity of the orders suspending trading in Canadian Javelin Ltd. on a number of grounds, just one of them being that the issuance of a series of consecutive trading suspension orders was illegal. Respondent also contended, *inter alia,* that there was no substantial evidence in the record to support the trading suspension orders and hence they must be set aside. In resolving the question of mootness, this Court is determining whether the court of appeals had jurisdiction to review the trading suspension orders generally, not merely with respect to the one issue on which Respondent prevailed. If this Court accepts the argument of the S.E.C. that only the history of prior consecutive trading suspension orders should be considered in determining whether this case is moot, the result will be that anyone seeking to challenge the validity of a single trading suspension order on the grounds of insubstantiality of the evidence or on any other grounds except the grounds on which Respondent prevailed in the instant case, would be foreclosed by the S.E.C.'s mootness argument. The S.E.C. states that it suspended trading in securities of a total of 941 corporate issuers during the twelve years preceding the decision of the court of appeals and that is the number of securities which should be considered in a determination of the probability that one of the securities owned by Respondent or one in his position will be the subject of a future trading suspension order.

With these considerations in mind, it is appropriate to insert a few numbers in the mathematical formula set forth in the S.E.C.'s brief. It should be noted that the S.E.C. always takes the higher number or the number most favorable to the S.E.C. For example, when it estimates that there are between 25,000 and 30,000 corporations that have publicly traded stock, it posits a "universe of 30,000 publicly traded issues." However, the burden is on the S.E.C. to show that this case is moot and not on Respondent to show that this case is not moot, and therefore the S.E.C. should be required to take the lower rather than the higher figure. Thus, assuming that there are between 10,000 and 15,000 corporations with publicly traded stock, it is appropriate to assume that there are 10,000 corporations with publicly traded stock and that Respondent owns securities issued by 150 of these corporations. Finally, the number of securities which have been suspended during the average year by the S.E.C. for the twelve years prior to the decision of the court of appeals is 941 divided by 12, which is 78.4. However, during the four years immediately preceding the decision of the court of appeals, the S.E.C. engaged in a rapidly accelerating program of trading suspensions and thus it is appropriate to consider the number of securities suspended from trading by the S.E.C. during this period, particularly since during the early years trading suspensions were relatively rare.[42] In the four years preceding the decision of the court of appeals, not counting the period between the time of the decision of the court of appeals and the end of 1976, the S.E.C. suspended trading in all securities of a total of 615 corporate issuers, or an average of 153.75 per year.[43] Rounding this off to 154, one finds

---

42. In 1964, the S.E.C. suspended trading in only one security, in 1965 only nine, and in 1966 only ten. In contrast, in 1973 the S.E.C. suspended trading in 236 securities, in 1974 in 168, in 1975 in 97, and in 1976, prior to the decision of the court of appeals, in 114. The S.E.C. suspended trading in another 16 securities in 1976 after the decision of the court of appeals.

43. According to Respondent's calculations, the S.E.C. suspended trading in securities of a total of 858 corporate issuers between 1964 and 1976. The

that under the formula in footnote 8 of the S.E.C.'s brief, a=10,000 - 150 = 9,850, b=150, and n = 154. Substituting these numbers into the S.E.C.'s formula, we find that P = .904. In other words, there is a more than 90% probability that trading will be suspended in one of the securities owned by Respondent in a given year, assuming that the trading suspensions continue at the rate prevailing prior to the decision of the court of appeals. This calculation conforms with actual experience because it can be seen from Appendix E that even not considering the trading suspensions of Canadian Javelin Ltd., during every year from 1970 through 1976 with the exception of 1975, at least one of the securities owned by Respondent was the subject of a trading suspension order. Furthermore, again not counting Canadian Javelin Ltd., during the years 1970, 1972, 1973, and 1974 at least one security owned by Respondent was the subject of a series of successive trading suspension orders. That is four out of seven years although according to the calculations of the S.E.C., the probability is only .236 that this will happen in a given year. Taking the more realistic figure of .904 as the probability of a security owned by Respondent being the subject of a trading suspension order during a given year and substituting that into the second formula proffered by the S.E.C., one comes up with a probability of .9999919 that one of the securities owned by Respondent will be the subject of a trading suspension order within the next five years. This is precisely what Respondent said, without the benefit of these mathematical computations, in his affidavit to the court of appeals when he stated (App. 153): "An elementary knowledge of probability theory establishes that based upon this, the likelihood is miniscule

---

brief for the S.E.C. states that the number is 941. It may be that the list provided by the S.E.C. to Respondent, as well as the list which is included in the appendix (App. 183-211), is not complete.

that the S.E.C. will never again suspend trading in any security in which I have an interest."

Of course, the S.E.C. does not accept the numbers or the reasoning just set forth. However, even using the S.E.C.'s numbers, fallacious as they may be, is not helpful to the S.E.C.'s position. Taking the equation offered by the S.E.C. and accepting the S.E.C.'s number of 30,000 publically traded issues and the number of 20 as the number of securities that will be subjected to consecutive suspension orders in the average year and reducing the number of securities owned by Respondent from 400 to 150, and again calculating the results, one finds that a = 29,850, b = 150, and n = 20, and that P = .096. This works out to a probability of .396 that one of the securities owned by Respondent will be the subject of series of successive trading suspension orders within the next five years.[44] Admittedly, this figure indicates a less than 50% chance but even this establishes a sufficiently substantial likelihood to preclude a claim by the S.E.C. that the case is moot. For example, published statistics indicate that nowadays the average American woman of childbearing age bears 1.9 children. From this, plus a consideration of other relevant factors, one might reasonably conclude that the average woman seeking an abortion has a less than 50% chance of becoming pregnant in the future. Nevertheless, this Court has invariably held that actions brought by pregnant women seeking abortions do not become moot nine months later and this Court has never seen the need to make the type of mathematical computations as to the probability of future pregnancy which are comparable

---

44. Respondent has made these calculations with an electronic calculator which does not have the capacity to handle some of the large numbers involved in these computations. Therefore, these computations may not be accurate to the last digit. However, using the same methods Respondent finds the figures given in the S.E.C.'s brief to be correct, at least from a mathematical point of view.

to those suggested in the brief by the S.E.C. In addition, it should be noted that the brief of the S.E.C. states (Brief pp. 18-19):

> "Moreover, application of principles of mathematical probability ideally would require information about the nature of respondent's portfolio. If the bulk of the securities respondent owns are listed on the New York Stock Exchange, or are of other well established and widely held corporations (such as many banks and insurance companies whose shares are traded over the counter), the practical likelihood of a suspension order may be small indeed since suspension of trading in such securities is extremely rare. On the other hand, if respondent's securities are predominantly those of less established issuers, there could well be a substantial probability that one of them will be subject to consecutive orders suspending trading within the next few years."

It so happens that the statement by the S.E.C. that the suspension of trading in securities of "well estblished and widely held corporations . . . is extremely rare," is false. On November 20, 1974, the S.E.C. suspending trading in American Telephone & Telegraph Co., Securities Exchange Act Release No. 11111, 5 SEC Docket 508 (November 20, 1974) (App. 185), and on January 24, 1975, the S.E.C. suspended trading in International Business Machines Corp., Securities Exchange Act Release No. 11208, 6 SEC Docket 189 (January 24, 1975). American Telephone & Telegraph Co. is the most widely held publicly traded corporation in the United States and International Business Machines Corp. is the largest corporation in the United States in terms of market value of publically held securities outstanding. Nevertheless, since it happens that the securities held by Respondent are "predominantly those of less established issuers", Respondent will not quarrel with this particular argument presented by the S.E.C. since the S.E.C. apparently is prepared to admit that this circumstance establishes that there is "a substantial probability that one of them will be subject to consecutive orders suspending trading within the next few years."

E

For all of the foregoing reasons it is abundantly clear that this case is not moot. The diverse claims the S.E.C. has made in an effort to get this Court and the court of appeals to declare this case to be moot all boil down to the assertion that when the S.E.C. voluntarily ceased issuing the series of orders suspending trading in Canadian Javelin Ltd., the case became moot. This argument is foreclosed by this Court's decision in *United States v. W.T. Grant Co.,* 345 U.S. 629, 632 (1953) which held that "voluntary cessation of allegedly illegal conduct . . . does not make the case moot" because to accept this argument would be to give the S.E.C. "a powerful weapon against public law enforcement" and the S.E.C. would be "free to return to [its] old ways. This, together with a public interest in having the legality of the practices settled, militates against a mootness conclusion." *Id.* Even in cases such as *Roe v. Wade, supra,* and *Sosna v. Iowa,* 419 U.S. 393, 399-403 (1975), where the plaintiff lost all interest in the outcome of the controversy shortly after the action was commenced, this Court has refused to declare the case to be moot. The case presented here is considerably less susceptible to a mootness argument since at present Respondent undoubtedly has a substantial interest in the outcome of this case. Indeed, were it not so, Respondent would not have been in a position to bear the enormous effort and expense required to appear before this Court and file this brief.

III

THE ISSUANCE OF A SERIES OF SUCCESSIVE TEN-DAY TRADING SUSPENSION ORDERS WHICH HAVE THE EFFECT OF SUSPENDING TRADING IN A SECURITY FOR A PERIOD EXCEEDING TEN DAYS IS A VIOLATION OF SECTION 12(K) OF THE SECURITIES EXCHANGE ACT

Section 12(k) of the Securities Exchange Act, 15 U.S.C. §78*l*(k), authorizes the S.E.C. "summarily to suspend trading in any security (other than an exempted security) for a period not exceeding ten days . . ." The S.E.C. contends that when Congress included the words "for a period not exceeding ten days" in the statute, it intended to give the S.E.C. the authority to suspend trading in a security for as long a period of time as the S.E.C. deems appropriate. Although the S.E.C. has never contended that this was the intent of Congress at the time it originally enacted the Securities Exchange Act in 1934, it claims that the failure of Congress to amend the statute during the intervening 44 years to even more expressly limit the suspension of trading in a security to "a period not exceeding ten days," establishes that Congress has acquiesced to the assumption of power by the S.E.C. to suspend trading in a security for longer time periods. This contention must be rejected for a number of reasons.

A

The authority to suspend trading in a security was originally given to the S.E.C. in 19(a)(4) of the Securities Exchange Act, 15 U.S.C. §78*s*(a)(4). Section 19(a)(4) was not included in the original drafts of the Securities Exchange Act but was added to the House version on May 4, 1934, 78 Cong. Rec. 8116 (1934), and to the Senate version on May 17, 1934. (In the House version, the provision was included as §18(a)(4) of the Securities Exchange Act.) There was no debate concerning §19(a)(4) in either the House or the Senate. The only debate concerning §19 occurred on April 30, 1934 and dealt with §19(b). 78 Cong. Rec. 8086-8093 (1934). Nevertheless, the purpose for which the trading suspension power was intended is obvious from its placement in the statute. This is explained in both the Senate and House reports. Senate Report No. 792, 73rd Cong., 2d Sess. 21 (1934) states:

> "Section 19. Disciplinary Powers over Exchanges.
>
> Subsection (a) authorizes the Commission when it deems such action necessary (1) to suspend for not more than 12 months or withdraw registration of an exchange which has violated the act or the rules and regulations thereunder or has failed to take adequate steps to enforce the same; (2) to suspend for not more than 12 months, or to withdraw the registration of a security of, an issuer who has failed to comply with the act or rules and regulations thereunder; (3) to suspend for not more than 12 months or expel a member or officer of an exchange who is guilty of a violation or of aiding a violation by acting for a person who, he has reason to believe, is engaged in a violation; and (4) summarily to suspend all trading in any registered security for a period not exceeding 10 days or with the approval of the President of the United States summarily to suspend all trading on a registered exchange for not more than 90 days. Orders issued pursuant to (1),(2), and (3) must be preceded by appropriate notice and opportunity for hearing; action under (4) is of an emergency nature and, therefore, may be exercised summarily."

With respect to its discussion of §19(a)(4), the language of the House report is identical. See House Report No. 1383, 73rd Cong., 2d Sess. 25. Thus, it is apparent that Congress included the trading suspension power in the Securities Exchange Act to enable the S.E.C. to bring about an immediate halt to the illegal or fraudulent sale of a security so as to give it time to institute suit or administrative proceedings or take other appropriate action before the occurrence of further injury to the investing public. Unfortunately, the S.E.C. did not use the trading suspension power in the way in which it was intended. Instead of being used as a stop-gap measure, it has become a remedy of last resort. During the first ten years of its existence, the trading suspension power was not invoked at all. The brief the S.E.C. has filed in this Court (Brief, p. 33, n. 14) states that during this period the policy of the S.E.C. was to institute deregistration proceedings pursuant to §19(a)(2) of the Securities Exchange Act. It is noteworthy that it was during this period of time that Mr. Justice Douglas was Chairman of the S.E.C. and the S.E.C. never resorted to the use of a summary trading suspension order. The brief for the S.E.C. indicates that around 1944 the S.E.C. abandoned its use of the relatively cumbersome deregistration proceedings under §19(a)(2) of the Securities Exchange Act and began to make use of the more expeditious summary trading suspension power authorized by §19(a)(4) of the Securities Exchange Act. However, this statement is inaccurate as is shown *infra.* The article by Goldstein and Mangrino, *supra,* 15 N.Y.L. Forum at 657-673 provides a complete chronological list of all 146 trading suspensions from November 24, 1974 until August 1, 1969 and gives the number of all Securities Exchange Act releases issued in connection therewith and other information.

Although the S.E.C. adopted in 1944 the practice of suspending trading in a security for a period exceeding ten days by the use of successive ten-day trading suspension orders, it was apparently prepared at one time to admit forthrightly that Congress had not expressly authorized this practice. For example, on April 16, 1959, the Chairman of the S.E.C., Edward N. Gadsby, addressed the American Society of Corporate Secretaries as follows

(Gadsby, "Current S.E.C. Legislative and Related Problems," 189 *Commercial &Financial Chronicle* 1863, 1903 (1959), cited in II Loss, *Securities Regulation* 184-185 (2d ed. 1961):

> "We have further recommended that Congress extend the Commission's existing authority summarily to suspend a security from trading on a national securities exchange for a period not exceeding 10 days when necessary in the public interest. Lately, this grant of power has been used to keep in effect a suspension of trading pending final disposition of delisting proceedings under Section 19(a)(2) of the Act. It has been useful where it has appeared that the current information available to the public concerning a security is misleading or is inadequate to permit investors to make informed judgments with respect to its purchase or sale, and it appears that the additional necessary information cannot be obtained and made available to investors until all the facts are elicited through the 19(a)(2) proceedings. These proceedings, because of their complexity often cannot be completed within a single 10-day period, and it has been found necessary to renew the suspension for successive 10-day periods. No express authority for such action is contained in Section 19(a)(4), and its proposed amendment codifies the current interpretation under which the Commission has acted.
>
> The present statutory power of suspension of trading applies only to transactions on a national securities exchange and does not explicitly extend to securities traded only in the over-the-counter markets. Among the Commission's recommendations is included a new Section 15(c)(4) which will give to the Commission comparable statutory power summarily to suspend trading in a security on the over-the-counter markets.
>
> The Commission has also proposed a new section which would authorize the Commission, in its discretion, to institute action on behalf of the United States to recover $100 per day in civil penalties for failure to file any required information or reports. A similar provision now

covers delinquencies in filing reports under Section 15(d), and its extension to other reports is designed further to strengthen the hand of the Commission in enforcing timely filings. The present remedies, principally that of mandatory injunction, have shown themselves to be effective only after substantial additional delay and after cumbersome technical litigation."

From this it is clear that the Chairman of the S.E.C. admitted that there was no authority to suspend trading for a period exceeding ten days under §19(a)(4) of the Securities Exchange Act and, accordingly, the S.E.C. had submitted a "proposed amendment which codifies the current interpretation under which the Commission has acted." However, this proposed amendment failed to pass in Congress. The proposed amendment to §19(a)(4), (H.R. 2480), provided the following (Hearings before a Subcommittee of the House Committee on Interstate and Foreign Commerce, 86th Cong., 1st Sess., on Securities and Exchange Commission Matters 92):

> "Sec. 20. Paragraph (4) of subsection (a) of section 19 of the Securities Exchange Act of 1934, as amended, is amended to read as follows:
>
> '(4) And if in its opinion the public interest so requires, summarily to suspend trading on any national securities exchange in any security registered pursuant to any provision of this title, for one or more periods no one of which shall exceed ten days, or with the approval of the President, summarily to suspend all trading on any national securities exchange for one or more periods no one of which shall exceed ninety days. No broker or dealer shall make use of the mails or of any means or instrumentality of interstate commerce to effect any transaction in, or to induce the purchase or sale of, any security, in which trading is so suspended pursuant to any provision of this clause (4), on a national securities exchange or otherwise."

At the same time, the S.E.C. proposed a new §15(c)(4) of the Securities Exchange Act which provided (*Id.* at 91-92):

> "Sec. 15. Subsection (c) of section 15 of the Securities Exchange Act of 1934, as amended, is amended by adding the following new paragraph:
>
> '(4) If in its opinion the public interest and the protection of investors so requires [sic], the Commission is authorized summarily to suspend trading, otherwise then on a national securities exchange, in any security (other than an exempted security) for one or more periods no one of which shall exceed ten days. No broker or dealer shall make use of the mails or of any means or instrumentality of interstate commerce to effect any transaction in, or to induce the purchase or sale of, any security in which trading is so suspended, otherwise than on a national securities exchange.'

The statement by S.E.C. Chairman Gadsby, who was accompanied by the other four commissioners as well as by future Commissioner Cohen and present Commissioner Loomis among others, *Id.* at 107, to the House Subcommittee as to the reasons for the proposed amendments, explained (*Id.* at 161-162, 163):

> *"Section 15—Extension of the Commission's authority to suspend trading to the over-the-counter markets*
>
> *Present law.*—Section 19(a)(4) authories [sic] the Commission, under certain stated conditions, summarily to suspend trading, for specified periods, in any security registered on a national securities exchange.
>
> *Problem.*—Section 19(a)(4) applies only to trading on a national exchange and the Commission has no comparable statutory power as to securities traded only in the over-the-counter market.

Remedy in the bill.—It is proposed to add a new section 15(c)(4) which will grant the Commission authority summarily to suspend trading in a security in over-the-counter markets similar to the authority to suspend trading on an exchange granted in the proposed amendment to section 19(a)(4). See section 20 below."

******

Sections 19 and 20—Expansion and clarification of the Commission's authority to suspend trading in any registered security on a national securities exchange

Present law.—Section 19(a)(2), which empowers the Commission, after opportunity for hearing, to deny, suspend, or withdraw the registration of a security on a national exchange, does not authorize the Commission to suspend trading in a security which still retains its registered status. Section 19(a)(4) authorizes the Commission, under stated circumstances, summarily to suspend trading on a national exchange in any registered security for a period not exceeding 10 days, or, with the approval of the President, summarily to suspend all trading on any national exchange for a period not exceeding 90 days.

Problem.—(1) During the pendency of proceedings under section 19(a)(2) to determine whether to deny, suspend, or withdraw the registration of a security on a national exchange, the Commission has exercised its summary power to suspend trading under section 19(a)(4). Since this power to suspend is limited to a period of 10 days, the Commission has followed the practice of issuing a series of consecutive orders under section 19(a)(4); but this practice has required a new determination every 10 days of the necessity of continuing the suspension under the standards of that section. Such periodic review and series of orders should be unnecessary to suspend trading during the course of a proceeding under section 19(a)(2).

(2) Generally, the power under section 19(a)(4) summarily to suspend trading in a particular security has been exercised where sudden changes of circumstances make it appear that the information available to the public about a

security is misleading or inadequate to permit investors to make an informed judgment with respect to the purchase or sale of the security, so that there is a possibility for fraud, and it appears that the additional necessary information can be obtained and made available to investors. Sometimes the necessary information cannot be obtained and made available in the 10-day period, and the Commission has had to renew the suspension for one or more additional periods not exceeding 10 days. However, section 19(a)(4) does not expressly provide such authority.

Remedy in the bill.—(1) The proposed amendment to section 19(a)(2) would eliminate the necessity of resorting to a series of successive 10-day suspensions under section 19(a)(4) during the pendency of a proceeding under section 19(a)(2), and would empower the Commission temporarily to suspend trading in a security pending determination of a proceeding under section 19(a)(2).

(2) The proposed amendment to section 19(a)(4) would codify the Commission's interpretation that it has the power to renew temporary suspensions for one or more additional periods not exceeding 10 days each."

As noted previously, these proposed amendments were killed in 1959. After having suffered a resolute rebuff in its efforts to obtain express Congressional authorization for its practice of suspending trading for successive ten-day periods, the S.E.C. came back five years later with a proposal which would not alter in any way the existing language of the statute and merely suggested the enactment of a new §15(c)(5) which did nothing more than extend to over-the-counter securities the S.E.C.'s authority to suspend trading in exchange listed securities. The S.E.C. now contends in this Court that the enactment of §15(c)(5), which is identical in all pertinent respects to §19(a)(4) except that it deals with over-the-counter rather than listed securities, demonstrates Congressional acquiescence to the assumption by the S.E.C. of the power to suspend trading in a security for successive ten day periods. The S.E.C. cites as primary authority for this contention a statement by the S.E.C. to a Congressional committee which said (Hearings on Investor Protection Before the Subcommittee of the House Committee on Interstate and Foreign Commerce, 88th Cong., 1st Sess. 219 (1963)):

> "Under Section 19(a)(4), the Commission has issued more than one suspension when, upon re-examination at the end of the ten-day period, it has decided that another suspension is necessary."

A reading of this sentence indicates that the S.E.C. was less than forthright. The sentence is ambiguous and can reasonably be interpreted to mean that the S.E.C. has on appropriate occasions issued as many as two consecutive trading suspension orders. This sentence says that the S.E.C. has issued "more than one suspension when . . . it has determined that another suspension is necessary." In short, the S.E.C. never advised Congress that in some cases it had suspended trading in a security for a year or more. Up until the time of the August 20, 1964 amendments to the Securities Exchange Act, the S.E.C. had invoked the trading suspension power with respect to securities of only 29 corporations, an average of less than one per year during the 30 years since the passage of the Securities Exchange Act and included in this are suspensions under §19(a)(2) rather than §19(a)(4). Thus, Congress cannot be expected to have had independent knowledge in 1964 of the S.E.C.'s practice of using the ten-day trading suspension power as a basis for suspending trading for much longer time periods since by then the S.E.C. had abandoned the forthrightness it displayed in 1959. However, assuming that a few members of Congress did read the statement of the S.E.C. and in addition realized that the S.E.C. had suspended trading for much more than one or even two ten-day periods, it cannot be said that a majority of both the House and the Senate, in enacting the 1964 amendment, was aware of the S.E.C.'s practice in this regard and acquiesced to it through the passage of the 1964 amendments to the Securities Exchange Act. Indeed, it is more reasonable to assume that precisely the opposite was the case. The statement by the S.E.C. is contained in small type in the voluminous transcript of the subcommittee hearing which is more than a thousand pages in length. It is possible that some members of Congress read the entire transcript and noticed the obscure passage upon which the S.E.C. now places great reliance, but it can hardly be said that a majority of the Senate and a majority of the House was cognizant of what was involved and passed the 1964 amendments to the Securities Exchange Act in full awareness of the implications now suggested by the S.E.C.

This is further demonstrated by the fact that when the 1964 amendments were debated on the floor of the House and the Senate, there was no mention whatever of even the fact that the 1964 amendments would extend the trading suspension power to over-the-counter securities, see 110 Cong. Rec. 17914-17927, 18180-18194, 18377-18389 (August 4-6, 1964), except for one sentence devoted to this provision by Senator Williams, 110 Cong. Rec. 13836 (August 6, 1964). In contrast, all of the other features of the 1964 amendments were discussed in detail. *Id.* In spite of the scant attention given to the grant to the S.E.C. of the authority to suspend trading in over-the-counter securities, this proved to be the power most frequently invoked by the S.E.C. of all of the arsenal of weapons available to it for the obvious reason that of the remedies available to the S.E.C., the trading suspension power is unique in that an aggrieved party is not entitled to notice and the opportunity for a hearing or even to a statement of the reasons for the actions of the S.E.C. It is also significant that in the course of the debates on the House floor,

William L. Carey, the then Chairman of the S.E.C., wrote a letter to the House Committee Chairman which stated (110 Cong. Rec. 18181 (August 5, 1964)):

> "Mr. Farbstein asked whether the failure of a foreign corporation to register or file reports under the bill would automatically mean that american investors and broker-dealers could not trade in that corporation's stock. The answer is categorically 'No,' as is made clear in the House committee report."
>
> "Mr. Farbstein also asked what steps the SEC would take if a domestic company refused to register or file reports as required by the bill. As you pointed out on the floor yesterday, we could move administratively, obtain a mandatory injunction to compel compliance by the issuer, or in cases of willful violation, seek criminal sanctions. These are our traditional remedies; as you will remember, injunctive and civil contempt remedies were finally resorted to in the Goldfine matter. As is the case with foreign corporations, noncompliance with the reporting or registration requirements of the bill does not automatically freeze trading by shareholders or broker-dealers.

Thus, the Chairman of the S.E.C. categorically stated that the failure of a foreign corporation to file its required reports would not make it illegal for U.S. broker -dealers to trade in its securities. In addition, the Chairman of the S.E.C. never suggested that the trading suspension power might be invoked as a remedy if a corporation became delinquent in its required filings. Yet, in the case presented here, one of the reasons given by the S.E.C. for suspending trading in Canadian Javelin Ltd., a foreign corporation, thereby making it illegal for U.S. broker-dealers to trade in its stock, was a delinquency in filing its 10-K report (App. 110). It is apparent from the House debates and from the House Committee Report that had the House been informed that the S.E.C. would exercise the trading suspension power in this manner, the 1964 amendments would have been defeated. Therefore, contrary to the contentions of the S.E.C., the legislative history of the 1964 amendments to the Securities Exchange Act makes it abundantly clear that the exercise of the trading suspension power in the instant case was not in accordance with the expressed intent of Congress.

B

The S.E.C. argues in its brief (Br. 22):

> "First, the statutory phrase 'for a period not exceeding ten days' cannot mean that there may be only one period of suspension for each security. Thus, if the Commission detects a manipulative scheme affecting a security and therefore suspends trading in that security for ten days, it must retain the power to suspend trading anew if, 30 days later, it detects yet another manipulative scheme. The phrase 'for a period not exceeding ten days' therefore can only be read as limiting the duration of a single suspension order, not as limiting the amount of time that a particular security may be subject to suspension of trading.
>
> But if trading may be suspended anew upon the discovery of a second manipulative scheme 30 days later, surely a new suspension order also could issue if the second scheme were uncovered only ten days after the first had been detected, *i.e.*, upon the eve of the expiration of the first suspension order. No statutory purpose would be served by requiring an intervening period during which trading would resume, when discovery of a second manipulative scheme independently warrants a second suspension in the public interest and for the protection of investors. Thus the phrase 'for a period not exceeding ten days' cannot reasonably be construed as barring successive suspension orders in all circumstances."

The S.E.C. can already be seen to be making several leaps in logic. It argues, as it did in the petition for rehearing in the court below, that surely the fact that the S.E.C.

has at some time in the past suspended trading in a security does not give that security an immunity from a future trading suspension order. It then goes from that premise to the assertion that if the S.E.C. has the authority to issue a subsequent trading suspension order it must have the authority to issue a subsequent order even if the second order follows the first order by only ten days. The S.E.C. claims that in the situation where a "second manipulative scheme" has arisen, surely a second suspension order can be issued only ten days after the first suspension order. From this point it takes another giant step in logic in the following paragraph of its brief when it says that although "new evidence of manipulative activity justifies a successive suspension of trading . . . nothing in the statute compels the Commission to consider only new evidence in evaluating the needs of the investing public." Now a pattern can be seen to emerge. In the following sentence the S.E.C. completes the circle by saying:

> "[I]t is consistent with the statute for the Commission, even in the absence of new evidence of fresh manipulative activity, to determine that existing conditions are such that the public interest and the protection of investors require a renewed suspension of trading."

Ergo, argues the Commission, all that is needed is a "new determination of the public interest . . . before issuing a successive order suspending trading" and, therefore, it follows that the S.E.C. may suspend trading for an indefinite period of time for any reason whatever which it finds consistent with the "needs of investors", without giving notice or the opportunity for a hearing and without making any statement as to the reasons for the trading suspension. In short, says the S.E.C., when Congress authorized it to suspend trading in a security for a "period not exceeding ten days," it clearly intended to vest in the S.E.C. the arbitrary authority to do anything it feels like when it comes to the matter of trading suspensions.

One of the many problems with the S.E.C.'s argument is that in the fifteen months which have passed since the decision of the court of appeals, no groundswell of support has developed for the S.E.C.'s view. Words have not been ringing through the halls of Congress denouncing the decision of the court of appeals and rallying support for an amendment to delegate expressly to the S.E.C. the power it claims it has always had. The Republic has not fallen. Indeed, noone seems to be concerned in the slightest about the perceived adverse consequences of the decision of the court of appeals, outside of the S.E.C. itself. For the past fifteen months the avenue has been open for the S.E.C. to request Congress to amend the statute and the S.E.C. has elected not pursue this route, for the obvious reason that Congress has never given and clearly has no intention of giving the S.E.C. the power to suspend trading in a security except "for a period not exceeding ten days."

An even more serious flaw in the S.E.C.'s argument concerns the premise of a "second manipulative activity." Remember that the S.E.C. uses this supposed "second manipulative activity" as a bridge to get from the Congressional authorization to issue a single trading suspension order to the possibility that two consecutive orders might be issued without violating the statute. However, one must wonder how this "second manipulative activity" could possibly arise. Supposedly, the S.E.C. suspended trading in the security at the outset because of a "first manipulative activity." Ten days have now passed and the S.E.C., for whatever reason, has not gone to court and has not instituted an administrative proceeding to bring to a halt this "first manipulative activity" and about this time "a second manipulative activity" comes to its attention. When did this "second manipulative activity" take place? Was it during the first ten-day trading suspension period? How is that posssible, since trading was suspended during that time? If the trading suspension has been ineffective in halting the second manipulative activity, what reason is there to believe that a subsequent trading suspension will do any better? In short, a trading suspension brings to an end all trading activity, manipulative or otherwise. If it has failed to do so, a further trading suspension will not do more. Cf. "The very fact that a series of contempt citations has failed to check the defendant's contemptuous acts . . . demonstrates that another citation is unlikely to do so." *Codispoti v. Pennsylvania,* 418 U.S. 506, 521 (1974) (Marshall, J., concurring in part). In short, when the S.E.C. claims that "when the disruptive conditions persist for more than ten days, suspension of trading under Section 12(k) remains the only effective protection immediately available to investors" (Br. 31), it is suggesting a purely hypothetical situation which is unlikely ever to arise and which most particularly did not arise in the instant case.

C

This brings one to another thing wrong with the S.E.C.'s argument. The S.E.C. speaks of the necessity of issuing successive orders suspending trading in a security in some cases. It never argues that it was necessary for the S.E.C. to exercise this authority in the instant case. It never says that there was a "second manipulative activity" which justified a second order suspending trading in Canadian Javelin Ltd. and clearly it could not say that there was a "thirty-seventh manipulative activity" which justified the thirty-seventh order suspending trading. In fact, the S.E.C.'s brief does not state that there was even a "first manipulative activity". The S.E.C.'s brief does purport to set forth the reason for the first trading suspension. It states that the suspension was ordered "because the Royal Canadian Mounted Police had commenced an extensive investigation into alleged manipulation of CJL common stock on the American Stock Exchange and several Canadian stock exchanges" (Br. 3). However, on the next page of its brief, when it states that it issued a "second order suspending trading," it fails to state the reason for this second order. Apparently, having justified the first trading suspension order, the S.E.C. does not feel the need to give an explanation of the reasons for any of the thirty-six subsequent successive trading suspension orders. Of course, later in its brief, the S.E.C. implies that the reason for the second trading suspension order might have been evidence of a "second manipulative activity," or might have been something else. What the S.E.C. is really arguing is that the facts of the particular case before this Court and the reasons for these particular trading suspensions is unimportant to any decision this Court might make because the only issue before this Court is whether there are circumstances, however remote and dissimilar from the facts and circumstances of this case, where the S.E.C. would be justified in issuing a series of successive trading suspension orders. However, this Court has observed in an analogous context that "[o]ne to whose conduct a statute clearly applies may not successfully challenge it for vagueness." *Parker v. Levy,* 417 U.S. 733, 756 (1974). In the case presented here, the Congressional prohibition on suspending trading in a security for a period exceeding ten days clearly applies since there was no evidence of a "second manipulative activity" or of any other reason which might justify a subsequent trading suspension. In fact, an examination of the memoranda which the S.E.C. has proffered as the "record" of this case demonstrate that there was no new reason for the subsequent trading suspension orders, assuming that there was a reason for even the first trading suspension order. Each trading suspension order is supported by a memorandum which supposedly provides the reason for the trading suspension. However, each memorandum has significant portions deleted by heavy black ink which prevented the court of appeals and now prevents this Court from having access to the full text of the memorandum. These black marks are indicated in the appendix filed by the S.E.C. in this Court by "***". This is actually a misrepresentation of the appearance of these memoranda as will be seen from an examination of the memoranda themselves. In any event, since the full memoranda are not avilable, one must look to the portions of the memoranda which the S.E.C. will permit Respondent and the judges of this Court to read in order to attempt to divine the reasons for the trading suspensions. However, the memoranda dated May 23, 1975, May 30, 975, June 16, 1975 and June 24, 1975 (App. 20, 22, 24, 26) are identical in every respect except the date. Similarly, the memoranda dated July 21, 1975 and August 1, 1975 are identical (App. 34-35, 37-38), as well as the memoranda dated August 21, 1975 and September 2, 1975 (App. 42-43, 45-46), the memoranda dated September 11, 1975 and September 23, 1975 (App. 48-49, 51-52), the memoranda dated October 1, 1975 and October 10, 1975 (App. 54-55, 57-58), and the memoranda dated February 5, 1976, February 12, 1976, February 26, 1976 and March 4, 1976 (App. 89-90, 92-93, 95-96, 98-99). An examination of the original record filed by the S.E.C. demonstrates that not only are these memoranda identical but they are actual photocopies of each other. Apparently the S.E.C. simply typed up a standard memorandum, made several photocopies, and simply inserted a new date whenever it decided to renew its trading suspension. In short, all the arguments made by the S.E.C. concerning the possibility of a "new manipulative activity" which might justify tacking a second trading suspension order on to a first order clearly do not apply to this case. Thus, it is apparent that the S.E.C. has violated §12(k) of the Securities Exchange Act by suspending trading in Canadian Javelin Ltd. for a period exceeding ten days without making a new determination that the suspension was necessary "in the public interest and for the protection of investors" and the arguments presented by the S.E.C. that there might exist circumstances under which a series of successive trading suspension orders would not be illegal would not affect the outcome of this case.

D

In its petition for rehearing in the court below the S.E.C. stated (Pet. for Rehearing, p. 3):

> "We wish to emphasize that the Commission does *not* contend that its ten-day summary suspension of trading in a stock may not be subject to court review by a person actually aggrieved. It does contend, however, that an order of the Commission renewing a summary suspension should be set aside only if it can be shown that the Commission abused its broad discretion."

Similarly, it is evident that the S.E.C. hopes that this Court will accept the proposition that there exist circumstances, however farfetched, under which a series of successive trading suspension orders would not be illegal and that this Court will vacate the decision of the court of appeals accordingly. The S.E.C. obviously realizes that all it need do is get its foot in the door in this matter, and it will be able to revert to its practice of issuing a series of successive trading suspension orders on a purely arbitrary basis and will at the same time for practical purposes be immune from any court challenge to the validity of these orders. If this Court accepts the proposition that an order suspending trading in a security may only be reversed upon a finding that there has been "an abuse of discretion", it will follow that a trading suspension order will become for practical purposes unreviewable because it will always happen that by the time a person seeking to challenge the validity of a trading suspension order succeeds in obtaining judicial review by the court of appeals, that order will have expired, and even if the court of appeals vacates the order on the grounds of "abuse of discretion", the decision will not have any bearing on whatever trading suspension order happens to be outstanding at that time because even assuming that the S.E.C. has continued to issue successive trading suspension orders, the court of appeals will not have before it the record of the new trading suspension order and, therefore, will not be in a position to determine whether the issuance of the current order is an abuse of discretion. Thus, the circumstances could not arise where court of appeals would actually vacate an outstanding trading suspension order.

Moreover, even assuming *arguendo* that a court of appeals might decide that the equities of the situation require that the current trading suspension order be vacated as well, the S.E.C. would always be able to conjure up a "new" reason for suspending trading in the security and would be able immediately thereafter to issue a new trading suspension order and several more months would pass before a court of appeals could rule on the validity of that trading suspension order. All the while the S.E.C. would be able to issue successive trading suspension orders uninterrupted and the person seeking to challenge the validity of these orders would be expending his efforts and financial resources in the ever fleeting prospect of bringing about the renewal of actual trading. Unless this Court is prepared to conclude that Congress does not intend that there should be any Congressional or judicial restraint against the issuance by the S.E.C. of trading suspension orders on a purely arbitrary basis, it must affirm the decision of the court of appeals to the extent that it enjoined the adoption and use of successive trading suspension orders.

E

In support of the proposition that when Congress included the words "for a period not exceeding ten days" in §12(k) of the Securities Exchange Act, it meant precisely the opposite of what it said, the S.E.C. cites as primary authority *Securities Regulation* by Professor Louis Loss. Since the S.E.C. itself has never articulated the reasons for which it suspends trading in a security, it quotes at length from what an outside observer such as Professor Loss found to be the reasons for trading suspensions. It ignores the fact that Professor Loss was writing in 1969, well before 1973 when the S.E.C. commenced its increasingly aggressive policy of suspending trading in securities. After devoting more than one page of its brief to quotations from Professor Loss, the S.E.C. asserts, "The Commission's long-standing and consistent construction is entitled to great weight."

It then cites a bunch of cases. However, none of the cases cited by the S.E.C. stand for the proposition which the S.E.C. is asserting in the instant case. Most of the cases cited by the S.E.C. held that an agency's interpretation *of its own regulations* was entitled to judicial deference. For example, in *Udall v. Tallman,* 380 U.S. 1, 16-17 (1975), this Court emphasized that there was "no statutory limitation involved". An exception to this is the most recent case cited by the S.E.C., *E.I. duPont de Nemours & Co. v. Collins,* 432 U.S. 46, 54-55 (1977). There, this Court dealt with the S.E.C.'s interpretation of a statute but the statute in question, namely §17 of the Investment Company Act of 1940, 15 U.S.C. §80a-17, authorized the S.E.C. to find, after an administrative hearing, that the "evidence establishes that . . . the terms of the proposed transaction, including the consideration to be paid or recedived, are reasonable or fair and do not involve over-reaching on the part of any person concerned . . ." Congress also provided the S.E.C. with the standards upon which to base this determination. Thus, Congress expressly delegated to the S.E.C. the authority to make a determination, and that determination was clearly entitled to judicial deference. In the instant case, however, Congress has delegated no such authority. It has authorized the S.E.C. to suspend trading in a security for "a period not exceeding ten days." Clearly, Congress did not intend to delegate to the S.E.C. the authority to decide that it was appropriate to suspend trading in a security for a period longer than ten days. Indeed, to paraphrase what the S.E.C. stated in a related context, under the S.E.C.'s interpretation, the words "for a period not exceeding ten days" would be surplusage.[45]

---

45. Under former §15(b)(7) of the Securities Exchange Act, 15 U.S.C. §78*o*(b)(7), the S.E.C. had the authority to "bar or suspend for a period not exceeding twelve months any person from being associated with any broker or dealer. . ." Respondent has been barred for life from being associated with any broker-dealer under this section. In his petition for writ of certiorari to review the decision of the court of appeals affirming that his petition for writ of certiorari to review the decision of the court of appeals affirming that bar, Respondent contended that the S.E.C. had exceeded its statutory mandate (Pet. No. 76-1547, p. 33). In response, the S.E.C. stated (Brief in opposition, p. 7): "Under petitioner's interpretation the word 'suspend' would be surplusage." However, under the S.E.C.'s interpretation, the words "for a period not exceeding twelve months" are surplusage. For example, in its proceedings against the former S.E.C. Chief Investigative Attorney who initially instigated the numerous proceedings against Canadian Javelin Ltd., the S.E.C. invoked a "bar" for a period of two years. *In the matter of Edward C. Jaegerman*, Securities Exchange Act Release No. 12905, 10 SEC Docket 726 (October 19, 1976). In the case of §15(b)(7), in 1975 Congress renumbered the statute as §15(b)(6) and amended it in such as a way as to codify the S.E.C.'s interpretation of what the statute said, or more accurately, what the S.E.C. believed the statute should say. With respect to the statute involved in the instant case, however, Congress has failed to amend the statute in such a way as to codify the authority which the S.E.C. claims it has.

The S.E.C. does not cite the decisions of this Court which are contrary to its position, of which there are many. Indeed, this Court seems to have said on a number of occasions that in particular the views of the S.E.C., as opposed to the views of other more reputable government agencies, are disentitled to judicial deference. See e.g. *Piper v. Chris Craft Industries, Inc.*, 430 U.S. 1, 41 n. 27 (1977); *Ernst & Ernst v. Hochfelder,* 425 U.S. 185, 199 (1976); *Foremost-McKesson v. Provident Securities,* 423 U.S. 232, 259-260 (1976). This is not a surprising result, because the S.E.C. can be seen invariably to adopt the view which gives the broadest possible scope to the federal securities laws and to the power and authority of the S.E.C. It is not surprising that sometimes the expansive views of the S.E.C. are not in accord with the intent of Congress as determined by the courts. In the case presented here no judicial deference whatever should be accorded to the views of the S.E.C. The judicial deference rule is applicable only in cases where "an agency has rendered binding, consistent, official interpretations of its statutes over a long period of time." *Piper v. Chris-Craft Industries, Inc., supra,* 430 U.S. at 41, n. 27. In the instant case, the S.E.C. has failed to cite any "binding, consistent, official interpretations, of the statute" whatever. All it says is that the S.E.C., for a long period of time, had followed the practice of issuing successive trading suspension orders and therefore it must be concluded that the S.E.C. thought about the matter and decided to interpret the applicable provisions of the Securities Exchange Act in such a way as to give the S.E.C. this authority. However, the fact is that the S.E.C. has never issued an official interpretation of the statute with respect to §12(k) of the Securities Exchange Act or its predecessor provisions. There are statements, such as the statement by the then Chairman of the S.E.C., Edward N. Gadsby, quoted *supra,* which indicate that there has been an official interpretation of the statute, but statements, speeches, and the like by individual commissioners of the S.E.C. are invariably prefaced with the words "the Securities and Exchange Commission, as a matter of policy, disclaims responsibility for any private publication or speech by any of its members or employees." In addition, it should be remembered that in his speech, Commissioner Gadsby stated, "[I]t has been found necessary to renew the suspension[s] for successive ten-day periods. No express authority for such action is contained in §19(a)(4). . . ." Clearly, no judicial deference should be accorded to the view now expressed by the attorneys from the Office of General Counsel of the S.E.C. appearing in this Court and who appeared in the court of appeals, when those views are not supported by any authoritative opinions of the S.E.C. itself. Indeed, one of the cases cited by the S.E.C. dealt with precisely this point. In *Investment Co. Institute v. Camp,* 401 U.S. 617, 628 (1971) this Court stated:

> "In *Burlington Truck Lines v. U.S.,* 371 U.S. 156, we said, 'The courts may not accept appellate counsel's *post hoc* rationalizations for agency action. . . . For the courts to substitute their or counsel's discretion for that of the agency is incompatible with the orderly functioning of the process of judicial review.' *Id.,* at 168-169. Congress has delegated to the administrative official and not appellate counsel the responsibility for elaborating and enforcing statutory commands. It is the administrative official and not appellate counsel who possesses the expertise that can enlighten and rationalize the search for the meaning and intent of Congress."

This citation alone would seem fatal to the S.E.C.'s entire presentation. The S.E.C. itself has never issued an authoritative opinion which purports to "enlighten and rationalize the search for the meaning and intent of Congress." In fact, the S.E.C. has been totally silent with regard to the qustion of the successive trading suspension orders. The "press release," as Securities Exchange Act releases were called in those days, cited in the S.E.C.'s brief, *In the Matter of Elastic Stop Nut Corp. of America,* Securities Exchange Act Release No. 3626 (November 29, 1944), merely announced a suspension of trading in that security for ten days. When that ten-day period expired, the S.E.C. did not issue an authoritative opinion stating that it interpreted §19(a)(4) of the Securities Exchange Act as giving it the authority to suspend trading for a further ten-day period. To the contrary, the S.E.C. was totally silent and did not even issue a release announce the continuation of the trading suspension. The procedure adopted by the S.E.C. at the time, which it also followed during the years prior to the November 18, 1976 decision of the court of appeals, was that a release was issued at the time of the initial trading suspension and generally no further releases were issued until the S.E.C. announced that trading would be allowed to resume.

One might wonder why the S.E.C. never had occasion to issue a statement as to the legal basis for issuing successive ten-day trading suspension orders. The answer is obvious. As the statement by S.E.C. Chairman Gadsby shows, the S.E.C. knew that it was on shaky legal ground when it issued successive trading suspension orders. It also knew that most people would assume that a government agency such as the S.E.C. was acting legally. Therefore, it simply avoided the issue and the public outcry which might have resulted from a formal statement that it believed it had the power under §19(a)(4) to suspend trading for as long a period of time as it deemed necessary and in most cases adopted the pragmatic procedure of not even issuing a Securities Exchange Act release when it continued a trading suspension. In this way, only the persons directly affected by a successive trading suspension order would have occasion even to become aware of the fact that the S.E.C. had exercised the power to suspend trading in a stock for a lengthy time period.

In 1956 the publication of the *SEC News Digest* commenced. In this publication, summary orders continuing a trading suspension were announced officially. *The Wall Street Journal* has also published brief announcements of the continuation of trading suspensions, but on a sporadic basis. However, the S.E.C. has never issued anything resembling a "binding, consistent, official interpretation of the statute" and rarely even a reason for continuing a trading suspension. This practice was criticized in the article by Goldman and Magrino as follows (Goldman and Magrino, *supra,* 15 N.Y.L. Forum at 656):

> "It is most strongly urged upon the Commission that the periodic extensions which are presently reflected only in the SEC News Digest, be made the subject of specific releases under the Exchange Act. These releases should, in themselves, report progress, if any, as to the then present status of the Commission's investigation and the facts thus far uncovered, thereby serving to provide the investment community with some basis for valuation and predictability."

F

The S.E.C. also argues (Brief p. 26) that "[w]here Congress has re-enacted or significantly amended a statute disapproving the agency's construction, Congress may appropriately be considered to have approved that construction as correct." However, the cases cited by the S.E.C. are all distinguishable from the instant case. For example, in *United States v. Correll,* 389 U.S. 299, 305-306 (1967) the Court noted that, "More than a dictionary definition is thus required to understand the provisions herein involved, and no appeal to the 'plain language' of the statute can obviate the need for further statutory construction."

Id. at 16. It then noted that "Congress heard a taxpayer plea for a change in the rule" and "[n]o such change resulted." *Id.* at n. 20. The matter was actively discussed by members of both houses of Congress. In the instant case, it is true that a written statement by the S.E.C. to the appropriate House committee did advise that on occasion the S.E.C. had found it necessary to suspend trading for more than one ten-day period. However, this statement was included in the small print of the hearings before a House and Senate subcommittee, noone contested the matter, it was never debated, and contrary to the representations in the S.E.C.'s brief (Brief, p. 29), the House Committee which "favorably reported on the amendment" said nothing about the possibility that the S.E.C. might suspend trading for more than one ten-day period. See House Report No. 1418, 88th Cong., 2d Sess. 24 (1964). The Senate Report, although more helpful to the S.E.C.'s position here, merely parroted what the S.E.C. had said in its formal statement proposing amendments to the legislation and again the matter was not contested or debated. See Senate Report No. 379, 88th Cong., 1st Sess. 66-67 (1963). As noted previously, the words of the proposed statute were plain and unambiguous and in contrast the words of the S.E.C. suggesting that there might be more than one trading suspension were unclear. It cannot be assumed that any member of the House or the Senate, much less a majority of both bodies, read the report and realized that this might mean that the S.E.C. might suspend trading in a security for a year or more or even for as long as thirteen years, all without notice or the opportunity for a hearing.

Moreover, even assuming that Congress was aware of the practices of the S.E.C., that would not help the position of the S.E.C. here because the practices of the S.E.C. were considerably different at that time. On this point, the brief for the S.E.C. misrepresents the facts. It states that after 1944 the S.E.C. rarely instituted proceedings under §19(a)(2). (Brief p. 33, n. 14). However, the fact is that from 1944 until 1964 the S.E.C. customarily instituted proceedings under §19(a)(2) of the Securities Exchange Act or under §8(d) of the Securities Act of 1933 ("Securities Act") simultaneously with a trading suspension under §19(a)(4), as the statement by S.E.C. Chairman Gadsby indicates, and subsequently published formal findings. For example, the S.E.C.'s first exercise of the trading suspension power resulted in the publication of twelve pages of formal findings reported as *In the Matter of Elastic Stop Nut Corporation of America,* 19 S.E.C. 412 (1945). Similarly, after the S.E.C.'s second exercise of the trading suspension power, *In the Matter of Red Bank Oil Co.,* Securities Exchange Act Release No. 3744 (October 16, 1945), the S.E.C. conducted hearings which resulted in an 18-page decision reported as *In the Matter of Red Bank Oil Co.*, 21 S.E.C. 695 (January 4, 1946) which ordered that the registration of Red Bank Oil Co. be suspended for twelve months pursuant to §19(a)(2). It is noteworthy that the S.E.C. invoked a §19(a)(4) suspension from October 16, 1945 until January 6, 1946, *Id.*, 21 S.E.C. at 697, and then invoked a §19(a)(2) suspension from then until January 3, 1947.

This pattern continued until the 1964 Amendments to the Securities Exchange Act. It is true that this procedure violated the express language of §19(a)(4) of the Securities Exchange Act, but there were substantial safeguards. Any time a trading suspension extended for more than ten days there was, in fact, the opportunity for a hearing. In the course of this hearing the corporation could be vindicated, if the trading suspension was unjustified. Due to the fact that the S.E.C. staff knew that it might be required to demonstrate that the trading suspension was justified in an adversary proceeding, it was more likely to exercise appropriate restraint and not to request a trading suspension without valid reason. The following are a few examples of how the S.E.C. proceeded in practice prior to the 1964 amendments.

Trading was suspended in Adolf Gobel, Inc. from March 3, 1953 until February 19, 1954 during which lengthy hearings were conducted which resulted in findings and opinion of the S.E.C. reported as *In the Matter of Adolf Gobel, Inc.*, 35 S.E.C. 535 (February 18, 1954) which ordered that trading would be allowed to resume. Trading was suspended in Bellanca Corporation (formerly Bellanca Aircraft Corporation) from April 24, 1957 until June 8, 1958 which resulted in findings and opinion of the S.E.C. reported as *In the Matter of Bellanca Corporation,* 38 S.E.C. 405 (June 2, 1958) which ordered the withdrawal of exchange registration in the corporation's stock. Trading was suspended in Cornucopia Gold Mines from July 28, 1958 until November 11, 1958. After the suspension was lifted and hearings pursuant to §19(a)(2) were completed, the S.E.C. issued findings and opinion which ordered the withdrawal of exchange registration of the corporation's stock. See *In the Matter of Cornucopia Gold Mines,* 40 S.E.C. 177 (August 11, 1960). Trading was suspended in The Bon Ami Company from February 11, 1959 until March 12, 1959 and subsequently the New York Stock Exchange removed the securities from listing and registration. In spite of the fact that this development left nothing before the S.E.C., it issued findings reported as *In the Matter of The Bon Ami Corporation,* 40 S.E.C. 933 (November 29, 1961) which set forth the factual basis for the proceedings against the corporation. Trading was suspended in Skiatron Electronics and Television Corporation on December 18, 1959 simultaneously with the commencement of stop order proceedings under §8(d) of the Securities Act. This trading suspension continued until October 12, 1960 and terminated following a decision of the S.E.C. to issue a stop order. See *In the Matter of*

Skiatron Electronics and Television Corporation, 40 S.E.C. 236 (October 3, 1960). Trading was suspended in Consolidated Development Corporation on February 12, 1960 in connection with a stop order proceeding under §8(d) of the Securities Act and this suspension continued until November 8, 1960 and terminated following a decision of the S.E.C. to issue a stop order suspending the effectiveness of the corporation's registration. See *In the Matter of Consolidated Development Corporation,* 40 S.E.C. 294 (October 27, 1960). Trading was suspended in Precision Microwave Corporation from April 4, 1962 until December 19, 1962 and in August, 1962 the S.E.C. instituted stop order proceedings pursuant to §8(d) of the Securities Act as well as deregistration proceedings pursuant to §19(a)(2) of the Securities Exchange Act. On May 22, 1964, the S.E.C. concluded these proceedings by ordering the suspension of the corporation's stock on the Midwest Stock Exchange for 30 days. See *In the Matter of Precision Microwave Corporation,* 40 S.E.C. 971 (1964). Trading was suspended in Atlantic Research Corporation from October 10, 1962 until November 16, 1962 at which time the corporation transmitted a report to its stockholders which was a factor leading to a decision of the S.E.C. to lift its "order temporarily suspending trading in the registrant's stock." However, the decision of the S.E.C. subsequently found that even this report failed to contain "an adequate, fair and candid statement of the facts . . . " and accordingly the S.E.C. issued a stop order. See *In the Matter of Atlantic Research Corporation,* 41 S.E.C. 733, 764 (December 6, 1963).

Atlantic Research Corporation was the last corporation which had its securities suspended from trading where the trading suspension terminated prior to the passage of the 1964 amendments to the Securities Exchange Act. The next security to be suspended from trading was that of Continental Vending Machine Corporation. That suspension commenced on May 8, 1963 and continued until June 2, 1976, a duration of more than thirteen years. The S.E.C.'s conduct in this proceeding stands in marked contrast to the actions of the S.E.C. prior to the 1964 amendments. At the termination of that trading suspension, the S.E.C. issued Securities Exchange Act Release No. 12505, 9 SEC Docket 787 (June 2, 1976) which stated that the reason for this prolonged trading suspension was that the corporation had been undergoing proceedings in bankruptcy and further stated that the suspension was being terminated because a court had determined that the common stock was worthless and would be cancelled. The release issued by the S.E.C. set forth no findings and opinion and made no statement that either the corporation or anyone else had committed any misconduct. The release failed to explain why the S.E.C. had found it necessary to suspend trading in this particular security for the extraordinary period of more than thirteen years but had not suspended trading for even a ten-day period in innumerable other securities of corporations which had undergone proceedings in bankruptcy. For many years there has been a rumor in Wall Street that the reason for the trading suspension in Continental Vending Machine Corporation was that this corporation, along with many other companies in the vending machine business, was Mafia controlled. However, the release issued by the S.E.C. failed to answer the question of the real reason for the S.E.C.'s prolonged trading suspension and it is apparent that the S.E.C. intends never to answer this question.

Clearly, Congress could not have anticipated this result when it enacted the 1964 amendments to the Securities Exchange Act. Even assuming *arguendo* that Congress was fully informed of the practices of the S.E.C. and acquiesced to its usurpation of power when it passed the 1964 amendments, all it did was agree that the S.E.C.

could continue its practice of continuing a trading suspension in connection with proceedings and hearings pursuant to either §19(a)(2) of the Securities Exchange Act or §8(d) of the Securities Act, that being the policy of the S.E.C. prior to the 1964 amendments, a policy abandoned shortly after these amendments were enacted. Incidentally, it should be noted that the termination of the suspension of trading of securities of Continental Vending Machine Corporation apparently came as a direct result of pressure brought to bear as a result of the proceedings instituted by Respondent challenging the suspension of trading in Canadian Javelin Ltd. Less than ten days after the June 2, 1976 release announcing the decision to terminate the trading suspension in Continental Vending Machine Corporation, the S.E.C. filed in this Court a brief in opposition to a petition for a writ of certiorari filed by Respondent which argued that the case was moot because "no order summarily suspending trading is any longer in effect." (Brief for S.E.C. In No. 75-1507, p. 2).

G

Another weakness in the S.E.C.'s presentation concerns the emphasis which the S.E.C. finds it necessary to place on the 1964 amendments to the Securities Exchange Act, as opposed to the 1934 enactment of the statute and the more recent 1975 amendments. As noted previously, the S.E.C. never says, and cannot say, that in passing the original version of the Securities Exchange Act in 1934, Congress intended to authorize the S.E.C. to suspend trading in a security for a time period exceeding ten days. Rather, the S.E.C. claims that when Congress extended the trading suspension power to over-the-counter securities in 1964, it acquiesced to the assumption by the S.E.C. of the power to suspend trading in a security for more than a period of ten days even though it used virtually the same language in the 1964 amendment, namely §15(c)(5) of the Securities Exchange Act, which had been used in 19(a)(4) of the original statute. However, the S.E.C. fails to explain how the enactment of §15(c)(5) in any way altered the meaning of §19(a)(4), which was not amended at that time. It has already been demonstrated *supra* that §19(a)(4) was intended as an emergency power and the strict ten-day limitation on its exercise was included for that reason.

One problem with the arguments of the S.E.C., in addition to the problems already pointed out, is that in 1975 both §15(c)(5) and §19(a)(4) were repealed and the new §12(k) was enacted. Recognizing the problem created by this development, the S.E.C. asserts that with respect to the 1975 amendments (Brief p. 34), "There is no indication that any substantive change was intended." This statement is rather curious considering the fact that on the next page of its brief the S.E.C. quotes from the report of the appropriate Senate Committee which states, *"With this change,* the Commission is expected to use this section rather than its 10-day suspension power in cases of extended duration" (emphasis added).

The contention of the S.E.C. is that the 1964 amendments to the Securities Exchange Act changed the meaning of the statute, although neither the House nor the Senate Report stated that a change was occurring beyond extending the S.E.C.'s trading suspension power to over-the-counter securities, and that the 1975 amendments to the Securities Exchange Act did not change the statute, although the Senate Report expressly states that the statute was being changed. The S.E.C. further contends that the words in the Senate Report, particularly the statement which said, "The Commission is expected to use this section rather than its ten-day suspension power in cases of extended duration," means something quite different from what the court of appeals found that it meant. The

S.E.C. contends (Brief p. 36) that this statement demonstrates that "the Committee knew that the Commission continued to possess the authority, which the Committee had approved in 1964 . . . , to issue successive trading suspension orders 'in cases of extended duration'." In other words, the S.E.C. contends that when the Senate report stated that, "The Commission is expected to use" §12(j) rather than §12(k) to suspend trading in a security for a period of extended duration, it nevertheless left open to the S.E.C. the alternative of using §12(k) in appropriate cases. Therefore, concludes the S.E.C., the suspension of trading of Canadian Javelin Ltd. under §12(k) for a period of more than one year was a valid exercise of the S.E.C.'s discretionary authority. In expressing this view, the S.E.C.'s brief states (Brief p. 36), "In other words, the Committee expressed a preference as to how the Commission should proceed, but it left the final decision as to the appropriate mode of enforcement in particular cases to the Commission's discretion."

In the next sentence of its brief, the S.E.C. stoops to total dishonesty. It states:

> "If the Committee had intended to terminate or circumscribe the authority it had earlier acknowledged to exist under predecessors of Section 12(k), it would have done so in the text of Section 12(k) itself; it cannot be presumed to have done so merely by including precatory language in a section of its report that discusses a different provision of the Act."

It has already been pointed out that the report issued by the Senate Committee concerning the 1964 amendment to the Securities Exchange Act can hardly be said to have acknowledged that the S.E.C. had the authority to suspend trading in a security for a lengthy time period. Thus, the first part of the above quoted sentence is misleading. The second part of the sentence, where the S.E.C. states that the decision of the court of appeals quoted from "precatory language in a section of its report that discusses a different provision of the Act," is an outright falsehood. The full pertinent text of the Senate report in question, which was quoted in the decision of the court of appeals, states (Senate Rep. No. 94—75, 94th Cong., 1st Sess. 106 (1975):

> "Section 8 of the bill would amend Section 12 of the Exchange Act by adding new subsections (j), (k), (l) and (m).
>
> Subsection (j) would provide a more logical placement of the authority the S.E.C. already has under present section 19(a)(2) to deny, to suspend the effective date of, to suspend for a period not exceeding twelve months, or to withdraw the registration of any security if it finds, on the record after notice and opportunity for hearing, that the issuer of such security has failed to comply with any provision of the Exchange Act or the rules and regulations thereunder. It would also make unlawful any trading in any such security by any broker or dealer. With this change, the Commission is expected to use this section rather than its ten-day suspension power in cases of extended duration.
>
> Subsection (k) would consolidate in one place the power the S.E.C. presently has under sections 15(c)(5) and 19(a)(4) of the Exchange Act to suspend summarily trading in any security (other than an exempted security) for a period not exceeding ten days. The S.E.C.'s power, with the approval of the President, to suspend summarily all trading on a national securities exchange would be continued and extended to include the power to prohibit trading in all securities, other than exempted securities, otherwise than on an exchange."

Thus it can be seen that, contrary to the representations of the S.E.C., the decision of the court of appeals quoted from a section of Senate Report No. 94-75 which discussed §12(k) of the Securities Exchange Act, not, as the S.E.C. claims, from "a section . . . that discusses a different provision of the Act." At this point it becomes apparent that the S.E.C. is engaging in a deliberate effort to confuse the Court by raising fictitious issues. This trend is also apparent on pages 32-33 of its brief, where the S.E.C. compares and contrasts trading suspensions under §12(k) of the Securities Exchange Act with deregistration proceedings under §12(j) of the Securities Exchange Act. It claims, for example, that "important protections are lost when the registration of a security is revoked pursuant to Section 12(j)." All this is very interesting, but it has no relevance to this case. Section 12(j) authorizes the S.E.C., *inter alia,* "to suspend for a period not exceeding twelve months, or to revoke the registration of a security . . . " It may be as the S.E.C. claims that the remedy of deregistration is too Draconian, but if that is the case, why cannot the S.E.C. simply suspend the registration of the offending security "for a period not exceeding twelve months." If the registration of a security is suspended, the corporation is still required to file 10-K and the other required reports and because of the last sentence of §12(j), a suspension of registration has precisely the same effect as a suspension of trading, as the S.E.C. itself admits (Brief p. 29). In practice, the only difference between suspension proceedings under §12(j) and §12(k) is that under §12(j) the S.E.C. is required to give "notice and opportunity for hearing" and to make findings "on the record" whereas under §12(k) it need not do so. It is apparent that the S.E.C. prefers to invoke §12(k) simply because it does not wish to go to the trouble of providing notice, giving potentially aggrieved parties the opportunity to be heard and making formal findings of fact, not to mention the embarrassment the S.E.C. would suffer if it were to turn out that the charges made in proceedings instituted under §12(j) were false.

In rationalizing this unwillingness to give aggrieved parties the opportunity to be heard, the S.E.C. asserts that, "It is impossible within a ten-day period, for the Commission" to complete an administrative proceeding. To be sure, if the S.E.C. adopts deliberate delaying tactics as it did in the administrative proceedings against Respondent, which lasted three years and three days, and as it has done in many other cases, see e.g. *Koss v S.E.C.*, 364 F. Supp. 1321, 1322-1323 (S.D.N.Y. 1973); *Arthur Lipper Corp. v. S.E.C.*, 547 F. 2d 171, 176, 184 (2d Cir. 1976), *rehearing denied* 551 F. 2d 915 (1977), *cert. denied*, __U.S.__ (1978), it will, in fact, find it impossible to complete proceedings within ten days. However, if it proceeds expeditiously, something which the S.E.C. has not recently been known to do but which nevertheless is not impossible, proceedings could be completed in ten days. On an every day basis, the S.E.C. asks federal district judges to proceed more expeditiously than the S.E.C. now claims it is possible for the S.E.C. itself to proceed. For example, in one of the cases involving Respondent, the S.E.C. staff requested permission to institute suit on December 27, 1974, obtained this permission on December 30, 1974, filed suit the same day, and requested and obtained from Judge Ward a temporary restraining order within a few hours after the suit was filed. No explanation is given for the fact that the S.E.C. claims it is "impossible" to do in ten days what the S.E.C. regularly asks judges to do in a few hours. The S.E.C. claims, for example, that it is impossible, within a ten-day period, for the Commission to "(a) conduct an investigation sufficient to determine whether an administrative proceeding pursuant to §12(j) ought to be instituted." One would have thought that when the S.E.C. resorts to the remedy of suspending trading in a security, it has sufficient command of the facts to know whether an administrative proceeding ought to be instituted. Similarly, the S.E.C. states that ten days is insufficient to "(b) provide the issuer with adequate notice of the alleged violations." Again, assuming the S.E.C. knows the facts, it is difficult to perceive a reason for the S.E.C.'s inability to notify the issuer of these facts. As for the claim that it is impossible for the S.E.C. to "(c) hold a hearing on the record before an administrative law judge," it would seem that the appropriate remedy would be for the S.E.C. to hire more administrative law judges or else judges of a better quality than it now employs. As to the claim that the time is insufficiently long to "(d) permit the administrative law judge to consider the matter prior to rendering an initial decision; and (e) review the initial decision rendered by the administrative alw judge," it should be pointed out that if the record is unclear and there is a substantial basis for believing that trading ought not to be suspended, a circumstance which would provide the most likely explanation for the inability of an administrative law judge and the S.E.C. itself to make findings of fact expeditiously, it would seem appropriate not to suspend the registration of a security until the full facts can be determined and to permit open market trading to continue. Admittedly, the S.E.C. will find it inconvenient if it is forced to do something in ten days which it is accustomed to doing in three years or more, but it must be remembered that stockholders have rights too and if the S.E.C. is unwilling to conduct hearings and make findings of fact as to the reasons for a suspension, individual investors should not be forced to suffer.

If the S.E.C. finds that ten days is too short a period of time to complete administrative proceedings under §12(j) of the Securities Exchange Act, its remedy is to apply to Congress for an amendment to the statute. Perhaps Congress would be willing to amend the statute so as to give the S.E.C. the right to temporarily suspend the registration of a security during the pendency of proceedings under §12(j). An analogous provision exists in §15(b)(5)(B) of the Securities Exchange Act, 15 U.S.C. §78*o*(b)(5)(B). In any event, none of this applies to the instant case, because the S.E.C. did not institute proceedings under §12(j) with respect to the securities of Canadian Javelin Ltd. In fact, as far as Respondent has been able to determine, the S.E.C. has never instituted proceedings of any kind under §12(j). What has obviously happened is that the S.E.C. has found §12(j) to be unsatisfactory, but rather than ask Congress for an amendment to the statute, it has undermined the purpose of the statute by utilizing §12(k) in a manner contrary to the expressed intent of Congress.

H

The S.E.C. argues that the court of appeals "did not grasp the significant differences between" §12(j) and §12(k) of the Securities Exchange Act (Brief p. 29). The S.E.C.'s principal argument on this point is that only securities registered with the S.E.C. may become the subject of deregistration proceedings. This argument, of course, does not apply to the facts of the instant case because Canadian Javelin Ltd. is, in fact, registered with the S.E.C.[46] What the S.E.C. is really saying is that in spite of the arsenal of weapons given to the S.E.C. by

---

46. The registration of Canadian Javelin Ltd. is purely voluntary, since it is a foreign issuer and therefore is exempt from the registration requirements. Canadian Javelin Ltd. is one of very few foreign issuers which file reports on Form 10-K. Normally, foreign issuers of securities who seek to have their securities listed on a stock exchange in the United States must agree to file financial information with the S.E.C. on Form 20-K. See CCH Fed. Sec. Law Rep. ¶32,221 [Exchange Act Binder]. Foreign issuers of securities not listed on a stock exchange may be required to file reports under S.E.C. Rule 12g3-2(b), 17 C.F.R. §240. 12g3-2(b). Canadian Javelin Ltd. came to file 10-K reports with the S.E.C. as a result of the injunctive action instituted by the S.E.C. on September 25, 1958. That action was concluded the same day with the consent by Canadian Javelin Ltd. that it would list its shares on the American Stock Exchange and would thereafter file financial reports required of United States issuers of securities. See transcript of hearing in *S.E.C. v. Canadian Javelin Ltd.*, 1958 Civil Action File No. 138-85 (S.D.N.Y.).

Congress, including the power to institute injunctive actions, administrative proceedings of various types and proceedings under §32(a) and §32(b) of the Securities Exchange Act, not to mention the power to transmit to the Attorney General a criminal reference, Congress has created a loophole by not giving power to the S.E.C. which is sufficiently broad. Indeed, when the first case was argued before the court of appeals on September 26, 1975, the attorney arguing orally for the S.E.C. used the term "loophole" to describe the statutory problem now discussed in the S.E.C.'s brief. The short answer to this is that if there is indeed a "loophole", the remedy is for the S.E.C. to ask Congress to fill it.

Contrary to the arguments of the S.E.C. (Brief p. 30-31), there is a rational basis for the decision of Congress not to authorize the S.E.C. to issue orders pursuant to §12(j) "in cases involving manipulation or fraud by third parties, in corporate crises, in situations where adequate financial information is unavailable and where markets have been disrupted by speculation based on rumors of doubtful accuracy." In a situation involving manipulation or fraud by third parties, the remedy of the S.E.C. is to go after those third parties by injunctive proceedings or, where those third parties are broker-dealers, by administrative proceedings pursuant to §15(b)(4) and §15(b)(6) of the Securities Exchange Act, rather than punish the innocent corporation, its officers and its stockholders by a prolonged trading suspension. Similarly, in cases of corporate crisis or where adequate financial information is unavailable, the remedy is for the corporation to notify the public of the situation or, failing that, the issuance of a Securities Exchange Act Release by the S.E.C. Congress has frequently made it clear that the philosophy of the Securities Exchange Act is one of full disclosure. If the full facts are unavailable and unknowable due to the fault of noone, a situation which might conceivably arise in a case of "corporate crisis," the Securities Exchange Act clearly does not authorize the S.E.C. to invoke the Draconian remedy of a prolonged suspension and/or deregistration, and for good reason. As far as "speculation based upon rumors of doubtful accuracy" is concerned, it is a fact of life that the securities markets are constantly influenced by rumors, some true and some untrue, and Congress was undoubtedly aware of this. Contrary to the representations of the S.E.C., the existence of rumors often has a beneficial effect on securities markets, as can be seen by the number of instances in which corporate officers have issued statements denying the truth of rumors, only to have these rumors proven true a few days later. Clearly, Congress had a sound rational basis for its decision to deny the S.E.C. the authority to suspend or revoke the registration of a security based on the S.E.C.'s determination that the market is influenced by "rumors of doubtful accuracy."

A reading of the full text of Senate Report No. 94-75, which expresses Congressional dissatisfaction with many aspects of the S.E.C.'s performance of its statutory duties, makes it abundantly clear that the decision of the court of appeals concerning legislative intent is correct. For example, in its discussion of Rule 15c2-11, Senate Report No. 94-75 at p. 48 stated, "The Committee expects, therefore, that, immediately upon enactment of S. 249, the Commission will exempt municipal securities from Rule 15c2-11." It is noteworthy that the Senate Report used the words "expects" in this sentence just as it used the words "expected" when it said, "The Commission is expected to use this section rather than its 10-day suspension power in cases of extended duration." It is obvious from the context that the S.E.C. could not contend that when Senate Report No. 94-75 states that, "The Committee expects . . . the Commission will exempt municipal securities from Rule 15c2-11," it did not, as the S.E.C.'s brief now claims with regard to analogous language (Brief p. 36), express "a preference as to how the Commission should proceed, but it left the final decision as to the appropriate mode . . . to the Commission's discretion."

I

Incidentally, the S.E.C. did not amend Rule 15c2-11, in spite of the express directive from Congress that it do so. This illustrates one final point. Congress has delegated to the S.E.C., an independent administrative agency, the authority to take certain action. If the S.E.C. exceeds that authority, Congress has no actual power to do anything about it. Regardless of what words Congress uses in its Senate and House Committee Reports, and regardless of how express its directives might be, as a practical matter the unbridled zeal of an administrative agency may only be tempered by judicial action such as the action the court of appeals took in the instant case.

This court has held that "an agency may not bootstrap itself into an area in which it has no jurisdiction by repeatedly violating its statutory mandate." *Federal Maritime Commission v. Seatrain Lines, Inc.,* 411 U.S. 726, 745 (1973). "[A]dministrative practice does not avail to overcome a statute so plain in its commands as to leave nothing for construction." *Norwegian Nitrogen Products Company v. United States,* 288 U.S. 294, 315 (1933). "Administrative construction over a long period of time is an available tool for judicial interpretation only when the statutory terms are doubtful or ambiguous." *United States v. Southern Ute Indians,* 402 U.S. 159, 173 n. 8 (1971); *Estate of Stanford v. Commissioner,* 308 U.S. 39, 42 (1939); *Norwegian Nitrogen Products v. United States, supra.* The S.E.C. argues in its brief that if Congress intended to limit the S.E.C.'s authority under §12(k) it should have done so "in the text of Section 12(k) itself;"

rather than through "precatory language in a section of" a Senate Committee Report. However, the S.E.C. fails to suggest any alternative statutory language which could more expressly limit the authority of the S.E.C. to suspend trading in a security for a period not exceeding ten days without creating a host of problems such as effectively immunizing a security from ever again being suspended from trading once a ten-day trading suspension order has been issued. The S.E.C.'s argument also ignores the fact that the present §12(k) adopts language which is identical in all pertinent respects to the original §19(a)(4) and both the House and the Senate Committee Reports stated in 1934 when that section was enacted that §19(a)(4) was intended to authorize the exercise of an emergency power with a duration strictly limited to ten days. There was no reason for Congress to feel the need to adopt even more express language than that found in §19(a)(4) when it enacted §12(k), if any is possible. Moreover, "Congressional inaction frequent betokens unawareness, preoccupation, or paralysis," *Zuber v. Allen,* 396 U.S. 168, 185-186 n. 21, 24 (1969).

The case presented here is clearly one where Congress has limited the authority of an agency to act, and in express terms. If the S.E.C. is allowed to prevail, it will mean that the S.E.C. and other government agencies will have broad latitude to interpret statutes as they see fit and there will be almost no limit to the extent to which an agency such as the S.E.C. could expand its own jurisdiction. Indeed, a number of members of the S.E.C. staff, including its publicity-hungry enforcement chief, Stanley Sporkin, have gone on record as stating that there is a deliberate policy of the S.E.C. to be continuously expanding its jurisdiction into new areas. Most of the recent judicial setbacks the S.E.C. has suffered have stemmed, not from an unduly restrictive attitude on the part of judges, as the S.E.C. commissioners and staff have often claimed, but because of the S.E.C.'s efforts to expand its jurisdiction so as for example, to enjoin activities heretofore never thought to have been prohibited by the Securities Exchange Act. If this Court allows the S.E.C. to prevail in the instant case, it will set a dangerous precedent and there will be virtually no limit to the raw power of the S.E.C. to take oppressive action.

IV

THERE IS NO SUBSTANTIAL EVIDENCE TO SUPPORT ANY OF THE TEN-DAY TRADING SUSPENSION ORDERS AND HENCE ALL OF THE ORDERS MUST BE VACATED

The petition for a writ of certiorari filed by the S.E.C. set forth two questions as being presented by this case. This Court granted the S.E.C.'s petition and denied Respondent's petition and, hence, the S.E.C. contends that the only questions involved in this case are the two questions presented by the S.E.C. and these questions are purely statutory in character, as a result of which the judges of this Court should not read the record and should not become familiar with the facts of this case, but rather should decide the abstract question of whether there might exist circumstances under which the S.E.C. could legally suspend trading in a security for successive ten-day periods. It is submitted, however, that this argument should be rejected. The case before this Court involves thirty-seven trading suspension orders of securities of Canadiàn Javelin Ltd. and related proceedings. The principal question before this Court is whether the S.E.C. acted illegally in issuing these thirty-seven trading suspension orders. It follows necessarily that the judges of this Court must read the record and must familiarize themselves with the facts and circumstances of these particular trading suspension orders in order even to reach the statutory questions which the S.E.C. has raised. The court of appeals has expressed agreement with this view. In the first decision involving trading suspension orders, *Sloan v. S.E.C.*, 527 F. 2d 11, 12 (2d Cir. 1975), the court of appeals stated:

> "We consider his blunderbuss attack frivolous except for its allegation that the 'tacking' of ten-day summary suspension orders by the S.E.C. for an indefinite period constitutes an abuse of that agency's authority and a deprivation of due process. Apparently this question has never been judicially considered and would seem not to be frivolous; see 2 L. Loss, Securities Regulation 854-55 (2d ed. 1961). We cannot decide it on the record before us. The record is entirely silent as to the reasons for the second series of suspensions, commencing in April of this year; we cannot tell whether they are based on substantial evidence, and hence cannot decide if they amount to an abuse of discretion by the S.E.C."

Following this, the court of appeals stated that it was dismissing Respondents' petition "without prejudice to this repleading after an administrative hearing before the S.E.C., from which judicial review might be sought" which would serve the purpose of "contributing to the record we now find insurmountably sparse." Thus, the court of appeals expressly stated that it needed to review a record which was not "insurmountably sparse" in order to determine the statutory question which the court of appeals eventually resolved in the second decision, *Sloan v. S.E.C.*, 547 F. 2d 152 (2d Cir. 1976). The S.E.C. did not seek review of the first decision of the court of appeals; it made no objection to the decision of that court at that time.

Subsequently, Respondent petitioned the S.E.C. for an administrative hearing. In spite of the representations made to the court of appeals that it was prepared to grant "some sort of administrative hearing," the S.E.C. denied this petition and consequently no administrative hearing was held. When Respondent then filed the second petition for review challenging the then current series of trading suspension orders, the S.E.C. did not file the record but rather filed a "certified list of items comprising the record." The S.E.C. did, however, provide Respondent with a copy of the record and Respondent included most of this record in his appendix to the appeal. Only in the manner did the court of appeals have the opportunity to read the record. In its decision of the second case, the court of appeals stated (Pet. App. B, p. 11a):

> "With respect to the first of these claims, an examination of the record discloses there was sufficient evidence of probable manipulation of CJL's common stock and of the false and fraudulent representations as to its soundness and value to justify the Commission's conclusion that the public interest and the protection of investors required summarily to suspend trading 'for a period not exceeding ten days' . . . "

Thus, the court of appeals did purport to review the record and determine that the first trading suspension order was valid. However, an examination of the record of the first trading suspension order (App. 11-12), makes it apparent that this determination by the court of appeals was clearly erroneous. The "informational memorandum" which provides the reasons given by the S.E.C. for the first trading suspension states (App. 12):

> "The trading suspension was prompted by the Royal Canadian Mounted Police having informed us that they were in the process of executing more than 40 search warrants in connection with their investigation of this matter."

Thus, the decision of the court of appeals was wrong because the S.E.C. never stated that it was suspending trading in Canadian Javelin Ltd. stock because "there was sufficient evidence ofprobable manipulation of Canadian Javelin Ltd.'s common stock and of the false and fraudulent representations as to its soundness and value." Of course, it appears that the court of appeals were merely being careless and was not terribly concerned with the reason for the first trading suspension, being more concerned with the statutory problem created by the fact that the S.E.C. had suspended trading for a period of more than one year by its practice of issuing successive ten-day trading suspension orders. Nevertheless, it is important to consider with care the reasons for the S.E.C.'s initial trading suspension and to determine whether the S.E.C. was merely being arbitrary or whether there was a justifiable basis for the trading suspension. A more complete statement than can be found in the memoranda included in the record of the facts and circumstances surrounding the trading suspension and the investigation by the Royal Canadian Mounted Police can be found at App. 176, which is a statement by a barrister appointed at the order of the Quebec Superior Court pursuant to a court ordered special general meeting of stockholders.

The particular facts of this case demonstrate that even in its initial suspension of trading of Canadian Javelin Ltd., the S.E.C. was acting on a purely arbitrary basis. Supposedly, the basis for the initial trading suspension was to provide the opportunity for disclosure to the American investing public that Canadian Javelin Ltd. and its officers were being investigated by the Royal Canadian Mounted Police. In the case of many corporations this might be considered to be a material fact although it must be noted that numerous corporations have been investigated by the United States Attorney General at one time or another and the S.E.C. has never been known to suspend trading in a security solely for that reason. In the case of Canadian Javelin Ltd., however, the investing public already knew that it was being investigated by the Royal Canadian Mounted Police. This was announced in an artaicle in *The Wall Street Journal* dated December 21, 1972, which stated that "The Royal Canadian Mounted Police, acting under warrants requested by the province, seized more than one hundred cases of documents from the downtown Montreal headquarters of Javelin and from the offices and homes of five Javelin officials" (App. 157). Interestingly, in spite of having suspended trading in Canadian Javelin Ltd. on many occasions, the S.E.C. did not suspend trading at the time of this article in *The Wall Street Journal.* The decision to suspend trading when similar circumstances arose on April 29, 1975 can thus be seen as having been arbitrary. Moreover, Canadian Javelin Ltd.'s problems with the government of the Newfoundland, which was the reason for the search of its offices (App. 176), are well known to the American investing public and go back to at least 1969. See *Bonime v Doyle,* 416 F. Supp. 1372, 1376 (S.D.N.Y. 1976).

When this case was before the court of appeals, the S.E.C. contended that its year-long trading suspension was necessary to complete an investigation which resulted in the filing of a civil suit against the principal stockholder and the directors of Canadian Javelin Ltd. (but not against Canadian Javelin Ltd. itself). In its petition to this court,the S.E.C. stated (Pet. 3-4), "The trading suspension was lifted in May, 1976, when the Commission's investigation had resulted in the filing of a civil action, *Securities and Exchange Commission v. Doyle, et al,* Civ. Action No. 76-1882 (S.D.N.Y.)." However, the memoranda filed by the S.E.C. to be included in the record of this case demonstrate that there was little in the way of an ongoing investigation into the affairs of Canadian Javelin Ltd. during the period of more than one year when trading was suspended. Similarly, the approximately 10,000 pages of material Respondent has examined as a result of a successful Freedom of Information Act request has disclosed virtually nothing concerning any investigation by the S.E.C. into the affairs of Canadian Javelin Ltd. during the 1975-1976 period. What the memoranda filed by the S.E.C. to demonstrate the reason for the trading suspension do show is that the S.E.C. was using the fact that a trading suspension was in effect as a negotiating tool to bring about the waiver of the assertion of various privileges by officers of Canadian Javelin Ltd., including the attorney-client privilege and the self-incrimination privilege. Essentially, the S.E.C. was offering to lift its suspension of trading in Canadian Javelin Ltd. stock provided that the management of Canadian Javelin Ltd. would cooperate with the S.E.C. Moreover, the event which brought about the termination of the trading suspension was not the filing of the injunctive suit by the S.E.C., as the S.E.C. now claims, but that the fact that in the Spring of 1976 an insurgent group of directors took over the management of Canadian Javelin Ltd. and agreed to cooperate with the S.E.C. The S.E.C. then intervened in proceedings in the Quebec Superior Court involving attempts by a group of stockholders and directors led by John C. Doyle, the principal stockholder in the company, to throw out the insurgent group of directors, which was led by William M. Wismer, a former Doyle ally and President of Canadian Javelin Ltd., which usurped control of Canadian Javelin Ltd. and which was undertaking measures to forestall a new election of directors due to the fact that the Doyle group had the votes. These proceedings are described in the report by the court appointed barrister (App. 159-177). The S.E.C. took the side of the Wismer group no doubt largely because of its hostility to Doyle arising from a number of circumstances including the fact that Doyle has been a fugitive from justice ever since he jumped bail in 1965 following an adverse decision of the court of appeals in *United States v. Doyle,* 348 F. 2d 715 (2d Cir. 1965), *cert. denied* 382 U.S. 483 (1965). See "John Doyle Tells Why He Fled to Canada," *The New York Times,* July 26, 1965. The change in management which arose from the revolt by the Wismer group from Doyle's control came as a direct result of the pressure applied by the S.E.C. through its year-long trading suspension since it was clear that the S.E.C. was not prepared to lift that trading suspension until it secured the cooperation of Canadian Javelin Ltd. Ironically, the decision of the S.E.C. which denied Respondent's request for an administrative hearing and which explained the reasons for the trading suspension included the purported reason that "Civil suits are pending in Canada involving a dispute regarding control of the company" (App. 110). The memorandum did not disclose the fact that the S.E.C. had intervened in these suits on the side of one of the parties.

As noted previously, the appendix filed by the S.E.C. misrepresents the memoranda which constitute the record of this case. In the first petition filed by Respondent for review of trading suspension orders, the S.E.C. adopted the practice of deleting material from its own internal memoranda by apparently putting a piece of white paper over the material it sought to excise and then making a photocopy which was then filed in court. As a result, it was impossible to determine how many lines of material were left out or, in some cases, if any material was deleted whatever. In the second case, the S.E.C. adopted the somewhat less objectionable practice of marking with heavy black ink through everything it did not want the court of appeals to read. At least this method enables someone who reads the record to determine how many lines of text had been deleted. In this Court, the appendix indicates deleted material by "***", which hides the fact that in some instances the deleted material occupies many lines of text. No explanation has ever been offered by the

S.E.C. as to the reasons for deleting this material or what information the deleted material might contain. It is obvious that the memoranda filed by the S.E.C. as the "record" of this case do not meet the substantial evidence test, and indeed they do not constitute evidence at all. With this in mind, it is appropriate to turn to the memoranda themselves to see what they actually say. The first memorandum (App. 12) states that the Royal Canadian Mounted Police have "advised that they are conducting an extensive investigation into what they believe to be a manipulation of Canadian Javelin Ltd.'s common stock . . . They have also indicated that several United States residents and broker-dealers may be involved in the manipulation."

The language of this paragraph is qualified by the words "believe," "may," and "indicated." If the Royal Canadian Mounted Police had stated unequivocally that there was a manipulation and what the manipulation consisted of specifically, that would be one thing. However, the record here shows no such statement and there is no evidence to support the claim that there was a manipulation. It should also be noted that the term "manipulation" is itself a vague term and the S.E.C. is in apparent disagreement with this Court and with *Webster's International Dictionary* (2d ed. 1934) as to the meaning of the term "manipulative." See *Ernst & Ernst v. Hochfelder, supra,* 425 U.S. 185, 199, n. 21.

Subsequent memoranda repeat the statement that the Royal Canadian Mounted Police "was conducting an extensive investigation into what it believed to be a manipulation of Canadian Javelin's common stock . . . " (App. 20, 22, 24, 26). Thereafter the wording was changed slightly and the memoranda state that the Royal Canadian Mounted Police "was investigating an alleged manipulation of Canadian Javelin Ltd's common stock. . . " (App. 28, 31, 34, 37, 40, 42, 45, 48, 51, 54, 57, 60, 63, 66, 68, 70,

72, 74, 77, 80, 83, 86, 89, 92, 95, 98, 101, 104, 107, 111). Ironically, when the S.E.C. issued an opinion which provided the only published explanation of the reason for suspending trading in Canadian Javelin Ltd., it did not include the reason that Canadian Javelin Ltd. was being investigated by the Royal Canadian Mounted Police concerning an alleged manipulation (App. 109-110). It should also be pointed out that all of the memoranda just cited all contain a statement that there was "a public announcement by the Royal Canadian Mounted Police . . . " In fact, the Royal Canadian Mounted Police is known to be an exceptionally closed-mouthed agency, rarely makes public announcements and did not do so in this case and the statement contained in almost all of the memoranda which are included in the record of this case that there has been a "public announcement by the Royal Canadian Mounted Police" was a lie. It should be noted that the term "lie" means a statement made with intent to deceive. The true fact was the statement contained in the initial memoranda which said that the Royal Canadian Mounted Police had advised the S.E.C. that it was conducting an investigation. Incidently, counsel for Canadian Javelin Ltd. apparently believe to this day that the seizure of the files by the Royal Canadian Mounted Police may have occurred at the request of the S.E.C. itself. It is clear from a variety of circumstances, some of which are not part of the record of this case, that the S.E.C. was working closely with the Royal Canadian Mounted Police. However, in order to avoid any acknowledgement of this relationship even in internal memoranda prepared by members of the S.E.C. staff, and explanation was given that there had been a "public announcement" when in fact no public announcement had been made. Respondent was able to determine that no public announcement had been made while this case was pending before the court of appeals.

The memoranda which constitute the record of this

case invariably state that there is taking place an investigation into a "manipulation." As one turns the pages of these memoranda, one waits with anticipation to be told what the manipulation consists of specifically. However, in the memorandum dated December 5, 1975 (App. 72), which purports to give the reason for the trading suspension order dated December 12, 1975, one learns for the first time that the investigation by the Royal Canadian Mounted Police "for the most part, relates to activities in Canada prior to the January 27, 1975 resumption of trading in the U.S." The sentence immediately preceding this statement is almost completely deleted, but it appears from the context that the deleted material sets forth a confidential communication between the Royal Canadian Mounted Police and the S.E.C. It is noteworthy that during the period prior to the January 27, 1975 resumption of trading in the U.S., trading was, of course, suspended by the S.E.C. and consequently it is not possible that there was a manipulation taking place in the United States which adversely affected the interest of U.S. stockholders. Therefore, the reason which the S.E.C. gave for its initial suspension of trading on April 29, 1975 ultimately proved to have had no effect on trading markets in the United States. In this regard, it is important to note that United States securities laws do not extraterritorial application. See Restatement (Second) of the Foreign Relations Law of the United States, §18. Cf. *Racaman v. Barish,* 408 F. Supp. 1189, 1195, n. 3 (E.D. Pa. 1975).

Commencing with the memorandum dated July 21, 1975 (App. 34) and ending with the memorandum dated March 4, 1976 (App. 98-99), every memorandum included in the record indicates that an investigation was being undertaken by the S.E.C. These memoranda all state:

"The investigation to date has revealed that from the commencement of trading on January 27, 1975 until the

Commission's trading suspension on April 29, 1975 CJV's stock has been continually manipulated on the Amex as well as several Canadian stock exchanges. The manipulation appears to involve Americans, Canadians and Panamanians. It also appears that John C. Doyle ("Doyle"), CJV's founder, former chairman of the executive committee and currently a director has been behind the manipulation."

However, none of these memoranda set forth what, if any, specific manipulative activity occurred. Aside of vague references to manipulative activity, the major theme of these memoranda concerns the efforts of the S.E.C. staff to investigate the affairs of Canadian Javelin Ltd. It appears that problems developed in the course of this investigation, most of which were related to the fact that Canadian Javelin Ltd. is a Canadian corporation, has no direct ties with the United States other than its listing on the American Stock Exchange and all of its officers, directors and accountants reside outside the territorial boundaries of the United States. As a result, the S.E.C. was not in a position to exercise its subpoena power and was forced to seek, unsuccessfully as it turned out, the cooperation of these individuals. The obvious *quid pro quo* for the arrangement proposed by the S.E.C. was that if the officers, directors, and accountants for Canadian Javelin Ltd. would cooperate by meeting with and giving sworn testimony before members of the S.E.C. staff and by agreeing to waive their Fifth Amendment rights and their attorney-client privilege, the S.E.C. would consider lifting the trading suspension. The memoranda trace the course of the ultimately futile efforts to secure the cooperation of Canadian Javelin Ltd. and associated persons. The May 6, 1975 memorandum (App. 14) states that the S.E.C. staff had met with counsel for Canadian Javelin Ltd. and had requested a press release. Since Canadian Javelin Ltd. is known to issue a press release on almost every occasion, it is obvious that the S.E.C. was not seeking just any press release, but rather wanted a press release which would admit guilt. Although the May 6, 1976 memorandum states, "We anticipate receiving their press release within a few days," and the May 12, 1975 memorandum repeats this statement (App. 17), the May 23, 1975 memorandum says (App. 20), "Company counsel previously indicted [sic] that they intend to submit an *appropriate* release but have not yet done so" (emphasis supplied). This sentence is repeated in the next three memoranda (App. 22, 24, 26). Note that the word "indicted" is used in each of these memoranda. By the time of the July 1, 1975 memorandum (App. 28-29), the S.E.C. staff had apparently abandoned its hope of obtaining from Canadian Javelin Ltd. a press release admitting culpability. This and the four preceding memoranda contain a statement that Canadian Javelin Ltd. is a "chronic violator" (App. 20, 22, 24, 26). The July 1, 1975 memorandum also indicates that by this time the S.E.C. staff had gotten around to taking depositions and exchanging information with the Royal Canadian Mounted Police (App. 28). This memorandum also states the significant fact that on June 27, 1975 the S.E.C. staff met with representatives of the American Stock Exchange who agreed to continue their own trading suspension "until the Commission is in a position to reveal the extent of the manipulation and its participants" (App. 28), a circumstance which apparently has not occurred to this day since the American Stock Exchange has continued its trading suspension even to the present.

The July 1, 1975 memorandum also states that the S.E.C. staff had met with "special counsel of the company" (App. 29). This reference is somewhat misleading because the "special counsel" to whom the memorandum obviously refers is one Meyer Eisenberg, a former employee of the S.E.C. who maintains his law office in Washington, D.C. and who was appointed by the order of United States District Judge Lloyd F. MacMahon at the request of the S.E.C. to represent Canadian Javelin Ltd. in proceedings before the Canadian courts. This appointment of special counsel took place as a result of an injunction obtained by the S.E.C. in *S.E.C. v. Canadian Javelin Ltd.*, 73 Civil 5074 (S.D.N.Y.). Litigation arising a result of Meyer Eisenberg's appointment, over the objections of Canadian Javelin Ltd., are alluded to in the memoranda dated December 19, 1975 (App. 75) thru March 4, 1976 (App. 78-81, 84, 86-87, 89-90, 92-93, 95-96, 98-99). Obviously, a meeting by the S.E.C. staff with Meyer Eisenberg under these circumstances was not likely to reveal any new information about Canadian Javelin Ltd.

According to the memorandum of July 1, 1975, the reason for meeting with Meyer Eisenberg was to request him to investigate several transactions involving Canadian Javelin Ltd. "during the height of the alleged manipulation" and to arrange for a meeting with Mr. Doyle (App. 29). This memorandum also states that:

> "The staff has traced Mr. Doyle's telephone in Nassau to have been frequently called by certain persons believed to have been directly involved with wash-trading during the relevant period. Furthermore, company counsel has not yet submitted an appropriate press release as was recently promised. The staff hopes to conclude the investigation shortly after it meets with Mr. Doyle."

The July 15, 1975 memorandum (App. 31-32) is identical to the July 1, 1975 memorandum. The July 21, 1975 and the August 1, 1975 memoranda (App. 34-35, 37-38) are different. They state:

> "Soon after the staff began issuing subpoenas, most of the U.S. residents who participated in the scheme fled to Panama. Recently an old time securities violator and close associate of Doyle refused to testify, invoking his 5th Amendment rights. Doyle has also recently indicated,

through counsel, that he is reluctant to testify in this matter.

The staff is communicating with the Quebec Securities Commission, the Grand Cayman police, and the Bahamian authorities and plans to meet with several company officials in the near future. It is anticipated that this investigation will conclude soon thereafter."

The August 1, 1975 memorandum (App. 40) states, for the first time, that the S.E.C. staff has "requested a meeting with the president of CJV, Canadian counsel for CJV, and the partner in charge of Lee Martin, the company's independent auditors. The staff has also been recently informed that Doyle is not receptive to a meeting with the staff." However, the next memorandum, dated August 21, 1975 states (App. 42-43):

> "Canadian counsel for CJV has informed the staff that approval of the board of directors is necessary in order for the president of CJV and its counsel to testify before the Commission and to furnish information concerning sensitive areas involving corporate activities. For this reason they have sought postponements concerning their appearances and they anticipate testifying within the next week or so."

The September 2, 1975 memorandum contains the same paragraph (App. 45-46), apparently forgetting that by that time more than a week had passed. The September 11, 1975 memorandum changes the text by stating that the scheduled appearances "have been postponed" (App. 49). Finally, the October 1, 1975 memorandum makes it clear that the efforts by the S.E.C. staff to obtain testimony and other evidence on this basis have proven futile. The memorandum states that on September 28, and 29, 1975 the board of directors of Canadian Javelin Ltd. met in Costa Rica and although it agreed to furnish information to the S.E.C. staff, it "refused to waive any attorney-client privilege" (App. 55). This arrangement was apparently unacceptable to the S.E.C. Cf. *S.E.C. v. Csapo,* 533 F. 2d 7 (D.C. Cir. 1976). This memorandum also states that neither the president of Canadian Javelin Ltd. nor Doyle nor his son intended to meet with the S.E.C. staff and that the "staff intends to pursue every available recourse to compel the testimony of these witnesses" (App. 55).

The text of the October 1, 1975 memorandum is repeated verbatum in the October 10, 1975 memorandum (App. 57-58), which constitutes the record of the order suspending trading dated October 15, 1975 (App. 56). October 15, 1975 was, coincidentally, the date of the first decision of the court of appeals reported at 527 F.2d 11 regarding the S.E.C.'s trading suspension orders. It is apparent that by this time the S.E.C.'s investigation, to the extent that it ever existed, had essentially ground to a halt. Succeeding memoranda deal with efforts by the S.E.C. staff to pursue various paths. The tone of these memoranda can be compared to the repeated assertion of Mr. Macaber, the Dickens character, that "something will turn up." The October 17, 1975 memorandum complains that Canadian Javelin Ltd. had disengaged its Washington, D.C. law firm of Steptoe & Johnson from representing it before the S.E.C. (App. 60). The memorandum implies that this occurred because Steptoe & Johnson had "recommended that CJV and its officers and directors cooperate with the staff in this investigation." It also complains that Canadian counsel for CJV had decided to retain counsel before meeting with the staff of the S.E.C. (App. 60). The next memorandum, dated October 31, 1975, says for the first time that Canadian counsel for Canadian Javelin Ltd., presumably the same counsel upon whom in earlier memoranda the S.E.C. claimed to have been relying to provide information (App. 14, 17, 20, 22, 24, 26), may himself "be involved in the manipulation" (App. 64). The memorandum which follows, dated

November 7, 1975 (App. 66), in addition to the two introductory paragraphs which have by now become standard in all these memoranda, does nothing more than repeat prior statements to the effect that the S.E.C. staff is attempting to meet with Canadian counsel for Canadian Javelin Ltd. Everything else in the memorandum is blacked out. The next memorandum, dated November 18, 1975, states that the attorney in question "no longer intends to discuss the matter with the staff" (App. 68). Finally, in the November 28, 1975 memorandum everything is blacked out with the exception of the standard two introductory paragraphs (App. 70). The next memorandum, which has been discussed *supra,* states that the Royal Canadian Mounted Police investigation concerns, for the most part, activities in Canadian prior to the resumption of trading in the United States (App. 72). The following memorandum, dated December 19, 1975, states for the first time that the S.E.C. Division of Enforcement has decided "that supervisory personnel at several U.S. broker-dealers should be interviewed in order to resolve any participation in the manipulation" (App. 74). No explanation is given as to why these broker-dealers had not been interviewed previously during the by now more than seven month period in which the suspension had been in effect. This memorandum also complains about a suit brought against Canadian Javelin Ltd., the S.E.C. and Meyer Eisenberg by a director of Canadian Javelin Ltd. The next memorandum, dated December 29, 1975, repeats prior material and refers to the fact that Meyer Eisenberg had been appointed by court order to represent Canadian Javelin Ltd. in that suit (App. 78). The January 9, 1976 memorandum repeats the by now three standard introductory paragraphs and adds nothing else (App. 80-81). However, the January 16, 1976 memorandum provides new material by stating that on January 14, 1976 the Royal Canadian Mounted Police had filed a criminal information against Doyle and four others in St. John's, Newfoundland (App. 83). From this it appears that the investigation by the Royal Canadian Mounted Police proved more productive than the investigation initiated by the S.E.C. The January 23, 1976 memorandum thereafter complains (App. 87):

> "To date, there has been no public release by the company concerning the RCMP investigation or the recent criminal informations filed in St. John's, Newfoundland. Moreover, CJV continues to refuse to cooperate with the S.E.C. staff."

The next four memoranda, dated February 5, 1976, February 12, 1976, February 26, 1976 and March 4, 1976 contained the three standard paragraphs and nothing else (App. 89-90, 92-93, 95-96, 98-99). The following memorandum, dated March 19, 1976 (App. 101-102), is highly significant. It states that on March 11, 1976 the S.E.C. approved the filing of an injunctive suit in federal court. This action was subsequently filed as *S.E.C. v. Doyle et al, supra*. However, since the complaint alleged that all of the named defendants were either persons who were not residents of the United States or corporations which had no ties with the United States and since Canadian Javelin Ltd. itself was not named as a defendant, it is not surprising that as it turned out none of the defendants appeared in that action until more than a year later. Indeed, it was not until a year after the complaint had been filed that the S.E.C. got around to attempting to effect service of process. The defendants in the suit filed by the S.E.C. were identical to the defendants in the criminal information filed in Canada except that the suit instituted by the S.E.C. added as defendants various corporations controlled by the individual defendants. In spite of the virtually insurmountable difficulties the S.E.C. must have known that it was facing in prosecuting that action, the March 29, 1976 memorandum states (App. 101), "The staff believes that with the filing of this complaint, the public purpose for which the suspension of trading of CJV stock was instituted on April 29, 1975 will have been amply served." The memorandum also states that the S.E.C. staff has the "present expectation that the suit will be filed . . . on or before the expiration of the current trading suspension" (App. 102). It turned out, however, that the S.E.C. did not institute suit as quickly as it thought it would be able to and the April 20, 1976 memorandum states that the lifting of the trading suspension was being held up for that reason (App. 111-112). Meanwhile, in an unexpected development, a Canadian court ordered a reorganization of the board of directors and the memoranda dated March 26, 1976 and April 2, 1976 reflect this fact (App. 104-105, 108). It is clear, however, that this development was not rationally related to the S.E.C.'s decision to continue the trading suspension, particularly since the April 2, 1976 memorandum states (App. 108), "New management has informed us that they wish to cooperate with the staff, waive an attorney-client privilege, and make available all CJV officers, directors and employees to the staff."

There was, however, one remaining matter which had gone unmentioned in all of these memoranda which was the fact that Respondent had been pursuing his judicial remedies for more than one year in order to force the suspension of trading to be lifted. In its first decision dealing with trading suspension, the court of appeals had, in effect, ordered the S.E.C. to give Respondent some sort of administrative hearing and on March 11, 1976 the S.E.C. had received a petition from Respondent conforming to the S.E.C.'s requirements. Because of this, rather than lift the trading suspension without responding to Respondent's petition, the S.E.C. decided to continue the suspension for one more ten-day period. The memorandum dated April 9, 1976, which discusses this decision, states (App. 119):

> "As the Commission will recall, the United States Court of Appeals for the Second Circuit, in October, 1975, rejected Mr. Sloan's attack on summary trading suspension based upon the Commission's representation that we would give a person who claimed to be aggrieved by such a suspension an opportunity to be heard (*Sloan v. Securities and Exhcnage Commisison,* C.A. 2 no. 74-2457). The court indicated at that time that such a hearing should result in a record which could later be reviewed on appeal if that became necessary."

As a result, the S.E.C. issued its last trading suspension order which was published in full text in the Federal Register (App. 109-110). It constitutes the only time the S.E.C. ever made a public statement as to the reasons for its year-long trading suspension of securities of Canadian Javelin Ltd. This order was couched in the same vague terms which are characteristic of the memoranda prepared by the S.E.C. staff but it gave different reasons for the trading suspension, such as the reason that Canadian Javelin Ltd. was delinquent in filing its 10-K report (App. 110). It dismissed the facts alleged in Respondent's affidavit in support of a request for an administrative hearing as "speculation" (App. 110).

From the above analysis, it should be clear that the orders suspending trading in Canadian Javelin Ltd. were unjustified, arbitrary, capricious, and were not supported by substantial evidence and, hence, must be set aside. What emerges from a reading of all the documents which the S.E.C. has included in the record is an unsubstantiated belief by unidentified members of the S.E.C. staff that persons connected with Canadian Javelin Ltd. have somehow engaged in a stock manipulation and this belief is coupled with the failure of Canadian Javelin Ltd. and certain associated persons to "cooperate" with the S.E.C.

staff. However, there exists no legal obligation for any person to "cooperate" with the S.E.C. The S.E.C. has vast powers, including the power to issue subpoenas and to institute actions for injunctive relief but no free government has ever devised a means, short of torture, which is prescribed by the Eighth Amendment, to create the power to compel persons to "cooperate." The S.E.C. apparently believes that the failure to cooperate is a sign of guilt. However, some of the world's largest corporations refuse to cooperate with the S.E.C. and refuse to comply with S.E.C. rules and nevertheless the S.E.C. does not suspend trading in their securities. For example, Hoffman LaRoche and Co., a Swiss pharmaceutical concern, has shares which are traded actively in the United States over-the-counter market at a current price of $44,500 bid —$48,000 offered per share. This corporation refuses to file the reports required by S.E.C. Rule 12g3-2(b), and although it follows the European practice of publishing its balance sheet in European newspapers once a year, it refuses to provide financial disclosure of the type required by the S.E.C. Nevertheless, the S.E.C. has not suspended trading in the shares of Hoffman LaRoche and Co. nor has it taken any other action against that corporation and is not likely to do so.

There is a broader issue involved here which goes beyond the specific trading suspension orders which happen to be involved in this case. In its petition for writ of certiorari, the S.E.C. stated (Pet. 5):

> "The decision below, by holding that the Commission has no statutory authority to issue consecutive suspension orders, eviscerates one of the principal tools available to the Commission for protecting the investing public against suspended fraud or manipulation of the market for particular securities."

What the S.E.C. is stating quite clearly is that it wants

the power to issue consecutive trading suspension orders. The S.E.C. claims that it needs this power for the purpose of "protecting the investing public against suspected fraud or manipulation of the market for particular securities." However, the record the S.E.C. has established generally in issuing trading suspension orders demonstrates that this is not the case. The reason most often given by the S.E.C. for a trading suspension is a delinquency by the corporation in filing its 10-K report. On the surface, this might seem to provide a valid reason for a trading suspension. However, it must be remembered that once a trading suspension order has been issued, Rule 15c2-11 comes into play and most of the securities which have been suspended from trading for the reason of a 10-K delinquency have never resumed trading. At the same time, the S.E.C. never institutes proceedings under § 32(b), 15 U.S.C. § 78*ff*(b), which is the Congressionally mandated remedy which provides for a fine of $100 for each and every day that a 10-K report is filed late. Thus, the S.E.C. never punishes the corporation and corporate officers who are actually responsible for the late 10-K filings but instead punishes the innocent stockholders by summarily suspending trading in their securities. The S.E.C.'s practice of suspending trading in securities *en masse* which are delinquent in filing their 10-K reports originated in Securities Exchange Act Release No. 10127, 1 SEC Docket No. 12, p. 7 (April 26, 1973) which announced the simultaneous suspension of trading in nine securities. This practice is continued with Securities Exchange Act Release No. 10138, 1 SEC Docket No. 15, p. 3 (May 7, 1973) (twelve securities); Securities Exchange Act Release No. 10321, 2 SEC Docket 232 (August 3, 1973) (five securities); Securities Exchange Act Release No. 10536, 3 SEC Docket 166 (December 4, 1974) (eight securities); Securities Exchange Act Release No. 10657, 3 SEC Docket 615 (February 26, 1974) (five securities);

Securities Exchange Act Release No. 10660, 3 SEC Docket 616 (February 27, 1974) (four securities); Securities Exchange Act Release No. 10662, 3 SEC Docket 617 (February 28, 1974) (five securities); Securities Exchange Act Release No. 10732, 4 SEC Docket 82 (April 11, 1974) (48 securities) and many others. In addition to releases which specified a delinquency in the filing of a 10-K report, a number of releases announced the suspension of trading in a group of securities on the grounds of a vague statement that "the subject issuers failed to comply with the reporting provisions of the Exchange Act resulting in a lack of current and accurate information available to the public." See e.g. Securities Exchange Act Release No. 10269, 2 SEC Docket 98 (July 5, 1973) (four securities). It is noteworthy that those releases which provided detailed information as to the degree of delinquency in filing a 10-K or other required report made it clear that not all companies were equally delinquent or had become delinquent during the same time period. For example, Securities Exchange Act Release No. 10536, 3 SEC Docket 166 (December 4, 1973) announced that trading in AIM Companies was being suspended because it had failed to file its 10-K annual reports for 1971, 1972 and 1973 as well as its 10-K quarterly reports for 1971, 1972 and 1973, whereas, at the same time, this release announced that trading in Mountain Equities Inc. was being suspended solely for failure to file its 10-Q quarterly reports for 1973. In short, what the S.E.C. did was merely take an arbitrary group of companies which were delinquent in filing their 10-K and 10-Q reports to various degrees and suspended trading in them simultaneously. Securities of other corporations which were equally delinquent were not suspended. The purpose of this was clearly to frighten corporations which were delinquent in their 10-K and 10-Q filings into bringing their filings up to date. The problem with this is that because of the haphazard methods of the S.E.C., corporations which were seriously delinquent in filing their 10-K and 10-Q reports often were not suspended from trading for a long time, whereas other corporations which had only become delinquent recently were suspended and as a result, it became impossible to predict when the S.E.C. would suspend trading in a security. It may be that the S.E.C. deliberately intended this result, since if a corporation knew precisely how delinquent it would have to be before the S.E.C. would suspend trading in its stock, it could simply defer filing its reports until a few days before the time to suspend had arrived. The drawback to this is that the scattershot methods adopted by the S.E.C. created a situation of instability and unpredictability in the securities markets, which is precisely what the existence of the S.E.C. was intended to prevent.

No better example of this can be found than in the trading suspensions of Canadian Javelin Ltd. which are the subject of the instant case. At this point it should be noted that Respondent does not contend that Canadian Javelin Ltd. is without sin. To the contrary, Respondent considers himself to be a victim of a securities fraud perpetrated by Canadian Javelin Ltd. and its officers, including Doyle and Wismer, among others. At the same time, had it not been for the S.E.C. and in particular the arbitrary way in which the S.E.C. applies its trading suspension power, Respondent would likely not have suffered serious financial loss from trading in Canadian Javelin Ltd. This is because of the fact that at the time that there was an active manipulation of the market in Canadian Javelin Ltd., the S.E.C. did not suspend trading although it had facts available which established that fraudulent conduct was taking place whereas later, after the manipulation had come to an end, the S.E.C. chose to suspend trading. If the S.E.C. had not had the power to suspend trading, Respondent would not have felt a false sense of security in believing that if an egregious fraud took place, the S.E.C. would suspend trading in Canadian Javelin Ltd. At the same time, had the S.E.C. not exercised its trading suspension power in November, 1973, by which time the market manipulation had come to an end, Respondent might have been able to recoup his losses during the course of normal trading activity. Finally, had the S.E.C. suspended trading at the height of the market manipulation, Respondent would have avoided a loss in excess of $123,000 plus brokerage commissions. This can be seen from facts which can be established from the record of the various court proceedings involving Respondent and Canadian Javelin Ltd. and from letters Respondent wrote to the S.E.C. itself during the height of the market manipulation.

Included as Appendix F and Appendix G to this brief are letters written by Respondent to S.E.C. staff attorney Larry Grimes of the Washington, D.C. office of the S.E.C. Larry Grimes was the attorney then in charge of the investigation of Canadian Javelin Ltd. These letters can be found in the files of the S.E.C. to which Respondent was given access pursuant to the Freedom of Information Act. This fact establishes that the S.E.C. received these letters. Nevertheless, the S.E.C. never responded to either letter even though, as the Freedom of Information Act material demonstrates, the S.E.C. almost routinely replies to letters of this sort. The second letter, dated August 10, 1973, stated, "The purpose of this letter is to make a formal complaint concerning trading activity in Canadian Javelin Ltd. ("CJV"), and to request that the Commission suspend trading in this security. I also request that the Commission investigate and conduct hearings concerning its trading activity. The reasons for this request are as follows:"

It can be readily seen from this letter and from the enclosures to the previous letter dated July 22, 1973 that an egregious fraud was occurring at this time. Specifically, a UPI news release dated June 20, 1973, which is included in Appendix F, stated that "Panama has postponed for at least two months, while it draws up a new mining code talks with Canadian Javelin Ltd. for a major mining concession, Commerce and Industry's Minister Fernando Manfredo said Wednesday." The release also quote Manfredo as saying, "We do not have sufficient information to support the claims of Canadian Javelin that this is the biggest copper deposit in the world" and that the Panamanian government "is now thinking about mining the copper reservers itself." Nevertheless, on June 22, 1973, only two days later, Canadian Javelin Ltd. issued a press release, which is included in Appendix G, which said that "Minister Fernando Manfredo's statement made it clear and confirmed that the company has delineated one of the world's largest copper mines" and that "the company is now moving from the exploration stage to that of construction." There is simply no way to reconcile these two conflicting statements. Canadian Javelin Ltd. was claiming that it was in the process of constructing one of the world's largest copper mines and that it possessed a concession giving it the right to commence this construction and at the same time a minister of the government of Panama was stating that Canadian Javelin Ltd. would have to wait two months before beginning negotiations for the major copper mining concession which Canadian Javelin Ltd. was claiming it already had. The fact is that Canadian Javelin Ltd. was claiming to own the mineral rights to an area of the Andes Mountains of Panama whereas the mineral rights were, in fact, owned by the government of Panama. This circumstance, which was pointed out by Respondent in his letters to the S.E.C. dated June 23, 1973 and August 10, 1973 was not generally known to the American investing public until the publication of an article in *The Wall Street Journal* dated October

25, 1973 entitled, "Now You See It: Canadian Javelin Doesn't Have Gold Rights In Panama, Nation Says; Firm Disputes That" and a further article in *The Wall Street Journal* dated October 30, 1973 entitled, "Canadian Javelin admits its announcement of Panama Mineral Rights was 'premature'." Subsequently, on November 29, 1973, the S.E.C. instituted suit against Canadian Javelin Ltd. and simultaneously suspended trading in its securities. The allegations of the complaint and the basis given for that trading suspension were precisely the facts and circumstances set forth in the two letters which Respondent had written to the S.E.C. three and four months earlier. The problem was that by the time the S.E.C. got around to suspending trading in November, 1973, the manipulation was over. The American Stock Exchange had instituted its own trading suspension on October 25, 1973. By the time of the S.E.C.'s trading suspension on November 29, 1973, the true facts had been published by *The Wall Street Journal* and more than a month had passed with no trading in Canadian Javelin Ltd. either on an exchange or in the over-the-counter market. Meanwhile, Respondent had suffered substantial losses. During the period from July 5, 1973 until July 26, 1973 the price of Canadian Javelin Ltd. rose from 7-1/8 to 14-5/8 on the American Stock Exchange. Respondent was short 33,400 shares. Respondent was thus caught in a short squeeze and was powerless to do anything about it other than write letters to the S.E.C. The meteoric rise in price of Canadian Javelin Ltd. occurred as a direct result of the fraudulent press release dated June 22, 1973 and a second fraudulent press release issued by Bison Petroleum & Minerals, Ltd., a subsidiary of Canadian Javelin Ltd., dated July 5, 1973, which is also included in Appendix G. After hitting a high of 14-5/8 on July 26, 1973, Canadian Javelin Ltd. leveled off and traded in the $13-14 range during the month of August. Due to the fraudulent state of the market which had existed at that time, Respondent did not buy or sell any Canadian Javelin Ltd. shares during this period but eventually got bought in on most of his short position, thereby sustaining substantial losses. The point is that the S.E.C. knew everything it needed to know to suspend trading in July or August, 1973, and had it done so Respondent and the investing public would have avoided serious financial losses. Instead, the S.E.C. allowed trading in Canadian Javelin Ltd. to continue through October 25, 1973, a period of great activity in the market for Canadian Javelin Ltd. during which Canadian Javelin Ltd. was often one of the ten most actively traded issues on the American Stock Exchange.

What happened here is typical of the *modus operandi* of the S.E.C. It is unusual for the S.E.C. to suspend trading during a period in which an actual manipulation is taking place. Indeed, Respondent is not aware of even a single instance where the S.E.C. has taken such an action. Instead, the S.E.C. does not act until the manipulation is over and with the benefit of 20-20 hindsight suspends trading because of a manipulation which took place at some time in the past. An example of this can be found in the S.E.C.'s own brief. On page 30, n. 11 of its brief, the S.E.C. cites as an example its suspension of trading in Power Conversion, Inc. Power Conversion Inc. was a notorious securities fraud. While the fraud was taking place, everybody knew about it but the S.E.C. did nothing. Eventually, the bubble burst and, as the brief of the S.E.C. notes, the price declined in less than two days from $39.75 to $5.00. With Power Conversion trading at $5 per share, the market manipulation was effectively over. Ironically, at that very point, the S.E.C. decided to step in and suspend trading. *The Wall Street Journal* subsequently reported that as a result of the S.E.C.'s suspension of trading in Power Conversion, Inc. four brokerage firms went into court ordered liquidation and another sustained losses in excess of $1,000,000.[47] The public is under the impression that the S.E.C. suspends trading when the price of a corporation's stock goes up without any corporate development justifying the price rise. This is because the S.E.C. often states that it suspends trading for this reason. However, the fact is that any time the S.E.C. suspends trading in a security for this reason, it waits to do so until the price has plummeted back down again. In short, apparently as a matter of policy, the S.E.C. does not take the unpopular action of suspending trading in a security at a time when the price is rising but rather suspends trading in a security at a time when the price is falling. As Respondent pointed out in his affidavit in support of his petition to the S.E.C. (App. 117-118), this was precisely the case each time the S.E.C. suspended trading in Canadian Javelin Ltd. In view of the notorious history of abuse of the trading suspension power on the part of the S.E.C., the S.E.C. should not be heard to claim as it does in this Court that the exercise of the trading suspension power is "one of the principal tools available to the Commission for protecting the investing public," when in fact the principal use for this "tool" is to bludgeon corporations and individuals into "cooperating" with the S.E.C. by consenting to injunctions and the like.

Under §25(a)(5) of the Securities Exchange Act, 15 U.S.C. 78*y*(a)(5), if the findings of the S.E.C. are not supported by substantial evidence, they must be set aside. Regardless of how this case is approached, the S.E.C. has not sustained the burden of proof as required by the Administrative Procedure Act, 5 U.S.C. §556(d), and clearly the findings and orders of the S.E.C. are not supported by

---

47. See *The Wall Street Journal*, "Volatile Issue: How Numerous Fingers Became Badly Burned Handling a Hot Stock," Jan. 2, 1973, p. 1 col. 6, p. 19 col. 5.

substantial evidence. Hence, the thirty-seven orders suspending trading in Canadian Javelin Ltd. must be vacated.

V

SECTION 12(K) OF THE SECURITIES EXCHANGE ACT, WHICH AUTHORIZES THE SECURITIES AND EXCHANGE COMMISSION "SUMMARILY TO SUSPEND TRADING IN ANY SECURITY" WHENEVER "IN ITS OPINION THE PUBLIC INTEREST AND THE PROTECTION OF INVESTORS SO REQUIRE" IS UNCONSTITUTIONAL

The decision of the court of appeals held that a single ten-day trading suspension did not violate the Constitution. It found it unnecessary to reach the question of whether a more lengthy trading suspension violated the Constitution in view of its resolution of the statutory question. If this Court agrees with the S.E.C. that the determiantion by the court of appeals of the statutory question was erroneous, it must proceed to a determination of the question of the constitutionality of the S.E.C.'s exercise of its trading suspension power.

The decision of the court of appeals stated (Pet. 14a-15a):

> "The petitioner also claims that his Constitutional rights were violated by the series of suspension orders because he was never afforded notice and an opportunity for a hearing. It is not necessary to deal with this point as a Constitutional violation, however, because the procedures adopted by the S.E.C. plainly transgressed the statutory provisions. For a single ten-day suspension no prior notice or hearing is required because the proceeding is summary in nature and because the emergency aspect of the order,

issued to protect the public interest and give protection to investors, makes it necessary."

There are several Constitutional problems involved in the S.E.C.'s exercise of its trading suspension power. A trading suspension effectively brings to a halt all trading regardless of whether or not interstate commerce is involved. Thus, the trading suspension power exceeds the power vested in Congress by the commerce clause of the Constitution and hence is unconstitutional. In addition, in cases such as *Fuentes v. Shevin,* 407 U.S. 67, 90-93 (1972) and *Mitchell v. W.T. Grant,* 416 U.S. 600 (1974), this Court has held that summary governmental action affecting property rights is unconstitutional unless an immediate hearing is available and even then in extraordinary situations. Other decisions make it clear that the "extraordinary situations" must involve an important governmental interest. For example, an important governmental interest has been held to exist when necessary to protect the public from contaminated food, from misbranded drugs, to aid the collection of taxes, or to aid the war effort. See *Calero-Toledo v. Pearson Yacht Leasing Co.,* 416 U.S. 663, 679 (1974). A question thus arises as to whether the need to suspend trading in a security is a sufficiently important governmental interest. It is submitted that the desire of a governmental agency to suspend trading a security, regardless of how strong that desire might be, does not reach the level of importance to the government as the need to collect taxes, for example. Moreover, it is difficult to imagine the kind of "extraordinary situation" which must exist for a trading suspension to be constitutionally valid. Certainly, there has been no showing that an extraordinary situation existed in connection with the trading suspensions which are the subject of the instant case. Therefore, these particular trading suspensions were unconstitutional. In addition, a trading suspension is unconstitutional because an aggrieved party is not entitled to a hearing. For example, in the instant case, Respondent requested that the S.E.C. provide him the opportunity for a hearing and this request was denied and had it not been for the prior decision of the court of appeals it would not even have been entertained. Therefore, the exercise of the trading suspension power, in this case at least, was unconstitutional.

Another constitutional defect to the trading suspension power is that it constitutes an unconstitutional delegation of legislative power. A trading suspension is a legislative act as defined in *Prentis v. Atlantic Coast Line Co.*, 211 U.S. 210, 226 (1908). In cases too numerous to cite, this Court has held that a delegation of legislative power to an administrative agency without appropriate standards is unconstitutional. See e.g. *Schechter Poultry Corp. v. United States,* 295 U.S. 495, 529 (1936). In the case of a trading suspension, the only standard provided by Congress is that the "public interest and the protection of investors so require." However, a determination of what constitutes the "public interest" is exclusively within the province of Congress. From this Court's court decision in *National Cable Television v. United States,* 415 U.S. 336, 342 (1974) it is clear that a delegation to an administrative agency of the authority to make a determination of what constitutes the "public interest" is unconstitutional. This was again explained in *Federal Energy Administration v. Algonquin SNG, Inc.,* 426 U.S. 548, 559, n. 10 (1976). In *National Cable Television, supra,* this Court held that the delegation to an administrative agency of the authority to take into consideration the "public policy or interest served and other pertinent facts," was sufficiently open-ended as to be an unconstitutional delegation of legislative authority. It is apparent that the delegation to the S.E.C. of the authority to determine what is "necessary in the public interest and for the protection of investors'' is even more open-ended and indeed Congress has provided no standards whatever. Indeed, the difficulty experienced by Congress in forcing the S.E.C. to limit the duration of its trading suspension orders demonstrates the existence of a fundamental constitutional defect in the delegation of the trading suspension power. Hence, the trading suspension power is an unconstitutional delegation of legislative power. The exercise of the trading suspension power is also unconstitutional in that it fails to provide for certain constitutionally protected rights such as the right to confrontation and cross-examination and, in addition, it is unconstitutional as being arbitrary and capricious. This can be seen from this Court's decision in *Greene v. McElroy,* 360 U.S. 474, 496-497 (1959), where this Court stated:

> ''Certain principles have remained relatively immutable in our jurisprudence. One of these is that where governmental action seriously injures an individual, and the reasonableness of the action depends on factfindings, the evidence used to prove the Government's case must be disclosed to the individual so that he has an opportunity to show that it is untrue. While this is important in the case of documentary evidence, it is even more important where the evidence consists of the testimony of individuals whose memory might be faulty or who, in fact, might be perjurers or persons motivated by malice, vindictiveness, intolerance, prejudice, or jealousy. We have formalized these protections in the requirements of confrontation and cross-examination. They have ancient roots. They find expression in the Sixth Amendment which provides that in all criminal cases the accused shall enjoy the right 'to be confronted with the witnesses against him.' This Court has been zealous to protect these rights from erosion.''

This decision puts its finger on the heart of the problem in dealing with the S.E.C. The members of the staff of the Division of Enforcement of the S.E.C., who are responsible for the trading suspension orders which are the subject of this case and who, for that matter, are responsible for the malicious prosecution of Respondent in two injunctive actions and one administrative proceeding, have demonstrated themselves to be masters of the "Big Lie" technique. The record of the cases in question shows that members of the S.E.C. staff are, indeed "perjurers and persons motived by malice, vindictiveness, intolerance, prejudice and jealousy." As Judge Haight observed in a recent case dealing with the activities of some of these same individuals, "It is a sad irony that representatives of a governmental agency dedicated to the prevention of fraudulent and misleading statements fell into this particular pattern of behavior." *United States v. Fields,* CCH Fed. Sec. Law Rep. ¶96,074 [current binder]. When Congress delegated to an independent administrative agency the power summarily to suspend trading in a security, it opened up the very possibility which has now arisen where the persons in a position to exercise that power can, if improperly motivated, cause serious harm to individuals and yet not be held accountable for their acts. One of the decisions of this Court has characterized the potential for misconduct on the part of the S.E.C. to the "intolerable abuses of the Star Chamber." *Jones v. S.E.C.,* 298 U.S. 1, 25-26 (1936). It has taken forty-four years from the time the S.E.C. was created by the enactment of the Securities Exchange Act of 1934 until the present date for the S.E.C. evolve into the agency it now is, but considering the broad powers given the S.E.C., of which the power summarily to suspend trading in a security is probably the one most rife with potential for abuse, it was inevitable that eventually power-hungry and improperly motivated individuals would get their hands on the reigns of this power and bring about the abuses which are the subject of this case. A few examples of the abuses created by the arbitrary exercise of the trading suspension power with respect to Canadian

Javelin Ltd. coupled with what Goldstein and Mangrino referred to as the S.E.C.'s "general but pragmatic policy of 'selective' enforcement" (Goldstein & Mangrino, *supra,* 15 N.Y.L. Forum at 640, n. 33) are appropriate.

As noted previously, Respondent was given access pursuant to the Freedom of Information Act to approximately 10,000 pages of material concerning the S.E.C.'s investigation of and trading suspensions in Canadian Javelin Ltd. An examination of this material, particularly with regard to requests by aggrieved parties for relief from the trading suspension orders demonstrates that the S.E.C. has acted in a most uneven-handed manner. More than 200 letters were received by the S.E.C. from persons protesting the trading suspensions. Many of these letters requested that the trading suspension be lifted and demanded a hearing. None of the requests for a hearing were granted. A number of letters asked to be provided with the reasons for the trading suspension. In response to these letters, the S.E.C. sent a copy of the press release announcing the initial trading suspension. Another common request was for information concerning how long the trading suspension would last. A typical response to this kind of letter is included as Appendix H to this brief.[48] (The name of the addressee of this letter is deleted in accordance with procedures adopted by the S.E.C. with regard to the dissemination of material under the Freedom

48. The inclusion of the memoranda as appendices to this brief is not improper. When this case was before the court of appeals, Respondent requested that 337 pages of material obtrained from the files of the S.E.C. pursuant to the Freedom of Information Act be included in the record (App. 148). The court of appeals took no action on this motion and consequently the material in question is not part of the formal record. However, this case is now before this Court and the question of whether this material should be included in the record may be reconsidered. Since all of the memoranda in question come directly from the files of the S.E.C., the S.E.C. is in a better position to determine their authenticity than Respondent and, therefore, cannot object to this procedure.

of Information Act.) It should be noted that this letter states that the S.E.C. "cannot predict when it will be lifted". Had the S.E.C. really suspended trading for a ten-day period as it claims, the answer to this question would be that the trading suspension expires in ten days or less. It is thus clear that the S.E.C. staff knew that the trading suspension was likely to last for longer than ten days. It is also interesting to note that this letter asserts that "important judicial remedies are available to investors." However, in the next sentence when it states that "recovery may be sought", it is obvious that the S.E.C. was contemplating a suit against the corporation which was the subject of the trading suspension order rather than a suit against the S.E.C. for wrongfully suspending trading.

Another type of letter can be found in Appendix I. This letter was from a broker-dealer that was experiencing capital problems because of the trading suspension. The broker in question owned 2,000 shares of Canadian Javelin Ltd. stock and wanted to sell these shares on the Montreal Stock Exchange, where Canadian Javelin Ltd. was actively traded in spite of the trading suspension by the S.E.C. Consequently, the broker in question sought a no-action letter. This request for a no-action letter was denied by the S.E.C. in a letter included as Appendix J. In marked contrast to this response is a memorandum included as Appendix K. This memorandum establishes that Stanley Sporkin has engaged in a criminal conspiracy to violate the Securities Exchange Act. The memorandum concerns a brokerage firm named Moses & Singer, which had a client who was holding shares of Canadian Javelin Ltd. in a restricted margin account while trading was suspended. (Moses & Singer, incidentally, is a New York City law firm, not a brokerage firm, and presumably had a brokerage firm for a client.) The memorandum states that "after consulting with Stan Sporkin," Moses & Singer was advised that it could deliver the securities against payment to a broker in Canada for sale by that broker for the account of the customer. However, §12(k) as well as former §15(c)(5) of the Securities Exchange Act provide that "no broker or dealer shall make use of the mails or of means or instrumentality of interstate commerce to affect any transaction in, or induce the purchase or sale of, any security in which trading is so suspended." The letter included in Appendix K makes it clear that the broker was in the position of asking its customer to sell the stock in order to be able to pay off the margin account. Thus, the broker in question was inducing its customer to make a sale of a suspended security in clear violation of the Securities Exchange Act and Stanley Sporkin was conspiring with the broker to bring about this violation, which in turn is a criminal violation of 18 U.S.C. §5 (criminal conspiracy).

A final and particularly egregious example of the harm resulting from the uneven application of the S.E.C.'s trading suspension orders can be seen from a no-action letter published as *Canadian Javelin Ltd.,* S.E.C. Division of Market Regulation (December 16, 1975), CCH Fed. Sec. Law Rep. ¶80,417 [1975-1976 Transfer Binder], a copy of which is included as Appendix L. This request for a no-action letter makes a one-sided statement of the facts, but, without complicating matters too much, the essential facts are that the brokerage firm of Edward & Hanly sued Respondent as a result of a transaction in Canadian Javelin Ltd. Edward & Hanly obtained an *ex parte* order of attachment and attached 1,000 shares of Canadian Javelin Ltd. in its possession which had been delivered to it by Respondent. Edwards & Hanly sued Respondent and Respondent counter-claimed for $13,000, representing the value of the securities converted by Edwards & Hanly. After a trial on the merits, Edwards & Hanly prevailed on its main case, but Respondent prevailed on his counter-claim for $13,000, the result being a judgement in favor of Respondent. On appeal, however, the appellate division reversed to the extent of dismissing the counter-claim. Edwards & Hanly then sought to sell the Canadian Javelin Ltd. shares in order to satisfy the judgment but was unable to do so because trading had been suspended. It then applied to the S.E.C. for a no-action letter permitting it to sell the 1000 Canadian Javelin Ltd. shares at a public auction at which it would then purchase these shares for resale on the Montreal Stock Exchange. The reason given by Edwards & Hanly for wanting to do this was that it had been informed that Respondent intended to appeal from the decision of the appellate court to the New York State Court of Appeals on the grounds of the unconstitutionality of the New York State Attachment Statute. Therefore, Edwards & Hanly wanted to sell the Canadian Javelin Ltd. shares prior to the termination of the trading suspension so as to moot any arguments Respondent might make to the court of appeals regarding the invalidity of the order of attachment. It so happened that at the time of this request for a no-action letter, the S.E.C. was also concerned about this particular 1,000 shares because Respondent was petitioning the court of appeals to lift the trading suspension, and in response to the S.E.C.'s argument in that court that the case was moot and that Respondent lacked standing to challenge the trading suspension orders, Respondent cited the circumstances pertaining to this 1,000 shares and the harm he was suffering as a result of the trading suspension. Thus, the S.E.C. had an interest in "mooting" the arguments raised by Respondent in the court of appeals. Therefore, the S.E.C. granted Edwards & Hanly a no-action letter in order to alleviate both of their problems with Respondent pertaining to this 1,000 shares. Shortly thereafter, Edwards & Hanly did in fact sell the Canadian Javelin Ltd. shares at a public auction and then re-purchased these shares and sold them on the Montreal Stock Exchange, in clear violation of §12(k) of the Securities Exchange Act and, as promised, the S.E.C. took no action. From this it is apparent that the staff of the S.E.C. has improperly if not illegally given preferential treatment to the client of Moses & Singer and to Edwards & Hanly by granting them permission to violate §12(k). It is submitted that this and other improprieties committed by the S.E.C. clearly demonstrate the unconstitutionality of §12(k) of the Securities Exchange Act.

CONCLUSION

The decision of the court of appeals, insofar as it vacated all but the first trading suspension order and ordered the S.E.C. to discontinue its practice of issuing successive trading suspension orders, should be affirmed. The orders of the S.E.C. suspending trading in Canadian Javelin Ltd. should also be vacated on the grounds of the lack of substantial evidence in the record to support them. This Court should declare §12(k) of the Securities Exchange Act to be unconstitutional. This Court may, in its discretion, remand the administrative proceeding against Respondent to the S.E.C. for reconsideration in light of this decision.

Respectfully submitted,

Samuel H. Sloan

APPENDIX A

PERTINENT STATUTES AND RULES

ADMINISTRATIVE PROCEDURE ACT

§556(d). Except as otherwise provided by statute, the proponent of a rule or order has the burden of proof. Any oral or documentary evidence may be received, but the agency as a matter of policy shall provide for the exclusion of irrelevant, immaterial, or unduly repetitious evidence. A sanction may not be imposed or rule or order issued except on consideration of the whole record or those parts thereof cited by a party and supported by and in accordance with the reliable probative, and substantial evidence. A party is entitled to present his case or defense by oral or documentary evidence, to submit rebuttal evidence, and to conduct such cross-examination as may be required for a full and true disclosure of the facts. In rule making or determining claims for money or benefits or applications for initial licenses an agency may, when a party will not be prejudiced thereby, adopt procedures for the submission of all or part of the evidence in written form.

Act of September 6, 1966, Pub. L. 89-554, 80 Stat. 386, 5 U.S.C. §556(d).

§558(c). When application is made for a license required by law, the agency, with due regard for the rights and privileges of all the interested parties or adversely affected persons and within a reasonable time, shall set and complete proceedings required to be conducted in accordance with sections 556 and 557 of this title or other proceedings required by law and shall make its decision. Except in cases of willfulness or those in which public health, interest, or safety requires otherwise, the withdrawal, suspension, revocation, or annulment of a license is lawful only if, before the institution of agency proceedings therefor, the licensee has been given—

(1) notice by the agency in writing of the facts or conduct which may warrant the action; and

(2) the opportunity to demonstrate or achieve compliance with all lawful requirements.

When the licensee has made timely and sufficient application for a renewal or a new license in accordance with agency rules, a license with reference to an activity of a continuing nature does not expire until the application has been finally determined by the agency.

Act of September 6, 1966, Pub. L. 89-554, 80 Stat. 388, 5 U.S.C. §558(c).

2a

SECURITIES EXCHANGE ACT OF 1934

§12(j). The Commission is authorized, by order, as it deems necessary or appropriate for the protection of investors to deny, to suspend the effective date of, to suspend for a period not exceeding twelve months, or to revoke the registration of a security, if the Commission finds, on the record after notice and opportunity for hearing, that the issuer of such security has failed to comply with any provision of this title or the rules and regulations thereunder. No member of a national securities exchange, broker, or dealer shall make use of the mails or any means or instrumentality of interstate commerce to effect any transaction in, or to induce the purchase or sale of, any security the registration of which has been and is suspended or revoked pursuant to the preceding sentence.

Act of June 4, 1975, Pub. L. 94-29, 89 Stat. 118, 15 U.S.C. §78 *l* (j).

§12(k). If in its opinion the public interest and the protection of investors so require, the Commission is authorized summarily to suspend trading in any security (other than an exempted security) for a period not exceeding ten days, or with the approval of the President, summarily to suspend all trading on any national securities exchange or otherwise, in securities other than exempted securities, for a period not exceeding ninety days. No member of a national securities exchange, broker, or dealer shall make use of the mails or any means or instrumentality of interstate commerce to effect any transaction in, or to induce the purchase or sale of, any security in which trading is so suspended.

Act of June 4, 1975, Pub. L. 94-29, 89 Stat. 118, 15 U.S.C. §78 *l* (k).

§15(c)(2). No broker or dealer shall make use of the mails of or any means or instrumentality of interstate commerce to effect any transaction in, or to induce or attempt to induce the purchase or sale of, any security (other than an exempted security or commercial paper, bankers' acceptances, or commercial bills) otherwise than on a national securities exchange of which it is a member, in connection with which such broker or dealer engages in any fraudulent, deceptive, or manipulative act or practice, or makes any fictitious quotation, and no municipal securities dealer shall make use of the mails or of any means or instrumentality of interstate commerce to effect any transaction in, or to induce or attempt to induce the purchase or sale of, any municipal security in connection with which such municipal securities dealer engages in any fraudulent, deceptive or manipulative act or practice or makes any fictitious quotation. The Commission shall, for the purposes of this paragraph, by rules and regulations define, and prescribe means reasonably designed to prevent, such acts and practices as are fraudulent, deceptive, or manipulative and such quotations as are fictitious.

Act of June 6, 1934, 48 Stat. 895; May 23, 1936, 49 Stat. 1377; June 25, 1938, 52 Stat. 1075; August 20, 1964, Pub. L. 88-467, 78 Stat. 570; December 30, 1970, Pub. L. 91-593, 84 Stat. 1653; June 4, 1975, Pub. L. 94-29, 89 Stat. 121, 15 U.S.C. § 78 *o*(c)(2).

§ 25(a)(1). A person aggrieved by a final order of the Commission entered pursuant to this title may obtain review of the order in the United States Court of Appeals for the circuit in which he resides or has his principal place of business, or for the District of Columbia Circuit, by filing in such court, within sixty days after the entry of the order, a written petition praying that the order be modified or set aside in whole or in part.

(2) A copy of the petition shall be transmitted forthwith by the clerk of the court to a member of the Commission or an officer designated by the Commission for that purpose. Thereupon, the Commission shall file in the court the record on which the order complained of is entered, as provided in section 2112 of title 28, United States Code, and the Federal Rules of Appellate Procedure.

(3) On the filing of the petition, the court has jurisdiction, which becomes exclusive on the filing of the record, to affirm or modify and enforce or to set aside the order in whole or in part.

(4) The findings of the Commission as to the facts, if supported by substantial evidence, are conclusive.

(5) If either party applies to the court for leave to adduce additional evidence and shows to the satisfaction of the court that the additional evidence is material and that there was reasonable ground for failure to adduce it before the Commission, the court may remand the case to the Commission for further proceedings, in whatever manner and on whatever conditions the court considers appropriate. If the case is remanded to the Commission, it shall file in the court a supplemental record containing any new evidence, any further or modified findings, and any new order.

Act of June 6, 1934, 48 Stat. 901; August 28, 1958, Pub. L. 85-791, 72 Stat. 945; June 4, 1975, Pub. L. 94-29, 89 Stat. 158, 15 U.S.C. §78 *y*(a).

§25(c)(2). The filing of a petition under this section does not operate as a stay of the Commission's order or rule. Until the court's jurisdiction becomes exclusive, the Commission may stay its order or rule pending judicial review if it finds that justice so requires. After the filing of a petition under this section, the court, on whatever conditions may be required and to the extent necessary to prevent irreparable injury, may issue all necessary and appropriate process to stay the order or rule or to preserve status or rights pending its review; but (notwithstanding section 705 of title 5, United States Code) no such process may be issued by the court before the filing of the record or the materials set forth in subsection (b)(2) of this section unless: (A) the Commission has denied a stay or failed to grant requested relief, (B) a reasonable period has expired since the filing of an application for a stay without a decision by the Commission, or (C) there was reasonable ground for failure to apply to the Commission.

Act of June 4, 1975, Pub. L. 94-29, 89 Stat. 158, 15 U.S.C. §78 *y*(c)(2).

§32(a). Any person who willfully violates any provision of this title, or any rule or regulation thereunder the violation of which is made unlawful or the observance of which is required under the terms of this title, or any person who willfully and knowingly makes, or causes to be made, any statement in any application, report, or document required to be filed under this title, or any person who willfully and knowingly makes, or causes to be made, any statement in any application, report, or document required to be filed under this title or any rule or regulation thereunder or any undertaking contained in a registration statement as provided in subsection (d) of section 15 of this title, which statement was false or misleading with respect to any material fact, shall upon conviction be fined not more than $10,000, or imprisoned not more than two years, or both, except that when such person is an exchange, a fine not exceeding $500,000 may be imposed; but no person shall be subject to imprisonment under this section for the violation of any rule or regulation if he proves that he had no knowledge of such rule or regulation.

Act of June 6, 1934, 48 Stat. 904; May 27, 1936, 49 Stat. 1380; June 25, 1938, 52 Stat. 1076; August 20, 1964, Pub. L. 88-467, 78 Stat. 580; June 4, 1975, Pub. L. 94-29, 89 Stat 162, 163, 15 U.S.C. §78*ff.*

(b) Any issuer which fails to file information, documents, or reports required to be filed under subsection (d) of section 15 of this title or any rule or regulation thereunder shall forfeit to the United States the sum of $100 for each and every day such failure to file shall continue. Such forfeiture, which shall be in lieu of any criminal penalty for such failure to file which might be deemed to arise under subsection (a) of this section, shall be payable to the Treasury of the United States and shall be recoverable in a civil suit in the name of the United States.

Former §15(c)(5). If in its opinion the public interest and the protection of investors so require, the Commission is authorized summarily to suspend trading otherwise than on a national securities exchange, in any security (other than an exempted security) for a period not exceeding ten days. No broker or dealer shall make use of the mails or of any means or instrumentality of interstate commerce to effect any transaction in, or to induce the purchase or sale of, any security in which trading is so suspended.

Act of August 20, 1964, Pub. L. 88-467, 78 Stat. 574, 15 U.S.C. §78 *o*(b).

Former §19(a). The Commission is authorized, if in its opinion such action is necessary or appropriate for the protection of investors—

* * * * * *

(4) And if in its opinion the public interest so requires, summarily to suspend trading in any registered security on any national securities exchange for a period not exceeding ten days, or with the approval of the President, summarily to suspend all trading on any national securities exchange for a period not exceeding ninety days.

Act of June 6, 1934, 48 Stat. 898, 15 U.S.C. §78*s*(a).

ALL WRITS ACT

§1651(a). The Supreme Court of the United States and all courts established by Act of Congress may issue all writs necessary or appropriate in aid of their respective jurisdictions and agreeable to the usages and principles of law.

Act of June 25, 1948, 62 Stat. 944; May 24, 1949, 63 Stat. 102, 28 U.S.C. §1651(a).

DECLARATORY JUDGMENT ACT

§2201. In a case of actual controversy within its jurisdiction, except with respect to Federal taxes other than actions brought under section 7428 of the Internal Revenue Code of 1954, any court of the United States, upon the filing of an appropriate pleading, may declare the rights and other legal relations of any interested party seeking such declaration, whether or not further relief is or could be sought. Any such declaration shall have the force and effect of final judgment or decree and shall be reviewable as such.

Act of June 25, 1948, 62 Stat. 964; May 24, 1949, 63 Stat. 105; August 28, 1954, 68 Stat. 890; July 7, 1958, Pub. L. 85-508, 72 Stat. 349; October 4, 1976, Pub. L. 94-455, Title XIII, §1306(b)(8), 90 Stat. 1719, 28 U.S.C. §2201.

FEDERAL RULES OF APPELLATE PROCEDURE

Rule 17(a). **Agency to File; Time for Filing; Notice of Filing.** The agency shall file the record with the clerk of the court of appeals within 40 days after service upon it of the petition for review unless a different time is provided by the statute authorizing review. In enforcement proceedings the agency shall file the record within 40 days after filing an application for enforcement, but the record need not be filed unless the respondent has filed an answer contesting enforcement of the order, or unless the court otherwise orders. The court may shorten or extend the time above prescribed. The clerk shall give notice to all parties of the date on which the record is filed.

RULES OF THE SECURITIES EXCHANGE COMMISSION

Rule 15c2-11. **Initiation or resumption of quotations without specified information.** (a) It shall be a fraudulent, manipulative, and deceptive practice within the meaning of section 15(c)(2) of the Act, for a broker or dealer to publish any quotation for a security or, directly or indirectly, to submit any such quotation for publication, in any quotation medium (as defined in this section) unless:

(1) The issuer has filed a registration statement under the Securities Act of 1933 which became effective less than 90 calendar days prior to the day on which such broker or dealer publishes or submits the quotation to the quotation medium: *Provided,* That such registration statement has not thereafter been the subject of a stop order which is still in effect when the quotation is published or submitted, and such broker or dealer has in his records a copy of the prospectus specified by section 10(a) of the Securities Act of 1933; or

(2) The issuer has filed a notification under Regulation A under the Securities Act of 1933 which became effective less than 40 calendar days prior to the day on which such broker or dealer publishes or submits the quotation to the quotation medium: *Provided,* That the offering circular provided for under Regulation A has not thereafter

become the subject of a suspension order which is still in effect when the quotation is published or submitted, and such broker or dealer has in his records a copy of such offering circular; or

(3) (i) The issuer is required to file reports pursuant to section 13 or 15(d) of the Act, or is the issuer of a security covered by section 12(g)(2) (B) or (G) of the Act, and

(ii) The broker or dealer has a reasonable basis for believing that the issuer is current in filing the reports required to be filed at regular intervals pursuant to section 13 or 15(d) of the Act, or, in the case of insurance companies exempted from section 12(g) of the Act by section 12(g)(2) (G) thereof, the annual statement referred to in section 12(g)(2) (G) (i) of the Act; and

(iii) The broker or dealer has in his records the issuer's most recent annual report filed pursuant to section 13 or 15(d) of the Act, or the annual statement in the case of an insurance company not subject to section 12(g) of the Act, together with any other reports required to be filed at regular intervals under such provisions of the Act which have been filed by the issuer after such annual report or annual statement; or

(4) Such broker or dealer has in his records, and shall make reasonably available upon request to any person expressing an interest in a proposed transaction in the security with such broker or dealer, the following information (which shall be reasonably current in relation to the day the quotation is submitted), which he has no reasonable basis for believing is not true and correct or reasonably current, and which was obtained by him from sources which he has a reasonable basis for believing are reliable: (i) The

exact name of the issuer and its predecessor (if any); (ii) the address of its principal executive offices; (iii) the state of incorporation, if it is a corporation; (iv) the exact title and class of the security; (v) the par or stated value of the security; (vi) the number of shares or total amount of the securities outstanding as of the end of the issuer's most recent fiscal year; (vii) the name and address of the transfer agent; (viii) the nature of the issuer's business; (ix) the nature of products or services offered; (x) the nature and extent of the issuer's facilities; (xi) the name of the chief executive officer and members of the board of directors; (xii) the issuer's most recent balance sheet and profit and loss and retained earnings statements; (xiii) similar financial information for such part of the 2 preceding fiscal years as the issuer or its predecessor has been in existence; (xiv) whether the broker or dealer or any associated person is affiliated, directly or indirectly with the issuer; (xv) whether the quotation is being published or submitted on behalf of any other broker or dealer, and, if so, the name of such broker or dealer; and (xvi) whether the quotation is being submitted or published directly or indirectly on behalf of the issuer, or any director, officer or any person, directly or indirectly the beneficial owner of more than 10 percent of the outstanding units or shares of any equity security of the issuer, and, if so, the name of such person, and the basis for any exemption under the federal securities laws for any sales of such securities on behalf of such person. If such information is made available to others upon request pursuant to this subparagraph, such delivery, unless otherwise represented, shall not constitute a representation by such broker or dealer that such information is true and correct, but shall constitute a representation by such broker or dealer that the information is reasonably current in relation to the day the quotation is submitted, that he has no reasonable basis for believing the information is not true and correct, and that the information was obtained from sources which he has a reasonable basis for believing are reliable.

(b) With respect to any security the quotation of which is within the provisions of this section, the broker or dealer submitting or publishing such quotation shall maintain in his records information regarding all circumstances involved in the submission or publication of such quotation, including the identity of the person or persons for whom the quotation is being submitted or published and any information regarding the transaction provided to the broker or dealer by such person or persons.

(c) The broker or dealer shall maintain in writing as part of his records the information described in paragraphs (a) and (b) of this section, and any other information (including adverse information) regarding the issuer which comes to his knowledge or possession before the publication of submission of the quotation, and preserve such records for the periods specified in Sec. 240.17a-4.

(d) For any security of an issuer included in paragraph (a)(4) of this section, the broker or dealer submitting the quotation shall furnish to the inter-dealer quotation system (as defined in paragraph (e)(1) of this section), in such form as such system shall prescribe, at least 2 days before the quotation is published or submitted, the information regarding the security and the issuer which such broker or dealer is required to maintain pursuant to said paragraph (a)(4) of this section.

(e) For purposes of this section:

(1) "Quotation medium" shall mean any "interdealer quotation system" or any publication or electronic communications network or other device which is used by brokers or dealers to make known to others their interest in transactions in any security, including offers to buy or sell at a stated price or otherwise, or invitations of offers to buy or sell.

(2) "Interdealer quotation system" shall mean any system of general circulation to brokers or dealers which regularly disseminates quotations of identified brokers or dealers.

(3) Except as otherwise specified in this section, "quotation" shall mean any bid or offer at a specified price with respect to a security.

(f) The provisions of this section shall not apply to:

(1) The publication or submission of a quotation respecting a security admitted to trading on a national securities exchange and which is traded on such an exchange on the same day as, or on the business day next preceding, the day the quotation is published or submitted.

(2) The publication or submission of a quotation for securities of foreign issuers exempt from section 12(g) of the Act by reason of compliance with the provisions of Sec. 240.12g3-2(b).

(3) The publication or submission of a quotation respecting a security which has been the subject of both bid and ask quotations in an interdealer quotation system at specified prices on each of at least 12 days within the previous 30 calendar days, with no more than 4 business days in succession without such a two-way quotation.

(4) The publication or submission of a quotation respecting a municipal security.

(4)(T) The publication or submission of a quotation respecting a security which, at least once each fifth business day, has been the subject of both bid and ask quotations at specified prices reported to, and published by, an interdealer quotation system—

(i) Which has reported to the broker or dealer who wishes to submit such a quotation that records of the system reflect that at least one registered broker or dealer has made, or

(ii) To which a registered broker or dealer who wishes to submit such a quotation has reported or represented that he has made both bid and ask quotations at specified prices on each of at least 12 business days within the previous 30 calendar days, with no more than 4 business days in succession without a reflection of the existence of such a two-way quotation.

This temporary subsection shall expire on April 30, 1977.

(g) The requirement in paragraph (a) (4) of this section that the information with respect to the issuer be "reasonably current" will be presumed to be satisfied, unless the broker or dealer has information to the contrary, if:

(1) The balance sheet is as of a date less than 16 months before the publication or submission of the quotation, the statements of profit and loss and retained earnings are for the 12 months preceding the date of such balance sheet, and if such balance sheet is not as of a date less than 6 months before the publication or submission of the quotation, it shall be accompanied by additional statements of

profit and loss and retained earnings for the period from the date of such balance sheet to a date less than 6 months before the publication of submission of the quotation.

(2) Other information regarding the issuer specified in paragraph (a)(4) of this section is as of a date within 12 months prior to the publication or submission of the quotation.

(h) This section shall not prohibit any publication or submission of any quotation if the Commission, upon written request or upon its own motion, exempts such quotation either unconditionally or on specified terms and conditions, as not constituting a fraudulent, manipulative or deceptive practice comprehended within the purpose of this section.

38 Fed. Reg. 18641, September 18, 1971, as amended at 41 Fed. Reg. 22826, June 7, 1976; 42 Fed. Reg. 13110, March 9, 1977, 17 C.F.R. §240.15c2-11.

APPENDIX B

LETTER FROM RESPONDENT TO S.E.C. DATED OCTOBER 21, 1975

Samuel H. Sloan
917 Old Trents Ferry Rd.
Lynchburg, Va. 24503

October 21, 1975

George A. Fitzsimmons
Secretary
Securities & Exchange Commission
500 N. Capitol Street
Washington, D.C. 20549

Re: Canadian Javelin Ltd.

Dear Sir:

I hereby demand that the Securities & Exchange Commission conduct an administrative hearing forthwith regarding the validity of the suspensions of trading in Canadian Javelin Ltd. I shall appear personally or through counsel at such a hearing. I assume that at the time of this hearing the S.E.C. will be prepared to go forward with proof showing that the suspensions of trading in question are justified. I wish to make it clear that I am challenging the validity of all suspensions of trading in Canadian Javelin Ltd. including those which may be in effect at the time of the administrative hearing or at the time the S.E.C. renders its decision.

In making this demand I am assuming that you are aware of the Per Curiam opinion of the United States Court of Appeals for the Second Circuit dated October 15, 1975 in *Sloan v. S.E.C.* 74-2457. The pertinant part of this opinion is as follows:

> "[T]he S.E.C. on this appeal has indicated that it is willing in fact to grant Sloan some sort of administrative hearing, thus satisfying any possible exhaustion requirement while also contributing to the record we now find insurmountably sparce.
>
> We therefore dismiss Sloan's appeal but without prejudice to his repleading after an administrative hearing before the S.E.C., from which judicial review may be sought."

Footnote 4 of the same opinion indicates that I should be given the opportunity to urge my objections before the S.E.C. For a statement of my objections I refer the S.E.C. to the two briefs I filed in this matter in the Court of Appeals. I do not believe it should be necessary for me to refile these identical briefs with the S.E.C. since the S.E.C. has already been served with an adequate number of copies and my arguments have not changed. However, I refer you to several court decisions which I believe provide further support for the arguments advanced in my briefs. These decisions are: *Schechter Poultry Corp. v. United States* 295 U.S. 495 (1935); *Panama Refining Co. v. Ryan* 293 U.S. 388 (1935); *Railroad Retirement Board v. Alton R.R.* 295 U.S. 330 (1935); *Standard Airlines v. CAB* 177 F. 2d 18 (2d Cir. 1949) and *National Cable Television v. United States* 415 U.S. 336 (1974).

Please advise me as to the date for this forthcoming hearing. I believe that the hearing should be held within the next one or two weeks since it is clear that the Court of Appeals considers further suspensions of trading to be of questionable validity unless a hearing has been conducted. Certainly, the S.E.C. should refrain from making any further orders of suspension of trading unless or until there has been a hearing. If the S.E.C. does not do so or if the S.E.C. indicates that a hearing may not be forthcoming in the reasonably near future, I shall be constrained to proceed accordingly.

Very truly yours,

Samuel H. Sloan

cc:

Diamond & Golomb
Counsel for Canadian Javelin Ltd.
99 Park Avenue
New York, N.Y.

United States Court of Appeals
for the Second Circuit
U.S. Courthouse
Foley Square
New York, New York

APPENDIX C

RESPONSE OF THE S.E.C. DATED NOVEMBER 7, 1975

Mr. Samuel H. Sloan
917 Old Trents Ferry Road
Lynchburg, Virginia 24503

Dear Mr. Sloan:

The Commission is in receipt of your letter dated October 21, 1975 in which you demand that an administrative hearing be held forthwith regarding the validity of the suspensions of trading in the securities of Canadian Javelin, Ltd.

Consistent with the *per curiam* opinion of the Court of Appeals in *Samual H. Sloan v. Securities and Exchange Commission*, 74-2457, you are invited to submit an appropriate application in support of your opposition to suspensions of trading in the common stock of Canadian Javelin. Your application should set forth in detail the factual matters you would offer to prove and your legal arguments in support of your position that the Commission is abusing its discretion by suspending trading in Canadian Javelin. Only in this way can a factual record be developed so that, in the event of further suspensions, a Court of Appeals could later determine whether those suspensions were an abuse of discretion. In your letter you refer us, for a statement of your objection to these suspensions, "to the two briefs I filed in this matter in the Court of Appeals." Those briefs are not suitable for this purpose and thus we invite you to file the type of petition set forth above.

Upon receipt of such a petition the Commission will determine whether the issues raised therein can be determined upon your affidavits or other written submissions in support of your petition or whether the issues can only be resolved in the context of an evidentiary hearing.

If I can be of any further assistance to you, please do not hesitate to contact me.

Very truly yours,

George A. Fitzsimmons, Secretary

APPENDIX D

FORM 211

NATIONAL QUOTATION BUREAU

INCORPORATED

CHICAGO
SAN FRANCISCO

116 NASSAU STREET
NEW YORK, N. Y. 10038
212-349-1800

BOSTON
LOS ANGELES

No quotation will be published until the broker-dealer seeking to insert the quotation furnishes the information requested in Parts 1 and 2 below, and if necessary, the information in Part 3, and duly executes and delivers this form.

PART 1

A. Exact name of the issuer and predecessor (if any).

B. State of incorporation.

C. Address of principal executive offices.

D. Complete title and class of security to be quoted.

E. Par or stated value of security.

F. Name and address of any transfer agent.

G. Number of shares outstanding of the security as of the end of the issuer's most recent fiscal year.

H. Price at which security is to be initially quoted. Bid .... Asked ....

PART 2

Check the item below which indicates the exemption from Rule 15c2-11 of the Securities Exchange Act of 1934 (the "34 Act") upon which you rely in submitting your quotation.

☐ A. The issuer has filed a registration statement under the Securities Act of 1933 (the "33 Act") which became effective less than 90 calendar days prior to the date hereof, and such registration statement has not been the subject of a stop order which is still in effect, and the undersigned has in its records a copy of the prospectus specified by Section 10(a) of the 33 Act; or

☐ B. The issuer has filed a notification under Regulation A of the 33 Act which became effective less than 40 calendar days prior to the date hereof, and the offering circular provided for under Regulation A has not become the subject of a suspension order which is still in effect, and the undersigned has in his records a copy of such offering circular; or

☐ C. (i) The issuer is required to file reports pursuant to Section 13 or 15d of the 34 Act, or is an issuer of a security covered by Section 12(g) (2) (B) or (G) of the 34 Act; and

(ii) the undersigned has a reasonable basis for believing the issuer is current in filing the reports required to be filed at regular intervals pursuant to Section 13 or 15d of the 34 Act, or, in the case of insurance companies, exempted from Section 12(g) of the 34 Act by subparagraph 12(g) (2) (G) thereof, the annual statement referred to in Section 12(g) (2) (G) (i) of the 34 Act; and

(iii) the undersigned has in his records the issuer's most recent annual report (on Form 10-K) filed pursuant to Section 13 or 15d of the 34 Act; or the annual statement of an insurance company not subject to Section 12(g) of the 34 Act; together with any other reports required to be filed at regular intervals under such provisions of the 34 Act which have been filed by the issuer after such annual report or annual statement; or

☐ D. The security of the issuer on which you are submitting a quotation has been the subject of both bid and asked quotations in an interdealer quotation system at specified prices on each of at least 12 days within the previous 30 calendar days with no more than four business days in succession without such a two-way quotation; or

☐ E. The security of the issuer of which you are submitting a quotation is admitted to trading on a national securities exchange (as registered under the 34 Act) and has been traded on such an exchange on the same day as, or on the business day next preceding, the day the quotation is published or submitted; or

☐ F. The security of the issuer of which you are submitting a quotation is a security of a foreign issuer exempt from Section 12(g) of the 34 Act by reason of comoliance with the provisions of Rule 12(g) 3-2(b) thereunder.

☐ G. None of the above.

If you have checked A or B above, supply a copy of the prospectus or offering circular to National Quotation Bureau with this Form 211.

If your answer was "G. None of the above", please supply the information specified in Part 3.

PART 3

A. Describe the nature of products or services offered by the issuer.

B. Describe the nature and the extent of the issuer's facilities.

C. Indicate the name of the Chief Executive officer and members of the Board of Directors of the issuer.

D. Attach a copy of the issuer's most recent balahce sheet and profit and loss retained earning statement.

E. Attach similar financial information for such part of the two preceding fiscal years as the issuer or its predecessor has been in existence.

F. State whether the undersigned, or any person associated with the undersigned, is affiliated directly or indirectly with the issuer.

G. State whether the quotation is being published or submitted on behalf of any other broker-dealer. If so, state the name of such broker or dealer.

H State whether the quotation is being submitted or published directly or indirectly on behalf of the issuer or any director, officer or any person, directly or indirectly, the beneficial owner of more than 10% of the outstanding units or shares of any equity security of the issuer. If so, state the name of such person and the basis for any exemption under the Federal securities laws for any sales of such securities on behalf of such person.

I certify that I have examined this form and, to the best of my knowledge and belief, it is true, correct and complete. I authorize the NATIONAL QUOTATION BUREAU, INCORPORATED *to furnish a copy of this questionnaire and any or all of the information contained in this form to the Securities and Exchange Commission or any other regulatory agency.*

Name of employee to contact regarding information contained herein________________ Phone________

Name and Signature of Partner or Officer________________

Firm Name ________________ Date________

Address ________________ Zip No. ________

NQB FORM 211

APPENDIX E

SECURITY POSITIONS OF SAMUEL H. SLOAN ON NOVEMBER 18, 1976

EQUITY

No. of Shares	Security	If ever suspended by the S.E.C., date the suspension commenced
439	A A A Enterprises	
450	A K Electric	
100	Aberle Industries	9/19/73
1200	Advance Metal Products Inc.	12/11/73
217	Airport Services Inc.	
1200	Airtronics International of Florida	9/28/73
1400	Albee Homes, Inc.	2/12/74
1807	Albro Industries Corp.	4/13/73
5	Allegeheny Airlines Inc.	
700	Allied Aero Industries	
430	Allied Management & Systems Corp.	9/28/73
1000	Amcourt Systems Inc.	10/31/74
8938	American Raceway, Inc.	6/2/71
46	Ancorp National Services	
850	Apollo Industries Inc. (Maine)	6/22/73 and 5/10/74
100	Apollo Industries Inc. (Utah)	
400	Applied Devices Corp.--new	2/3/72, 5/15/73 and 2/26/74
600	Applied Synthetics Corp.	5/7/73
100	Associates International Inc.	1/30/74
300	Atek Industries Inc.	12/11/73
1	Athey Products Corp.	
1940	Atlas Credit Corp. Warrants	
60	Automated Reference Corp.	
100	Avien Inc.	11/13/74
200	Basic Sciences Inc.	
100	Beckley Industries	
500	Bio-Pure Inc.	
4	Burlington Development & Const. Co.	
200	CM Industries Inc.	
4000	Cadgie Taylor Co.	

13	Canadian Javelin Ltd.	3/13/71, 3/7/72, 11/29/73, 1/13/75 and 4/29/75
3210	Carolina Caribbean Corp.	11/13/74
7275	Carousel Fashions	
1000	Cavanagh Communities Corp.	
14	Central Railroad of New Jersey	
754	Clayco Petroleum Corp.	
1100	Celopatra Wig Creations	
600	Computer Applications Inc.	
1500	Computer Graphics Inc.	
100	Cracker Barrel Supermarkets, Inc.	
100	Cryo-Therm Inc. Units of Contingent Interest	
500	Custer Channel Wing Corp. Class B	4/26/73 and 2/28/74
100	D E I Industries Inc.	5/21/73
200	D S I Systems Series A Preferred	
3500	Daryl Industries Inc.	
200	Demetrios Inc.	
100	Dextra Corporation	1/27/72 and 4/11/74
9750	Dialog Computing Inc.	
400	Diapulse Corp. of America	8/3/73
3959	Document Systems Inc.	
490	Donut Kastle Inc.	
490	Donut Kastle Inc.	
600	Dorothy Perkins Cosmetics	
3	Drew National Corp. preferred	
1050	Electrospace Corp.	3/12/74
300	Environmental Services Inc.	8/3/73
3500	Equity National Industries Inc.	
250	Fisco Inc.	6/17/74
450	Four Seasons Equity Corp.	7/17/72
21995	Four Seasons Nursing Centers of America Inc.	5/13/70 and 7/17/72
68	Franklin National Bank	5/13/74, 5/15/74, 5/16/74 and 5/25/74
1035	Galaxy Group Inc.	
526	Gammas Process Co.	2/21/74
43	Gold Ribbon Foods	
136	Greatamerica Corp.	
100	Greater Continental Corp.	9/27/73
300	Gro-Plant Industries Inc.	
365	Grove Press Inc.	
500	Gulf Leasing Corp.	
5	Harver Educational Services	
6000	Hemisphere Hotels common	4/11/74
5500	Hemisphere Hotels warrants	4/11/74
5	Hollywood Color Labs	
16	Hugoton Gas Trust Units	

10250	Hydron Europe, Inc. subscription warrants	
300	Inland Systems Inc.	5/7/73
323	International banknote Co. preferred	
200	International Systems Associates, Ltd.	7/11/73
1815	Jama Productions	
40	The Laand Corporation (a/k/a Geolectrics Corp.)	
400	Laser Sciences Inc.	2/27/74
150	Leader International Industries	8/13/74
400	Lilac Time Inc.	1/5/73
100	Living & Learning Centers	
600	Lyntex Corp.	7/26/73
25	Macrose Industries Corp.	
150	Management Computer Systems Corp. warrants	
17	Manhattan Continental Development Corp.	4/22/76
28	Maxson Electronics Corp. warrants	
150	Mega Systems Inc. (Formerly Data Network Corp.)	4/11/73
200	Multitech Inc.	7/6/73
550	Multivox Corporation of America	
38	N M S Industries	
1475	National Tape Corp.	8/31/71
400	Old Town Corp.	5/22/73
2010	Operation Match Inc.	
600	Pan American Industries	
400	Photon Inc.	3/26/73
100	Pickwick Organization Inc.	5/15/73
1	Playboy Enterprises	
50	Professional Data Services Inc.	
200	R A I Inc.	
6	R E D M Corp.	
750	Republic Color Inc.	
200	Rocky Mountain Industries Inc.	
1939	Sabre Inc.	
1150	Sav-On Inc.	5/23/73
100	Sawyer-Adecor International Inc.	4/11/74
600	Saxony Industries Inc.	
5075	Scienscope Inc.	
400	Scientific Control Corp.	6/28/73
300	The Seaboard Corp.	10/18/73
1048	Seaferro Inc.	6/13/73
5220	Sherwood Diversified Services—new	
1725	Sherwood Diversified Services—old	
200	Space Plastics Inc.	
10602	Speedata, Inc.	
200	Stanwick Corp.	
525	Stenocomp Inc.	
5850	Stirling Homex Corp. common	11/21/72

50400	Stirling Homex Corp. preferred	11/21/72
20000	Storybook Village, Inc.	
25	Structural Plastics Corp.	
4075	Syntonic Technology (Control Data) warrants	
200	Tele-Broadcasters Inc.	
200	Telescript C S P, Inc.	
100	Texas International Speedway common	
2000	Thermatrol of New York, Inc.	
160	1325 Union Corp.	
350	Toledo National Insurance Co. Class B	
200	Topper Corp.	2/9/72
38000	Trans World Airlines warrants	
100	Triex International Inc.	12/15/72
50	U. N. Industries	
43	United Reserve Underwriters	
63	United States Crown Corp.	4/11/74
600	[illegible]ndotronics Corp.	
100	Venture Concepts Inc.	
16398	Viatron Computer systems Corp.	
200	Vista Petroleum Corp.	
200	Webcor Inc.	
300	Wentworth Manufacturing Company	
255	Wilson & Co. warrants	
2962	Wilson Sporting Goods 10-15-78 warrants	
12	Wing Aircraft Co.	
100	Witt Tax Centers Inc.	
2900	World Wide Realty & Investing Corp.	4/5/73

SHORT POSITIONS

200	Resorts International Corp. Class B

DEBT

$8000	Administrative Systems (cv. deb.) 8% of 1983	4/26/73
$100	Belock Instrument Corp. 6% of 1975	6/22/65
$1000	Esgro, Inc. (cv. deb.) 6% of 1988	
$101000	Paul Hardeman, Inc. (cv. deb.) 5-1/2% of 1978	
$800	Michigan International Speedway 8% of 1978	
$19000	T M A Co. (cv. deb.) 6-1/2% of 1982	6/12/73
$56000	Texas International Speedway (cv. deb.) 8% of 1984	
$3000	Viatron Computer (cv. deb.) 6-1/4% of 1989	

APPENDIX F

LETTER FROM SAMUEL H. SLOAN TO S.E.C. STAFF ATTORNEY DATED JULY 22, 1973 AND ENCLOSURES

July 22, 1973

Larry Grimes
S.E.C.
Washington, D.C.

Dear Mr. Grimes,

Enclosed is a clipping from the Montreal Gazette of June 21, 1973, and the original UPI news release dated June 20, 1973. The American Stock Exchange halted trading immediately upon publication of this article, apparently at the request of the company. To the best of my knowledge it was not reprinted anywhere in the U.S. The company has never released a statement clarifying the differences between this news article and statements previously issued by Canadian Javelin. I have gone to great lengths to determine the accuracy of this and a great many other news articles concerning Javelin. The American Stock Exchange has not been particularly helpful. They have spoken to me on the telephone, but they refused to reply in writing to the two letters I wrote them concerning Javelin, a copy of one which is enclosed.

Recently there was a news article published in the Wall Street Journal (July 6, 1973), which stated that Bison Petroleum and Minerals had acquired a 200,000 acre mineral concession from the Government of Panama. This statement was untrue. Apparently Bison did purchase an existing mineral concession from Pavonia, S.A. another subsidiary of Javelin. The terms of the purchase and the price paid have not been disclosed.

As a shareholder of Canadian Javelin I am concerned by the numerous conflicting statements concerning Canadian Javelin and the fact that I am unable to obtain a resolution to these conflicts. I remember in the not so distant past, Javelin claimed to own the timber rights to 300,000,000 acres of forest land in Newfoundland. This claim turned out to be based on fictitious documents provided by an undisclosed Lichtenstein corporation. I would appreciate any help you could provide in resolving these conflicts.

Very truly yours,

SHS/aq

Javelin copper deal delayed by Panama

PANAMA CITY — (UPI) — Panama has postponed for at least two months, while it draws up a new mining code, talks with Canadian Javelin Ltd. for a major copper mining concession, Commerce and Industries Minister Fernando Mangredo said yesterday.

The minister also reported the government is renegotiating a petroleum concession granted last month to Texaco and indicated it might break off talks with a Japanese consortium headed by Mitsui for another copper-mining deal.

Manfredo made his remarks at a luncheon of the Foreign Correspondents Club of Panama.

A draft proposal submitted by Canadian Javelin last May 7 to develop the rich Cerro Colorado copper deposit, considered by some geologists as the world's biggest, was shelved and the company was told it would have to await the approval of a new code before negotiations could resume, Manfredo said.

"We should have this new code within two months," the minister said.

TWO FEATURES

He said two new features of the draft now being considered by Panama's legislative commission call for a government representative on the board of directors of foreign mining companies operating in Panama and periodic revision of certain terms of their concessions.

"Whatever decision the board of that company takes can affect the country and therefore the country should be represented," Manfredo said.

"The presence of a government representative, who will have voice but no vote, also will mean that the government will be more aware of the company's operations in the country."

COPY SENT OVER UPI NEWSWIRE

Sylilis Mr.
Repeating per your request Javelin 6-20
Night Ld
By J. Paul Hyatt

Panama City (UPI)—Panama has postponed for at least two months, while it draws up a new mining code talks with Canadian Javelin Ltd. for a major copper mining concession, commerce and industries Minister Fernando Manfredo said Wednesday.

The minister also reported the Government is renegotiating a petroleum concession granted last month to Texaco and indicated it might break off talks with a Japanese Consortium headed by Mitsui for another copper mining deal.

Manfredo made his remarks at a luncheon of the Foreign Correspondents Club of Panama.

A draft proposal submitted by Canadian Javelin last May 7 to develop the Rich Cerro Colorado Copper Deposit, considered by some Geologists as the worlds biggest, was shelved and the company was told it would have to await the approval of a new code before negotiations could resume, Manfredo said.

"He should have this new code within two months," the Minister estimated.

He said two new features of the draft now being considered by Panamas Legislative Commission call for a government representative on the Board of Directors of foreign mining companies operating in Panama and periodic revision of certain terms of their concessions.

"Whatever decision the board of that company takes can affect the country and therefore the country should be represented," Manfredo said.

"The presence of a government representative, who will have voice but no vote, also will mean that the government will be more aware of the company's problems," he said. "It will not be an obstacle for the companys operations in the country."

Although Manfredo began his remarks on Cerro Colorado by saying, "We do not have sufficient information to support the claims of Canadian javelin that this is the biggest copper deposit in the world," later on he added, "I am convinced that there is a great deposit there."

The Minister denied that the Texaco exploration concession had been rejected. He said one clause dealing with arbitration that ran contrary to the tenets of the 1972 constitution on the subject "has objected to" by the legislative commission.

He also acknowledged that there had been some "Misinterpretations" of a clause giving Texaco an option to build a transisthmic pipeline for the exclusive purpose of pumping its own crude oil from the Atlantic, where the concession is, to the Pacific Ocean.

"Some members of the commission interpreted this to mean that the pipeline would be used for commercial ends, but this is clearly not authorized in the language of the clause," he said.

Negotiations with the Japanese consortium to mine copper at the Petrouilla area, which appeared near completion last month, are continuing, Manfredo said. He added, however, that the government "is now thinking about mining the copper reserves itself."

The minister said Panama has asked for the opinions of government mining specialists in Peru, Chile, Mexico, Canada and South Africa on the draft of its new mining code.

April 19, 1973

Mr. Charles Stevens
American Stock Exchange
86 Trinity Place
New York, N.Y.

Dear Mr. Stevens:

It has come to my attention that Canadian Javelin Ltd. did not hold an annual meeting for the year 1972. This fact was confirmed to me by their attorneys Steptoe and Johnson. Their last annual meeting was held on June 22, 1971 based upon the proxy materials which are on file in your library. I have been a shareholder of record of this company for more than a year and I am extremely anxious to receive some sort of financial information and to attend their annual meeting regardless of where it is held. I understand that this failure to hold an annual meeting is both a violation of Canadian Corporation Laws and the rules of the American Stock Exchange. Could you please advise me in writing as to what steps you have taken to correct this problem.

I wrote the American Stock Exchange concerning this company on March 14, 1973. So far my letter has not been answered. Therefore I am sending you a copy of this letter by hand and ask that you give it your immediate attention. I note that Canadian Javelin has still not sent its annual report for 1972 to its shareholders.

Very truly yours,

BY HAND

APPENDIX G

LETTER FROM SAMUEL H. SLOAN TO S.E.C. STAFF ATTORNEY DATED AUGUST 10, 1973 AND ENCLOSURES

Received Aug. 14, 1973
Division of Enforcement

Larry Grimes
Securities and Exchange Commission
Washington, D.C.

Dear Mr. Grimes,

The purpose of this letter is to make a formal complaint concerning trading activity in Canadian Javelin Ltd. ("CJV), and to request that the Commission suspend trading in this security. I also request that the Commission investigate and conduct hearings concerning its trading activity. The reasons for this request are as follows:

1. On June 20, 1973 the Government of Panama through its Minister of Commerce and Industry, Fernando Manfredo made a formal announcement to members of the press that it was terminating its negotiations with Canadian Javelin Ltd. I spoke to the Director of Mineral Resources of Panama in person on July 27, 1973 and by telephone on Aug. 8, 1973, and he advised me that this situation has not changed. This fact has not been disclosed to the public nor is it generally known.

2. Canadian Javelin has issued a statement that "The government of Panama has in no way suggested that the burden on Canadian Javelin Ltd." under a proposed new mining code would be heavier than under present regulations. This carefully worded statement avoids, but does not dispute the statement by Fernando Manfredo and tries to create a false impression that nothing has changed

with respect to the situation in Panama.

3. Due to the political situation in Panama particularly with respect to the Panama canal it seems unlikely that negotiations will resume in the near future. Panama on one well publicized occasion threatened to attack the Canal Zone.

4. It appears that the approximately $14,000,000 Canadian Javelin claims to have spent on the Panamanian drilling operation as stated in their balance sheet will have to be written off as a loss.

5. Canadian Javelin has widely circulated information that it has delineated an area of 2.2 billion tons of copper bearing minerals. I spoke to George Mickum, council for the company and asked him to tell me either what calculations were involved in producing this figure or what qualified geologist has made this computation. Mr. Mickum refused to answer me and questioned my motives in raising such an issue. I feel this is the routine sort of question that any securities analyst would ask. Mr. Mickum stated that the basis for these calculations has been reviewed and received the approval of the S.E.C. and if there were any questions concerning the basis for these calculations he was sure that the S.E.C. would suspend trading in CJV immediately. He also stated that representatives of the S.E.C. had visited the drilling sight, had received detailed information concerning the nature and extent of the drilling, and was satisfied that nothing irregular was taking place.

6. In spite of the assurances by Mr. Mickum that nothing was irregular there is a question in my mind as to whether his statements are accurate. I visited the drilling sight in Panama and neither the geologists employed there nor the geologists employed by the government of Panama to investigate and analyze the results of the drilling had any idea where 2.2 billion ton figure came from. Furthermore the S.E.C. office of Mining Engineering has adivsed me

that they have no information to back up this figure and they dispute directly some of Mr. Mickum's statements.

7. I have received numerous telephone calls from stock brokers who have heard that CJV has an immense copper find in Panama and is about to release the news that they have obtained financing for the construction and development necessary for this project. I also received a call an individual who claimed the stock would go to between $100 and $500 a share. I believe that these kind of calls indicate that the public has been greatly misled concerning the nature of Javelins work in Panama.

8. On April 1, 1971 the Commission issued release No. 125 which placed a burden upon brokers to use due diligence before effecting transactions in this security. I believe that I have satisfied this requirement but that many brokers have generally ignored this release.

9. Due to the nature of the recent trading activity in Canadian Javelin many brokers are unable to consumate the transactions into which they have entered. As a result there is a substantial fail position in the street so much so that brokers have become unable to effect buy-ins. As a result it appears that a number of brokers will suffer a severe financial loss. It also appears that if the present situation is allowed to continue CJV will trade at a substantially higher price in the immediate future which will further aggrevate the loss of these brokers and will be detrimental to the protection of the public.

10. It is generally known and agreed the CJV has engaged in fraudulent and deceptive practices for more than 20 years and that the chairman of the company has been convicted and sentenced for ignoring the registration requirements of the 1933 and 1934 Acts. The situation in Panama is not dissimilar to the situation which has existed in the past in Newfoundland, Labcrador, Julian Lake, and Lake Wabush in which the company made wild projections which never came to fruition. In light of the history of this

company it would seem reasonable to assume that the statements of the Government of Panama are accurate.

11. I note that even respectable financial reporting services have made misstatements concerning the financial condition of CJV. For example Standard & Poor's reports that CJV earned 3 cents last year whereas in reality it reported a substantial loss.

12. I have been informed by PICKANS MATHER & CO which is the managing agent for LAKE WABUSH property from which CJV receives all of its income, approximately $4.5 million per year, that due to problems CJV is having Pickans Mather does not make any money payments directly to CJV but rather uses the money to pay creditors, lawyers, and others to whom CJV owes money. For this reason I question the accounting methods which are used to calculate the income of CJV.

I enclose various correspondence and news releases to support the above statements.

Very Truly Yours,

C.C. Stephen Girard
American Stock Exchange

LETTERHEAD OF
CANADIAN JAVELIN LIMITED
Executive Offices — 1115 Sherbrooke St. West
Suite 2703, Montreal 110, Quebec

June 22, 1973

PRESS RELEASE
FOR RELEASE MONDAY A.M.

Mr. John C. Doyle, Chairman of the Executive Committee of Canadian Javelin Limited, in charge of the Company's Cerro Colorado copper deposit in Panama, stated today from Panama that Minister Fernando Manfredo's statement made it clear and confirmed that the Company has delineated one of the world's largest copper mines. He stated the Company is now moving from the exploration stage to that of construction. He also explained that the Company has been consulted and provided with drafts of the new Mineral Code under consideration, and further has been asked for its suggestions. Mineral Code under consideration, requested Mr. H. J. Price (former Superintendent of Anaconda's Chuquicamata mine in Chile, the world's largest existing copper mine) and now General Manager of Canadian Javelin's Cerro Colorado copper deposit, to act as consultant and to assist and advise the Government on the provisions of the new Code. In no way has the Government suggested that the burden on the Company would be heavier than that provided under the present exploration contract that assures the Company's rights to exploit the copper under the present Mineral Code.

It has been the policy of Canadian javelin to include Government representatives on the Board of Directors of the Company, as was done in the development of its Wabush iron ore mines. The company official stated that it would be particularly appropriate in Panama where the Company has enjoyed a very good and co-operative relationship with the Government. Elements of importance, due to the size of the Cerro Colorado copper project in the Republic of Panama, are available labour, a potential increase in Panamanian export trade balances and the environmental aspect singular to the mine which is located near the summit of the central mountain range, equal distance from both oceans (30 miles from both the Atlantic and the Pacific). The mechanics of disposing of 62,000,000 tons of tailings per year with which it is planned to fill the pestilential swamp bordering the oceans and thereby improve local living conditions.

The Company executive pointed out that the mine power supply to be installed will be greater than the total present electrical generating capacity of Panama. He stated that the physical task to be accomplished may be compared to the Panama Canal in that in the first fifteen years of operation it is expected that the total material extracted in this open pit mine will be greater than the total yardage excavated in building the Panama Canal itself.

The Chairman stated that the size of the Cerro Colorado deposits their company engineers had calculated in early June, 1973, was approximately 2,271,000,000 tons, indicated by drilling. The Cerro Colorado ore body appears to be the world's largest copper deposit. This is based on the fact that the Chuquicamata copper mine in Chile, generally considered to have been the world's largest, had an original size, according to published records, of 2,000,000,000 tons. Many hundreds of million tons have been mined during its fifty-seven years of operation. The Company official stated that the Company has been advised by one of the world's foremost geological consulting firms, Watts, Griffis and McOuat Ltd., Toronto, Canada, that the potential reserves are expected to be in excess of 3,000,000,000 tons. These geologists, along with other consultants. have been retained by Javelin to assist the Company staff in preparing the mining plan.

Mr. Doyle also revealed that the Company has now completed Hole 106 which, based on published records, is the longest continuous vertical intersection of copper mineralization in the history of mining. The test hole, when terminated four-fifths of a mile deep in the earth (approximately 4,400 feet) was still in good copper mineralization of commercial grade.

The Company official further stated that the Cerro Colorado copper deposits have attracted the attention of the world's foremost mining and fabricating companies. He said serious discussions have been held and are continuing between the Company's representatives and Noranda Mines Ltd., Placer Development Ltd., of Canada, De Beers Consolidated Mines Ltd., Anglo-American Ltd. of South Africa, who are the world's largest producers of diamond and gold and amongst the biggest producers of copper, Standard Oil of Indiana, British Hynoch Metals Ltd., a company jointly owned by British Insulated Callender's Cables Limited, the world's largest user of elemental copper, and Imperial Metal Industries Ltd., a subsidiary of Imperial Chemical Industries Ltd., Outokumpu Oy of Finland, Norddeutsche Raffinerie A.G., Germany's largest refiner and producer of copper, Pechiney of France, Rio Tinto Patino, Madrid and many others. These discussions, while not finalized, have resulted in assuring the company of long term sales of blister and copper concentrates that would be sufficient to sustain mining and processing at a rate of more than 100,000 tons per day.

He also pointed out that most of these companies have agreed with Javelin that the immense size of these deposits indicates a desirability of the establishing of a copper smelter in Panama. The establishment of this smelter in itself requires changes in Panamanian regulations governing mineral development.

Finally, Mr. John C. Doyle pointed out that a group of consultants working on the project led by Wright Engineers Ltd. of Vancouver, Canada, are sizing equipment, completing the pricing and determining all relevant economic and cost factors. This work is scheduled to be completed early in August of 1973 and the Company expects to be ready shortly thereafter with the financing and marketing completed to enable the establishment of a mining and milling installation which, when fully operative, would have a capacity of 176,000 tons per day. Recent bulk smapling of the minerals to be mined during the first fifteen years have been tested by Lakefield Research Laboratories, Lakefield, Ontario. These tests have assayed an average grade of .81% copper, with additional minor contents of gold, silver and molybdenum. These metals, with large scale mining, should add substantial dollar values to the copper production.

There is now at Cerro Colorado a technical staff of Panamanian and Canadian engineers, geologists, drillers, and approximately three hundred Panamanian construction and exploration employees.

July 23, 1973

Dow Jones & Co.
22 Cortlandt St.
New York, N.Y. 10007

Dear Sirs,

On July 5, 1973 you carried a news article on the Dow Jones News Service concerning Canadian Javelin Ltd. The information in this article was repreated in the Wall Street Journal on July 6, 1973. The information contained in this article was untrue. I spoke to the Minister of Commerce and Industry in Panama, Fernando Manfredo, on the telephone in Panama on July 5, 1973 to confirm the story contained in this article. He said that the statement was untrue and furthermore that under the present Panamanian mining code no outside company could engage in mining activities in Panama. I enclose a copy of a UPI news release, dated June 20, 1973 which confirms this fact.

After learr.ing that the information contained on the broad tape was untrue I immediately contacted your New York and Montreal offices to express my concern. Their position was that the Dow Jones was essentially correct and they would not print a retraction or a clarification. This position was not justified by the facts. According to them Bison purchased the concession, not from Panama but from another subsidiary of Javelin. In fact they said, this was not a purchase at all but merely a transfer of an existing right.

They acknowledged that Javelin does not have the right to mine copper in Panama.

Since the publication of this untrue article, Javelin has become one of the most actively traded securities on the American Stock Exchange. You are no doubt aware of the damage caused to shareholders and purchasers of any security which has been the subject of false and misleading press releases. You are further, no doubt aware of your responsibility as a reputable news agency to verify the accurancy of the stories you print. In addition you are doubtless aware of the incalculable damage which has been done to Javelin shareholders in the past as a result of false, misleading and deceptive news articles published by you in your news services. Javelin was suspended by the S.E.C. in 1971 and again in 1972, in the later case as a direct result of a feature article which you carried a few days before the suspension.

Because of your flagrant disregard for the rights of Javelin shareholders to receive accurate information concerning their company. I am considering taking legal action against your agency. Prior to so doing I would like to give you this opportunity to clarify your position with regard to the issues I have raised. I would appreciate your response as soon as possible.

[Letterhead of Canadian Javelin Ltd.]

August 3, 1973

I have duly received from Mr. Steven L. Gerard of the American Stock Exchange Inc. a copy of your letter to him of July 23rd and a copy of his reply thereto dated July 31st, 1973. I note that Mr. Gerard has sent you a copy of our Annual Report, recent press releases and reprints of recent newspaper articles.

It appears that you have received all the information available to shareholders of the Company generally. However, we have no record of your attendance at the Company's annual meeting held on May 9th, 1973. If there is any information furnished to shareholders or in press releases which you have not received, I shall be glad to make same available to you.

I have been advised that you arrived in the Republic of Panama on Friday morning July 27th last and that you visited Canadian Javelin's Cerro Colorado copper properties on July 28th. The Company will, therefore, hold you responsible for the authenticity of any information which you may see fit to disseminate.

Yours truly,

W.M. Wismer,
President

WMW/nc
cc Mr. Steven L. Gerard,
American Stock Exchange Inc.

Dow Jones Newswire Item

—CANADIAN JAVELIN UNIT SAYS IT ACQUIRED 200,000 ACRE MINERAL CONCESSION IN PANAMA - July 5, 1973

CANADIAN JAVELIN UNIT—PANAMA CONCESSION - July -5, 1973

Montl -DJ- Bison Petroleum & Minerals Ltd. 61 PC owned by Canadian Javelin Ltd. said it has acquired a 200 00-acre mineral concession from the government of Panama.

Bison said the concession is known to contain gold, silver and other metals.

The agreement carries the right to proceed further to another agreement for actual exploitation.

Canadian javelin said that with its wholly-owned subsidiaries and majority-owned Bison it holds 600,000 acres of mineral concessions in Panama.

Bison also said it negotiated an agreement in principle with A.I.S. resources Ltd. Montreal for participation by A.I.S. in financing of an exploration and development program on the mineral concession. Details will be announced after approval by regulatory authorities.

APPENDIX H

LETTER FROM S.E.C. TO UNIDENTIFIED INVESTOR REGARDING TRADING SUSPENSION IN CANADIAN JAVELIN LTD.

June 5, 1972

Thank you for your letter of May 24, 1972, requesting information on the subject company.

Enclosed for your information are copies of Securities Exchange Act of 1934 Release Nos. 9111, 9125, and 9528 concerning the Commission's actions with respect to Canadian Javelin Ltd.

We would like to point out that the Commission considers very carefully many factors prior to suspending trading in any security. A suspension of trading is ordered only when it is deemed appropriate and in the interest and protection of the investors. The suspension of trading in the stock of Canadian javelin, Ltd., is still in effect and we cannot predict when it will be lifted. You may be assured that when the Commission deems it appropriate and in the public interest, the suspension will be lifted and trading will be resumed at which time a public release will be issued.

You ask what rights you may have in this matter. It should be noted that important judicial remedies are available to investors. However, recovery may be sought only through the assertion of claims by investors before an appropriate court which usually involves the services of an attorney.

Thank you for your interest in writing.

Sincerely yours,

Frank J. Donaty, Jr., Chief
Section of Complaint Processing
By: Ruby E. Johnson,
Complaint Processor

Enclosures

APPENDIX I

LETTER REQUESTING NO ACTION LETTER

October 10, 1974

Mr. Richard J. Morrisey
Room 392
Division of Market Regulation
Securities and Exchange Commission
500 North Capitol Street
Washington, D.C. 20549

Re: *Canadian Javelin, Ltd.*

Dear Mr. Morrisey:

In February and March of this year we corresponded with the Staff concerning the ownership by our client, Interstate Securities Corporation, of 2,000 shares of Canadian Javelin, Ltd. Trading in Canadian Javelin stock on the American Stock Exchange and in the OTC market was suspended on November 23, 1973 by order of the Commission. This suspension as you know is still in effect.

Interstate, a registered broker dealer, purchased the Canadian Javelin stock, for its own account as principal, early in November 1973, for its own account as principal, early in November 1973 at approximately $11 per share. The suspension causes the stock to be subject to a 100% haircut for purposes of Interstate's NYSE minimum capital computation.

Meanwhile, the stock is, and has been, actively traded on the Montreal Stock Exchange even though the price has steadily declined. This state of affairs works a hardship on our client and we question its necessity in light of the active interest in the stock in Canada by people who by now presumably are aware that trading has been suspended in the U.S. On Interstate's behalf, we request that the Commission permit it to sell the 2,000 shares on the Montreal Exchange.

Thank you.

Sincerely,

MOORE AND VAN ALLEN

Robert W. King, Jr.

RWK, jr/kw

cc: Mr. Glen R. Shipway

APPENDIX J

LETTER DENYING REQUEST FOR A NO ACTION LETTER

November 5, 1974

Robert W. King, Jr., Esq.
Moore and Van Allen
Attorneys at Law
Johnston Building
Charlotte, North Carolina 28281

Dear Mr. King:

This is in response to your letter of October 10, 1974 in which you request permission for your client, Interstate Securities Corporation, a registered broker-dealer, to sell as principal 2,000 shares of the common stock of Canadian Javelin, Ltd. Trading in the common stock has been suspended by order of the Commission since November 29, 1973. Reference is also made to your correspondence with the staff in February and March of this year.

On July 17, 1974 final judgments of permanent injunction were entered against Canadian Javelin and others (*Sec. v. Canadian Javelin, et. al.* (S.D.N.Y.), SEC Litigation Release No. 6441, *SEC Docket*, July 30, 1974, 620-1), requiring, among other things, that Canadian Javelin file with the Commission reports, and amendments thereto, as required under the Securities Exchange Act of 1934 (the "Act"). We have been informed by Canadian Javelin that this information is expected to be filed with the Commission in the near future. At that time the necessity for the trading suspension will be reviewed by the staff and the Commission. In view of the foregoing, and the specific prohibitions of Section 15(c)(5) of the Act, we are not in a position at this time to take further action on your request.

Sincerely yours,

Richard John Morrisey III
Attorney

RJM:mcv:11-4-74

cc: Lewis, Klein, Spirer, King, Morrisey, Digest Files, Records, Subject File, Atlanta Reg. Office

APPENDIX K

OFFICE MEMORANDUM
SECURITIES AND EXCHANGE COMMISSION

January 9, 1974

TO: Files
FROM: Sig Schoedel, Attorney, Division of Enforcement

SUBJECT: Canadian Javelin

Mr. Michaelson of the brokerage firm Moses & Singer, NYC raised the question on January 2nd, 1974 whether stock of Canadian Javelin, now suspended from trading, can be sold in Canada where a market for that stock still exists. Moses & Singer has a customer carrying stock of Canadian Javelin in a margin account which is restricted because its debit balance exceeds Regulation T's 50% loan value. The account also requires maintenance margin at this time.

After consulting with Stan Sporkin, I telephoned Mr. Michaelson and advised him of our staff's informal position which would permit Moses & Singer to deliver Canadian Javelin stock against payment to a Canadian broker provided that ohe sale order was initiated by the customer in Canada entirely on his own, and that Moses & Singer's participation in the transaction was confined to delivery against payment. I also advised Mr. Michaelson that his firm would have to abide by the withdrawal provisions of Reg.T which require that at least 70% of the payment received from the Canadian broker must be used to reduce the customer's debit balance in his margin account.

cc: Ken Spirer, Room 303

APPENDIX L

NO ACTION LETTER OF THE SECURITIES AND EXCHANGE COMMISSION, DIVISION OF MARKET REGULATION REGARDING THE SALE OF SHARES OF CANADIAN JAVELIN LTD. WHILE TRADING SUSPENSION IS IN EFFECT

Securities and Exchange Commission, Division of Market Regulation. December 16, 1975. (Available January 15, 1976). Correspondence in full text.

[*SEC Staff Reply*]

This is in response to your letter of September 24, 1975, and subsequent telephone conversations concerning a proposed sale of 1,000 shares of the common stock of Canadian Javelin, Ltd. ("Canadian Javelin") by your client. We understand the following facts to be pertinent:

Canadian Javelin is a Canadian company, many of whose shareholders are United States citizens. On November 29, 1973, the Commission suspended all trading in the United States in the securities of Canadian Javelin pursuant to Sections 15(c)(5) and 19(a)(4) of the Securities Exchange Act of 1934 (the "Act"). The trading suspension has been ordered by the Commission for additional ten day periods, most recently pursuant to Section 12(k) of the Act, as amended by the Securities Acts Amendments of 1975 (P.L. 94-29, June 4, 1975), and is still in effect. You state that Canadian Javelin common shares are still traded in Canada.

Your client, Edwards & Hanly, is a registered broker-dealer. Samuel H. Sloan & Co. ("Sloan"), a registered broker-dealer, purported to sell short 4,000 shares of Canadian Javelin common stock through Edwards &

Hanly. Edwards & Hanly was notified by the American Stock Exchange that Sloan's sales were allegedly improper, whereupon Edwards & Hanly bought in the 4,000 shares of Canadian Javelin common stock for Sloan's account. These transactions resulted in a debit balance in Sloan's account of $6,611.42.

Sloan thereafter delivered 1,000 Canadian Javelin shares to Edwards & Hanly, which attached the shares as security for Sloan's debit balance under an Order of Attachment issued by the New York Supreme Court, New York County. Since September, 1973, the Canadian Javelin shares have been held by the Sheriff of New York County. On May 27, 1975 the New York Supreme Court, Appellate Division, First Department, granted a judgment in the sum of $5,662.50 to Edwards & Hanley. Sloan has appealed from this decision.

Edwards & Hanly desires to sell the attached Canadian Javelin shares in Canada for the purpose of staisfying its judgment against Sloan. It is proposed that, pursuant to New York law, the Sheriff of New York County will conduct a public auction to sell the stock. Edwards & Hanly proposes to bid for the stock up to a limit approximating its current market price in Canada, and, if the firm is the successful bidder, it would immediately attempt to sell the shares in Canada. If another bidder purchased the shares at the auction, Edwards & Hanly would, as judgment creditor, receive the net proceeds of the sale.

Section 12(k) of the Act, as amended, authorizes the Commission summarily to suspend trading in any security for a ten day period and provides that no broker or dealer shall make use of the facilities of interstate commerce to effect any transaction in, or induce the sale or purchase of, any security in which trading is so suspended. In our opinion the proposed purchase and sale of Canadian Javelin shares would be transactions effected by a broker-dealer within the meaning of Section 12(k) of the Act.

Nonetheless, if Edwards & Hanly limits its activities to purchasing the Canadian Javelin shares at a sheriff's public auction and thereafter to selling such shares in Canada, or to receiving the net proceeds of the auction of such shares (in the event that the shares are purchased by another bidder), the staff will not recommend that the Commission take enforcement action under Section 12(k) of the Act. Edwards & Hanly must be acting in good faith at all times, and, along with the other parties to the proposed sale, have no connection with the activities announced by the Commission as the basis for suspending trading in Canadian Javelin securities. Finally, in deciding whether to engage in such conduct, Edwards & Hanly must consider all other relevant provisions of the federal securities law.

[*Letter of Inquiry*]

In accordance with our telephone conversation, we wish, on behalf of our client, Edwards & Hanly, to request a no-action letter from the staff of the Commission in connection with a proposed sale by our client of 1,000 shares of common stock of Canadian Javelin Ltd. in Canada. We are advised that trading in said stock is suspended in the United States.

The facts upon which we base our request for such a no-action letter are as follows:

On July 17, 1973, Samuel H. Sloan, d/b/a Samuel H. Sloan & Co. purported to sell, through Edwards & Hanly, 2000 shares of Canadian Javelin common stock. An additional 2,000 shares of Canadian Javelin were purported to be sold on July 25, 1973. As is well known to the Commission, Mr. Sloan was, at that time, engaged in the improper short-selling of Canadian Javelin stock through many brokerage firms.

Edwards & Hanly was notified by the American Stock Exchange of Mr. Sloan's improper activities and proceeded to buy in the 4,000 shares of Canadian Javelin for Mr. Sloan's account and risk. The mandatory buy-in resulted in a debit balance in Mr. Sloan's account with Edwards & Hanly of $6,611.42.

The mandatory buy-in of Mr. Sloan's account was accomplished without notice to Mr. Sloan for reasons, again, known to the Commission. Following the buy-in, Mr. Sloan inexplicably delivered 1,000 shares of Canadian Javelin to Edwards & Hanly with the request that the delivery be against immediate payment. The cashier at Edwards & Hanly, not knowing about the buy-in the day before, accepted the stock. Thereafter, communications were had within Edwards & Hanly. The fact of the buy-in and the loss was established, and Edwards & Hanly determined to assert a lien on the 1,000 shares of Canadian Javelin as security for the loss it sustained.

Thereafter, Edwards & Hanly caused an Order of Attachment to be issued by the Supreme Court, New York County, for the purpose of attaching the 1,000 shares of Canadian Javelin stock as security for the debt. Since September, 1973, the 1,000 shares of Canadian Javelin in question have been held by the Sheriff of New York County under said Order of Attachment.

Following lengthy litigation between Edwards & Hanly and Mr. Sloan concerning Edwards & Hanly's claim and certain counterclaims asserted by Mr. Sloan, on May 27, 1975, the Appellate Division, First Department, entered an order granting Edwards & Hanly a judgment in the sum of $5,662.50. The decision of the Appellate Division is reported at 48 A.D. 2d 644, 368 N.Y.S. 2d 218 (First Department, 1975).

It should be noted that Mr. Sloan, simultaneously with pursuing litigation in the State Courts, pursued the same litigation in the Federal Courts. His complaint against Edwards & Hanly in that forum was dismissed by order of Judge Bonsal, see CCH 73-74 Transfer Binder, Paragraph

94,579 (S.D.N.Y. 1974).

Mr. Sloan has appealed the order of the Appellate Division to the New York State Court of Appeals and the order of Judge Bonsal to the United States Court of Appeals for the Second Circuit.

Since Edwards & Hanly now has a judgment in its favor, it wishes to execute upon the 1,000 shares of Canadian Javelin currently held by the Sheriff of New York County, and to sell the same to partially satisfy the judgment in question.

As is apparent from the foregoing recitation, Edwards & Hanly has been forced to become involved in expensive and protracted litigation with Mr. Sloan and, apparently, Mr. Sloan intends to continue the litigation with continuing expense and inconvenience. If, however, Edwards & Hanly is permitted to sell the shares of stock which have been attached and thereby to satisfy its judgment, many of the real and fictitious issues which Mr. Sloan proposes to raise in further litigation will be obviated. For example, Mr. Sloan wants to attack the Constitutionality of the New York Attachment Statute, which an execution and sale of the stock would render moot.

By reason of the foregoing, Edwards & Hanly believes that the sale of the stock in question at the present time is necessary to avoid continuing substantial expenditures of legal time and effort in litigating with Mr. Sloan, as well as to realize some recovery on the judgment in its favor, which has taken so long to obtain.

Should the staff of the Commission determine that it would take no action should Edwards & Hanly sell the stock, the Sheriff of New York County, under New York law, would conduct a public auction to sell the stock. Edwards & Hanly would bid for the stock up to a limit approximating its current price in Canada, and if Edwards & Hanly were the successful bidder, the stock would be transmitted to Canada for immediate sale. Of course, should another party desire to compete in bidding for the stock, the ultimate proceeds would, nonetheless, be received by Edwards & Hanly as judgment creditor.

For the foregoing reasons, we respectfully request, on behalf of Edwards & Hanly, that the staff of the Commission issue a no-action letter so as to permit Edwards & Hanly to sell the stock in question and, hopefully, to terminate time-consuming and frivolous litigation with Mr. Sloan.

Printed in Dunstable, United Kingdom

91226250R00145